TOTALIVING

PITTI IMMAGINE

LONGWOOD
C O L L E G E

LIBRARY

Longwood College
Farmville, Virginia 23909-1897

A center for learning. A window to the world.

TOTAL LIVING

EDITED BY MARIA LUISA FRISA _ MARIO LUPANO _ STEFANO TONCHI

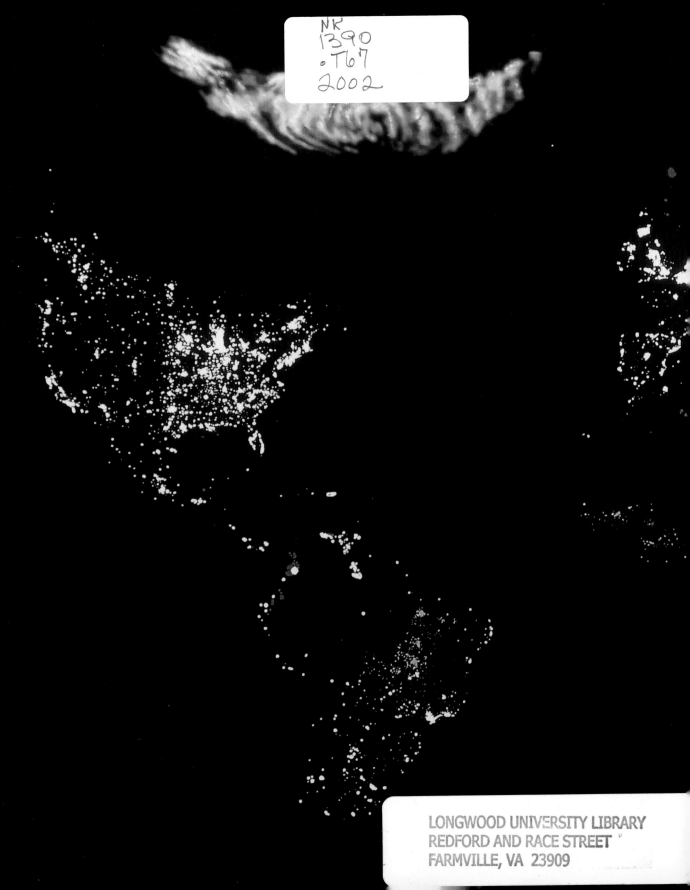

__ __ ← **EARTH AT NIGHT**, COLOR-CODED IMAGE FROM SATELLITES OF THE AMERICAN DEFENSE METEOROLOGICAL SATELLITE PROGRAM. PHOTO © W.T. SULLIVAN III/SCIENCE PHOTO LIBRARY, LONDON __ __ DOUG AITKEN, *RISE*, 1998. CIBACHROME MOUNTED ON PLEXIGLASS, 76.2 X 89 CM. COURTESY COLLECTION WALKER ART CENTER, MINNEAPOLIS; JUSTINE SMITH PURCHASE FUND, 1999

WORLD LIGHTS AND CITY LIGHTS __ Light energy motion. Development money power. Lots of light at important points of the world seen by night. America Europe Japan, concentrations of manifest energy. Few points elsewhere, and Africa hardly even appearing.

Not even astronauts are so lucky as to be able to observe in the magic spell of distance from Earth and all at once, such an impressive array of technology and image. The nocturnal view is more fascinating than the daytime one, where between green zones only the deserts are conspicuous, a reversed world. It only takes one of California's frequent blackouts to gauge the weakness of that prestigious contraption of light, hence of human capacities and power.

That monument to light on the Santa Monica hills, the Getty Center, power money culture, is permanently illuminated. The sun on its windows or on the 16,000 tons of Roman travertine, or the computer that regulates the artificial light. Again from the hills, the Case Study House #22, a sign of Angeleno uncertainty between where inside and outside, watches the lights of the city in the plain below. A thousand films of love or crime have depicted that regular expanse of lights stretching as far the eye can see, the uneasy lure of a city held to be a possible model for the twenty-first century, the provincial metropolitan village that becomes a world city of the angels.

Los Angeles, the original hub of boundless surrounding villatopolises, is a paradigm of mutation: a hard city of quartz, a city living in fear of earthquakes, a Latin metropolis. Everyone racks their brains to think of ways of regulating its rambling sprawl, of improving mobility between the links in its chain, its intricate tangle of highways and the urban, rural, suburban and periurban mosaic that crosses administrative boundaries and is host to wealth and conflict, simple life and consumer temples. **MS**

CASE STUDY HOUSE # 22, LOS ANGELES, 1960, DESIGN PIERRE KOENIG, PHOTO JULIUS SHULMAN. FROM LESLIE JACKSON, *ARCHITECTURE AND INTERIORS OF THE 1950S*, LONDON: PHAIDON, 1994

___ JIM CARREY IN *THE TRUMAN SHOW*, 1998, DIRECTOR PETER WEIR. PHOTO © INTERPHOTO/GRAZIA NERI ___ ___ **SEASIDE, CITY LOCATED ON THE FLORIDA COAST BETWEEN PENSACOLA AND PANAMA CITY**, PLAN SHOWING PARTITION INTO 80-ACRE LOTS, 1985, URBAN DESIGN ANDRES DUANY AND ELIZABETH PLATER-ZYBERK

SEASIDE, FLORIDA __ Designed and as neat and tidy as a movie set, genuine and phony, this little town came into being in 1981. Those seeing *The Truman Show* without knowing that it iss set in a real town, believe it really is a movie set. The idea was inspired by that guru of neo-traditionalists, the Luxembourger architect Léon Krier, who personally suggested the avenues between the houses, and who in 1989 built a house there. (The "ridiculous" – according to American architect Michael Sorkin – consultant to Prince Charles of England, he will build a village in Great Britain in the "New England" style.) Designed to be inexpensive, after a decade it costs ten times more. It is an attempt – like the villas in the Los Angeles sprawl whose new urbanism, here as in Celebration, is meant to be a compact and "urban" alternative – to realize the American Dream.

A small community, its architects maintain that the variety of its styles makes it different from the usual planned communities. Deemed attractive but whimsical, idiosyncratic and claustrophobic, like other forms of "community trap," it has about two hundred and fifty houses, narrow roads for forced pedestrian use, and small squares.

The houses are like lovely hotel rooms. A seaside resort, visitors come for a week and only about twenty families seem to live there all year round. As an "answer" to the failings of big cities and their urban sprawls, this new urbanism does not look effective. But its combative advocates attempt to spread its model. **MS**

MAISONETTES IN A SUBURBAN SPRAWL __ New suburbs on the Los Angeles model are mushrooming here and there, isolated in the landscape. From the city to the old utopia of the suburb and on to the "technoburb" of cars in a nation of tarmac.

The pioneer spirit. Leave your imprint on a new community, in a new place, with new friends. You have toiled all your life for this house. The American Dream: to own your own home, which is part of your identity. We create family values in the most desirable of environments. Anybody who doesn't agree with my values must keep out of here, otherwise they might jeopardize my interest in a comfortable life in the company of people living on the same income as mine. Advertising and a good many inhabitants say identical things.

Others don't see it like that. Everyone here wants to tell you what to do. The people from the apartment block are tremendously aggressive, with nothing to do but be obsessed by the question of security. A barren atmosphere, a garden of Eden turned into merchandise. They miss all the true dimensions of life, the challenge and conquest, diversity and wonder. Here "walls grow in the residents' minds just like they do outside their houses." **MS**

__ **A LAWN FOR EVERY HOUSE**, STILL FROM *EDWARD SCISSORHANDS*, 1990, DIRECTOR TIM BURTON. © 1990 TWENTIETH CENTURY FOX; 2000 TWENTIETH CENTURY FOX HOME ENTERTAINMENT, INC.

__ __ **EAST BAY SUBDIVISION NEAR SAN FRANCISCO, CALIFORNIA**, PHOTO ALEX S. MACLEAN __ __ **PROTOTYPE FOR SOUTHERN CALIFORNIA HOMES, INC.**, LOS ANGELES, 1947, DESIGN
EDWARD BARNES AND HENRY DREYFUSS, PHOTO JULIUS SHULMAN. FROM PETER GÖSSEL, ED., *JULIUS SHULMAN: ARCHITECTURE AND ITS PHOTOGRAPHY*, COLOGNE: TASCHEN, 1998

kate spade
NEW YORK
shoes   handbags   paper

THE LAWN __ Domestic symbol and national icon, an area for strolling into situations of play, work or rest, the lawn represents a zone of uncertainty, a sort of borderline between public and private space, between building and landscape, between dream and reality.
The ambivalence of the lawn arose in the early fifties, when television first showed suburban life, of which the lawn is an indispensable icon. The lawn is thus identified as a synonym of domestic harmony and a mirror in which to reflect the public image of private situations. And again, together with fast food chains, highways and the movie industry, a sign capable of unifying the American landscape.
Not until the first half of the eighties did a few films begin to scratch the surface of this idyllic iconography. *Blue Velvet* by David Lynch (1986) opens with a long subjective shot, where the camera moves across and scours the lawn to reveal its obscure secrets and hidden fantasies. **LP**

CELEBRATION __ The Disney group's Celebration Company project, approved in 1993, shows a division of land into 355 sites, lake and lakeside, golf club, avenues and boulevards, Presbyterian church, schools, parks, downtown, plaza, public offices, an inn, and spaces for future residential and business developments.

The fairy-tale Disney world is made glorious reality. Celebration is a small town – a "village" – for 20,000 inhabitants near Orlando, Florida, and almost joined to the old Epcot theme park that had been intended as an experimental ideal city of the future.

A Disney world for all. Not the childlike one a few minutes away. Not the Vegas "Disney for adults," but a real place in which to live, work and socialize; the mythic "neighborhood" cherished by the traditional strictly American lifestyle in contrast with life in big cities.

Types of houses affordable by all were expressly ruled out. The presence of poor people is not contemplated, thus naturally contradicting the idea of community. Like other high income "privatopias," Celebration looks more like an anti-community niche.

In a "post-neotraditionalist" design, like other instances of a rather different new urbanism, Celebration is an élite town, even though it is aimed at the middle classes and sports an "egalitarian" morphology of homes of mixed values and in six different *styles* – from Mediterranean to colonial. People, it has been said, go there in search of something unattainable in American life today: a better place to live.

Like it or not, and unlike the great urbanists, Disney has succeeded in realizing an urban utopia.

Celebration is a new town *sui generis*. It has even been praised for its chronicles of local life. And they say that to understand it as an inhabited place, we should drop the yardstick used for other Disney operations. **MS**

Above, **Lucy redecorates:** In her new New York pad, Lucy goes as "contemporary" as TV will allow, installing up-to-the-minute modulars with chic, acutely pitched seats, vertigo'd (or not) arms and shadow, buttonless tufting in the manner of Ed Wormley. The straight-edged draped coffee table adjusts upward for makeshift Manhattan dining. Door moldings are squared, not arched, as in the old apartment, wall decorations all but absent. The deep window embrasure behind the piano is framed by pleated pelmet and drapes, which can be drawn over the criss-crossed organdy under-curtains.

Right, **Lucy's furaner:** A schism in the modular sofa (powered by the set director with a rudman, in the earlier episode, left and growing embonforse for Lucy regarding old and new. This armchair from scene two is suddenly resurrected, the armless modular gone. Two ashtrays.

L C R C R O.
D C R T R

TEXT **FRANCES McCUE**
PHOTOGRAPHS **JASON SCHMIDT**
ILLUSTRATIONS **WOUTER DOLK**
PRODUCTION **EMILIO PIMENTEL-REID**
CAPTION HELP **MARK McDONALD**

With her over-lipsticked mouth, pencil-arched eyebrows, and dusky voice, Lucy Ricardo brought the first situation comedy to television. She was an unlikely heroine: a postwar housewife married to a Cuban bandleader, an exuberant perpetrator of style and self-conviction. Never the plain homemaker, her dresses lifted starched collars into midair and her cigarette trousers (for more casual work) marked slim, sure fits. If Lucy's clothes had flounce, they also had class. If her humor was clownish, it was also perfectly timed and wincing.

This was the early 1950s. The show's set was, at first, simple: a New York apartment with a living/dining area, bedroom, nursery, and kitchen. Constrained within the narrow panorama of the show's three rolling cameras, this trompe l'oeil set gradually took on the brash hodgepodge style of its exuberant heroine: the bedroom gained built-in twin beds and sleek shelving; louvered shutters

opened onto the kitchen; the main room sported its low coffee table and ultramodern couch like emblems of the affordable contemporary, all of it gathered and deployed with Lucy's characteristic bravado.

It wasn't easy. Like Buster Keaton, Lucy worked against constraints. While Keaton ran the wrong direction on the roof of a train, Lucy railed against other odds — her fusty neighbors Fred and Ethel (funny, supportive and completely without taste), and husband Ricky, who held the purse strings and didn't care at all about interior design or fashion. Just as Keaton had the power to turn the simplest props into comedic hinges, Lucy wrangled furniture into comic obstructions, forcing it into the house against Ricky's wishes. She stuffed a whole sectional couch into the kitchen until she could convince him to accept it. Her persistence, and ability to win, was both funny and liberating.

In 1950s America, however, the life of a homemaker was anything but liberating. Lucy's comedy was also an escape act. She spent afternoons shaking the dust mop over the mantle and moving the furniture to enhance clutter, all to convince Ricky that their small apartment was crowded and unhealthy. At last he relented and the Ricardos packed up and moved to the suburbs — a rambling Connecticut farmhouse.

The Connecticut house had exposed beams, a large hearth and firewood cabinet. Giving up on her aspirations toward the modern, Lucy ushered in braided rugs, a hutch, and pewter knickknacks. "It's an Early American style," she claimed to Ethel, as if she had traded in her New York life for an older aesthetic. Even the contemporary couch from the apartment was gone, replaced by a dowdy sofa, that sour mix of colonial and Victorian styles that blighted so many households in the 1950s.

No longer was Lucy the finagler who wallpapered and painted the Mertz's apartment in a desire to improve it. In one telling act of desperate renovation, Lucy and Ethel tore apart then relaid all the bricks for a barbecue their husbands had spent the afternoon building, searching for Lucy's lost wedding ring. Here, Lucy's efforts were not to enhance décor, but to find the symbol of the Ricardo's marriage and, ultimately, to save her from Ricky's wrath. In the end, the barbecue became a tilted altar to both Lucy's innovation and her devotion, a suburban totem leaning toward the hideous.

Above, **"Vix as austra vero" (I can hardly call these things my own):** Lucy puzzles over how to fit the now-displaced chic into her new old house, replete with beamed ceilings and roughly bouldered hearth. The Kagan-esque sofa and chairs from the previous scene here reveal more period detail: the sofa seat's sinuous concave curve, the lines of sports-car-like stitching and tufting, and, high, Jughettorically conical legs — anxiousness Manhattan immigrants. The rectangular drop-leaf tension, but its days are numbered.

Above, **Connecticut Conquistadores:** Here Canaan WASP meets L.A. ranch, the sofa suspiciously similar to the dowdy chintz number in apartment number one, now garnished with a dust ruffle. The mantelpiece sports a pewter plate, Paul Revere tankards and other mini-valives to and of the Founding Fathers. At far left, a "Colonial" rocker, probably from Ethan Allen and, at far right, a glimpse of round rag rug and Dutch shoes hung with knickback shoes. No lamps, four ashtrays.

Right, **I Love Lucy Logo:** The bosomy heart — airbrushed with the same pneumatic ethos of Ford and Frederick's of Hollywood — nestles in a following satin backdrop validated from Hollywood promo photos of Lana Turner and other starlets.

"I Love Lucy" - Courtesy of CBS Broadcasting, Inc.

___ "LUCY RICARDO: DECORATOR," TEXT FRANCES MC CUE, PHOTO JASON SCHMIDT. PAGES FROM *NEST*, NO. 4, SPRING 1999 ___ **THE CUNNINGHAM FAMILY IN** *HAPPY DAYS*, TELEVISION SERIES CREATED IN 1974. PHOTO © YORAM KAHANA/SHOOTING STAR/GRAZIA NERI

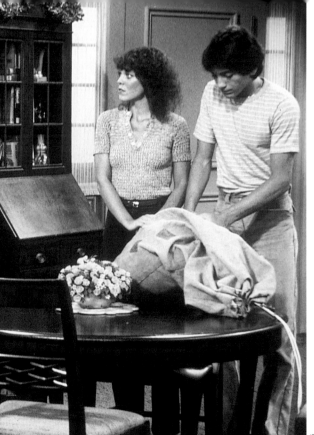

THE GOODLIFE

Photographed
by
STEVEN MEISEL

Fashion Editor: *BRANA WOLF*   Hair: *EUGENE SOULEIMAN FOR AVEDA*   Make-Up: *PAT McGRATH FOR AVEDA*
Models: *CAROLYN MURPHY & CHANDRA NORTH & MYKA & CHRIS BROWN & JUSTIN CHRISTENSEN & COLIN EGGLESFIELD & THE KIDS*

Nella pagina accanto. Per Carolyn e per il ragazzo. Camicia a righe e jeans: T-shirt e pantaloni: tutto Moschino Jeans. Per i bambini. Camicie scozzesi, gola, pantaloni, abitino e maglietta: tutto C.K. Jeans Kids.

470

"THE GOODLIFE," PHOTO STEVEN MEISEL, FASHION EDITOR BRANA WOLF. PAGES FROM *VOGUE ITALIA*, NO. 566, OCTOBER 1997

"THE GOODLIFE." PHOTO STEVEN MEISEL. FASHION EDITOR BRANA WOLF. PAGES FROM *VOGUE ITALIA*, NO. 566, OCTOBER 1997

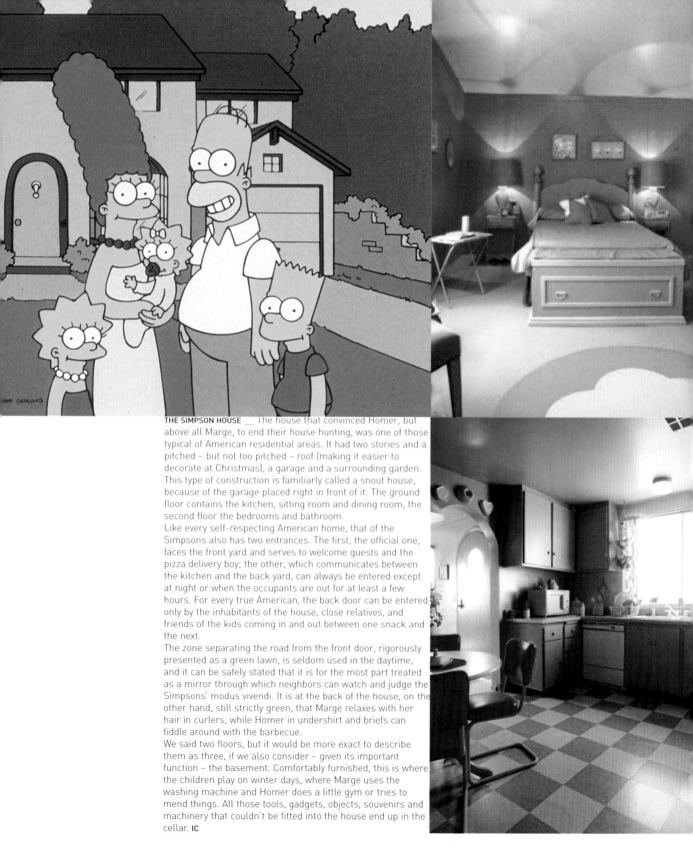

THE SIMPSON HOUSE ___ The house that convinced Homer, but above all Marge, to end their house hunting, was one of those typical of American residential areas. It had two stories and a pitched – but not too pitched – roof (making it easier to decorate at Christmas), a garage and a surrounding garden. This type of construction is familiarly called a snout house, because of the garage placed right in front of it. The ground floor contains the kitchen, sitting room and dining room, the second floor the bedrooms and bathroom.

Like every self-respecting American home, that of the Simpsons also has two entrances. The first, the official one, faces the front yard and serves to welcome guests and the pizza delivery boy; the other, which communicates between the kitchen and the back yard, can always be entered except at night or when the occupants are out for at least a few hours. For every true American, the back door can be entered only by the inhabitants of the house, close relatives, and friends of the kids coming in and out between one snack and the next.

The zone separating the road from the front door, rigorously presented as a green lawn, is seldom used in the daytime, and it can be safely stated that it is for the most part treated as a mirror through which neighbors can watch and judge the Simpsons' modus vivendi. It is at the back of the house, on the other hand, still strictly green, that Marge relaxes with her hair in curlers, while Homer in undershirt and briefs can fiddle around with the barbecue.

We said two floors, but it would be more exact to describe them as three, if we also consider – given its important function – the basement. Comfortably furnished, this is where the children play on winter days, where Marge uses the washing machine and Homer does a little gym or tries to mend things. All those tools, gadgets, objects, souvenirs and machinery that couldn't be fitted into the house end up in the cellar. IC

___ MODEL HOME FOR CELEBRATION, A "PERFECT CITY" IN FLORIDA. PHOTO © ENRICO FERORELLI/GRAZIA NERI

Close encounters of the furred kind: Teletubbies (left) and their HQ, shot by paparazzi who dodged the BBC's ban on publicity for the puppets

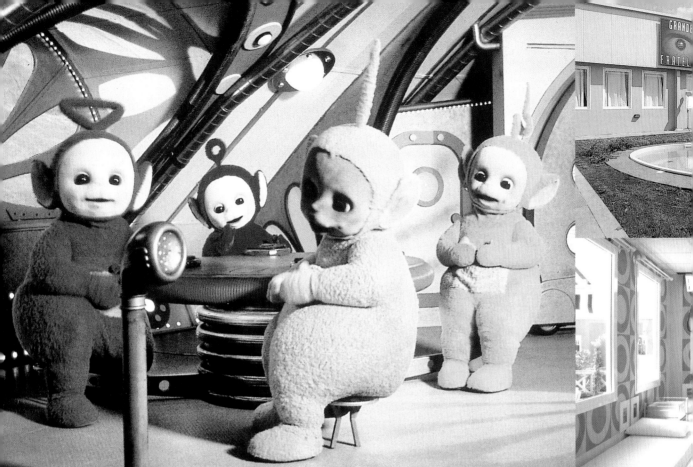

TELETUBBIES ___ *Teletubbies* is the BBC and Ragdoll Productions program for toddlers aged between 9 and 17 months. The lead roles are played by four alien-looking puppets – Po, Laa Laa, Dipsy and Tinky Winky – who have antennas on their heads and a TV screen set in their tummies. Onto these are projected and re-projected a second time – to satisfy the babies' desire for repetition – scenes of real children and adults filmed in a variety of leisure activities. The puppets live in Teletubbyland in the Teletubbies' house, the Tubbytronic Superdome. In reality this is a structure situated in the English Warwickshire countryside, where real actors dressed in colored fur tracksuits perform. Other elements of their environment are a vacuum cleaner (the Noo Noo), flowers, rabbits, a sun-child, a windmill, a toaster, a creamer and a loudspeaker-receiver emitting songs and lullabies. The program, say its producers, is responsible and amusing, conceived to develop the aptitudes of tiny tots, their listening capacities and their imagination. It makes them feel at home with technology and teaches them simple movements: like standing up, walking, climbing steps, jumping up and down, and, through the narrator, simple words suitable for describing simple experiences. Despite the program's success, a lot of criticism has been provoked by the commercial initiatives and merchandising associated with it. The objections have been particularly vociferous in the United States, where a promotional agreement on the Teletubbies was signed between Burger King and Itsy Bitzy Entertainment Co., just after a report released by the American Academy of Pediatrics claimed that the increasing use of television is recorded as a significant factor in the rising number of people suffering from obesity, a socially important phenomenon in that country. **AT**

_ _ THE BIG BROTHER HOUSE IN CINECITTÀ, 2000. PHOTO © DANILO CERRETI/STUDIO PIEMME/MUCI _ _ INTERIOR OF THE BIG BROTHER HOUSE IN CINECITTÀ, 2001. PHOTO © NEW E.R.A. _ _ THE CONFESSIONAL IN THE BIG BROTHER HOUSE, AMERICAN VERSION. PHOTO © CORBIS SYGMA/GRAZIA NERI

___THE FURNISHED FÜRNI HOUSE, STILLS FROM THE FILM *FIGHT CLUB*, 1999, DIRECTOR DAVID FINCHER

FIGHT CLUB __ A change in life every now and then is a good thing. . . . Choosing how to live is now possible at last. The dream scenes that we used to gaze at through windows are here, within everybody's reach . . . To furnish your everyday life just come and see us . . . We call it democratic design. **Ikea**, 1998

Fight Club has been described as a fascist movie, at various levels: the space monkeys and the terrorist commando, organized by Tyler Durden (a violent Brad Pitt liberator) are clearly paramilitary and fascist with their black uniforms and shaved heads, and in their blind obedience to their leader's laws and discipline. The reference to evolution is fascist, with a violence that can liberate and purify subjects from the fascism of the brands and goods that create the needs that inform our society.

"Like many others, I too had become a slave of the Ikea nest trend. People I know, who in the old days used to go to the bathroom with a porn glossy, nowadays take in an Ikea catalog," says the narrator, a mild and frustrated Edward Norton, as the empty apartment in the space of a long shot conforms to his darkest desires, sweeping straight from the picture of the catalog to the picture that the catalog has of him. To be unfinished, like a house full of condiments but with no food. In *Fight Club* the insomniac narrator eats mustard with a knife, wearing boxer shorts, a shirt and tie with a penguin pattern on them: the penguin being his animal guide.

"I had quite a decent stereo, a wardrobe that was just beginning to be really respectable. I only needed a little more to be complete," complains the narrator. But Durden philosophizes: "You have to be incomplete or the things you possess will end up possessing you. Martha Stewart is only polishing the handles on the Titanic." **AT**

Novitá!

Office

Vanity

Dining

olation, intimacy, fantasy.

The Comfort Unit....
Roll up service carts mean you
never have to leave bed

___ __ ANDREA ZITTEL, **THE A-Z BED BOOK**, CATALOGUE PRODUCED IN COORDINATION WITH *TRANSCRIPT (A JOURNAL OF VISUAL CULTURE)*, UNIVERSITY OF DUNDEE, SCOTLAND. © ANDREA ZITTEL 1995. PHOTO COURTESY ANDREA ROSEN GALLERY, NEW YORK

Text Dodie Bellamy   Photographs David Levinthal

Cold War Barbie

BARBIE DINING ROOM/SNACK PLAY SET __ With this set Barbie and Ken can sit down and have a wonderful, candlelight dinner followed by a delicious slice of Raspberry Shortcake for dessert – all the while overlooking the lights of the city glimmer in the distant valley. There's no doubt about it, the Barbie Dining Room set has everything you need for lots of fun! Includes dining table, chairs, candle holder, candles, dinnerware and pretend food pieces. Colors may vary. Product may not be exactly as depicted.
From the **Mattel** Web site
http://www.quikbuy.com/barbie.html

__ __ **"COLD WAR BARBIE,"** TEXT DODIE BELLAMY, PHOTO DAVID LEVINTHAL. PAGES FROM *NEST*, NO. 1, 1997 __ __ **BARBIE DINING ROOM, SNACK PLAY SET** PRODUCED BY MATTEL. (HTTP://WWW.QUIKBUY.COM/BARBIE.HTML)

Disegno pagina: Cappotto di pelle con trengli da plica, Sportmax. Borsa Anol Lagerfeld Gallery. Tulle pagina precedente. Chemisier di chiffon a pois. Cotone. Accli Pages e Agent Reba.

Impresa pagina: Cappotto dreased ti lana Calvi Walnuti da clema Max Mara. Slah pagina precedente. Abito di chiffongaldi di pellapeltina. Roberto Cavalli. Gioielli di data ti Cartier

Pull V-neck di cashmere a costine con maniche a sbuffo e pantaloni di seta moirée, Cesare Fabbri. Collier a cuore, Chopard

___ **"SERIES 5. LIFE,"** PHOTO STEVEN MEISEL, FASHION EDITOR LORI GOLDSTEIN. PAGES FROM *VOGUE ITALIA*, NO. 599, JULY 2000

A jacket Tiffany for bianco. col. azzurra, Petit pois Valentino Studio, Borsa Karl Lagerfeld Paris, collant rosso, décolleté in vernice, e guanti in tela, Max Mara.

Guanti di ninna infine di cotta plastico e press grembiule di insulin bagno di Hollis gilted, Helm & Tiffany, Borsa Karl Lagerfeld Paris, collant Wolford, décolleté in vernice, Max Mara.

Tiffany & Co. Manicure Gina Viviano for Cloutier.

LAURIE SIMMONS ___ *Kaleidoscope House* is a doll's house designed by artist Laurie Simmons and architect Peter Wheelwright.

Commissioned by Bozart Toys to join a line of artist toys now on the market, *Kaleidoscope House* started as a modernist reconsideration of the good old Victorian doll's house. Its interiors are enclosed by transparent polycarbonate walls that change color according to the rainbow spectrum.

To furnish the rooms a range of furniture is available, designed by names that include Karim Rashid, Jonathan Adler and Ron Arad. There is also a miniature contemporary art kit to choose from, with works by Cindy Sherman, Peter Halley, Carrol Dunham and others.

Kaleidoscope House is the product of interests long shared by its two creators in the various aspects of domestic life, but also of personal experience with their respective children. So it is not surprising that Simmons and Wheelwright decided to put themselves into the house, too. After all, aren't we really both the producers and the products of the space we occupy? **EDC**

___ LAURIE SIMMONS, *KALEIDOSCOPE HOUSE # 1*, 2000, COLOR PHOTOGRAPH, 40.5 X 61 CM. COURTESY THE ARTIST ___ ___ LAURIE SIMMONS AND PETER WHEELWRIGHT, *KALEIDOSCOPE HOUSE*, 2000

___ ___ **CASE STUDY HOUSE # 22**, LOS ANGELES, 1960, DESIGN PIERRE KOENIG, PHOTO JULIUS SHULMAN. FROM *JULIUS SHULMAN: ARCHITECTURE AND ITS PHOTOGRAPHY*,
COLOGNE: TASCHEN, 1998

PIERRE KOENIG __ "It was the panorama that demanded a contemporary style," recalls the client for Pierre Koenig's celebrated house, which from the Hollywood hills commands a sweeping view of Los Angeles. *Less is more* carried to the extremes of hedonistic abandon is that "contemporary style," which originated in California in the forties as the principal expression of a modern alternative to traditional residential architecture. In the postwar building rush, it was not construction principles that singled out one trend from another. They had a modular composition and the prefabrication of units in common, but not the demands of taste. The Case Study House program was launched in 1945 by the California magazine *Arts & Architecture* in support of the modern outlook, if not its creation. The aim was to propose models of high quality living but at a reasonable cost by appointing architects of different ages and degrees of renown. By the late fifties, and in the face of economic requirements that had changed considerably, with the Case Study House #22 Koenig came close to the conclusion of a victorious cycle. A few years before, when the outcome of that architectural dispute had already become clear, it had been defined thus by modern circles: "The design of houses is today in a state of pleasant confusion. . . . Pleasant because we want our houses to be pleasant. It might be said that current fashion is pleasure itself." (Emerson Gable in the introduction to *A Treasury of Contemporary Houses*, published in 1954). **RD**

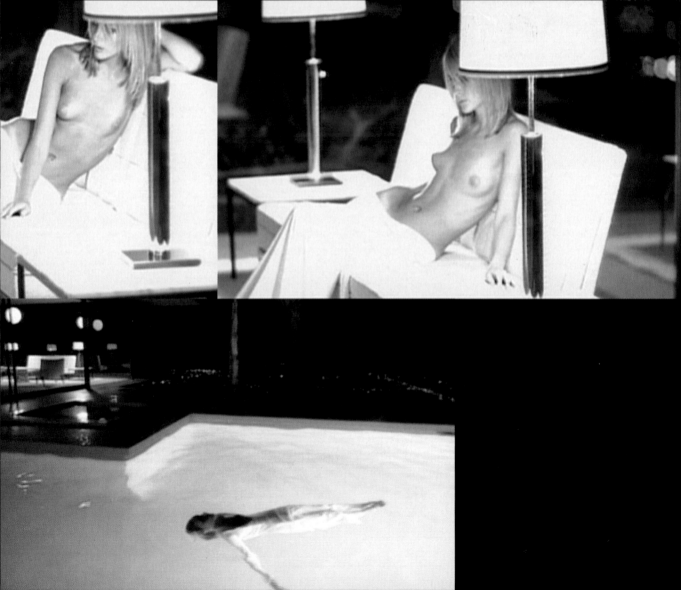

___ ___ **THE ARCHITECT JOHN LAUTNER, RIGHT, SHOWING CLIENT PAUL SHEATS THE MODEL OF THE HOUSE'S FIRST DESIGN, 1960**. FROM BARBARA-ANN CAMPBELL-LANGE, *JOHN LAUTNER*, COLOGNE: TASCHEN, 1999

SERIES
1
L.A.

____ **"SERIES 1 L.A.,"** PHOTO STEVEN MEISEL. PAGES FROM *VOGUE ITALIA*, NO. 595, MARCH 2000. LOCATION **SHEATS/GOLDSTEIN HOUSE**, BEVERLY HILLS, LOS ANGELES, 1963, 1980-1994, DESIGN JOHN LAUTNER

___ _"**SERIES 1 L.A.**," PHOTO STEVEN MEISEL. PAGES FROM *VOGUE ITALIA*, NO. 595, MARCH 2000. LOCATION **SHEATS/GOLDSTEIN HOUSE**, BEVERLY HILLS, LOS ANGELES, 1963, 1980-1994, DESIGN JOHN LAUTNER

ABITO LUNGO DI MOUSSELINE A
POIS, DONALD DEAL. OCCHIALI LI-
LY ET CIE, BEVERLY HILLS; OREC-
CHINI, COLLANA DI PIETRE, BRAC-
CIALETTO E ANELLI: MARTIN KATZ
LTD; COLLANA DI PLEXIGLAS A
BOULES E BRACCIALE CON PIETRE,
BILL BLASS; BORSA LAMBERTSON
TRUEX; SCARPE DOLCE & GABBANA.

TASCHEN __ Only Angelika and Benedikt Taschen offer books about the natural sciences next to others that are soft porn. Unconventionality and attractive prices are the hallmark of their products, which manage to be competitive in a global publishing market dominated by the big corporations. Taschen has shops and offices in London, Madrid, New York, Paris and Tokyo. But its head offices are in Cologne, in a nineteenth-century building converted into a sort of exhibition space, with works by Helmut Newton and Martin Kippenberger.

Taschen publishes books on art, design, architecture, interior design and cinema, without worrying about distinctions between high and low culture, between leading lights in the star system and practically unknown authors. In this way their monographs on great twentieth-century architects like Richard Neutra or Antoni Gaudí have the same glamour as that of Betty Page; just as Nobuyoshi Araki, Roy Stuart, Richard Kern and other erotic publications vie with pop stars like Salvador Dalí, the best-selling book of the eighties. That, moreover, is precisely how the Taschen adventure began, thanks to the intuitions of its founder, Benedikt. It was he who in the eighties used a family loan to buy forty thousand copies of an American book on Magritte, which he later sold in Germany at three times the price. Since then Taschen has increasingly pinned its faith on the selling power of images, without bothering about linguistic and geographic distances. And when they also moved into Los Angeles, the Taschens bought a typical Taschen icon: Chemosphere, a mushroom house on the Hollywood hills overlooking the lights of the Universal City. **LP**

___ __ **HOUSE FOR LEONARD MALIN (CHEMOSPHERE)**, HOLLYWOOD, CALIFORNIA, 1960, DESIGN JOHN LAUTNER. FROM BARBARA-ANN CAMPBELL-LANGE, *JOHN LAUTNER*, COLOGNE: TASCHEN, 1999

___ ANGELIKA AND BENEDIKT TASCHEN IN CHEMOSPHERE, PHOTO JOHN MIDGLEY. FRONT AND BACK TASCHEN CATALOGUE COVER, FALL/WINTER 2001-2002 ___ COVERS OF BOOKS
PUBLISHED BY TASCHEN, FROM THE FALL/WINTER 2001-2002 CATALOGUE

0 5 1

___ BARBARA MAC LAMPRECHT, *NEUTRA: COMPLETE WORKS*, EDITED BY PETER GÖSSEL, WITH PHOTOS BY JULIUS SHULMAN, COLOGNE: TASCHEN, 2000, VOLUME 1. 32 X 41 X 5 CM

INSIDE PALM SPRINGS

IN THE FREY

Albert Frey designed 200 buildings
in the middle of the California desert.
With their sharp edges and modern
lines, they're a graphic metaphor for
this season's hottest prints.

Photographs by Marcus Mâm.
Styled by Elizabeth Stewart.

Albert Frey came to
America in 1930 from
Zurich and moved to Palm
Springs in 1934. There, he
developed an architectural
style now known as "desert
modernism." Throughout his
75-year career, he used
inexpensive industrial
materials to sleek, elegant
advantage. In 1963 he
blasted through three tons
of rock to build his small
home, now a museum, and
lived there until his death
in 1998. Carolina Herrera's
graphic silk dress, $2,000,
sets off Frey's minimalism.
At Carolina Herrera, 954
Madison Avenue. Earrings,
Ben-Amun. Belt, DKNY.
Shoes, Versace.

___ "IN THE FREY," PHOTO MARCUS MÅM, STYLING ELISABETH STEWART. PAGES FROM *FASHIONS OF THE TIMES - THE NEW YORK TIMES MAGAZINE*, PART 2, SPRING 2001

City Hall, above, which Frey completed in 1952, was (along with the Loewy House) one of his favorite buildings. Jersey top, $145, and stretch cotton miniskirt, $160, Sportmax. At MaxMara stores. Sunglasses, Morganthal Fredericks. Earrings and bracelet, Kenneth Jay Lane. Handbag, Judith Leiber. Belt, Sportmax.

Frey designed this Ralph's supermarket, left, in 1960, when it was called the Alpha Beta. While the store awaits the bulldozer, Palm Springs preservationists are trying to stop demolition. Shop — or protest — in your silk trench coat, $540. At BCBG Max Azria, 770 Madison Avenue, or call (888) 636-2224. Brooch in hair, Ben-Amun. Handbag, Tod's. Shoes, Jimmy Choo.

Hair: Alex Dizon for Artist by Timothy Priano. Makeup: Lisa Storey for Independent NY. Fashion assistant: George Kotsiopoulos. Model: Juliana McCarthy.

159

Catch the aerial tram leading up Chino Canyon at the Tramway Station which Frey, a student of Le Corbusier, built in 1963. For the trip, students of fashion may want to slip into Iceberg's viscose rayon top, $276, and pants, $355. At Iceberg, 772 Madison Avenue and Beverly Hills. Earrings, Ben-Amun. Necklace, DKNY. Shoes, D & G by Dolce & Gabbana. Handbag, Tod's.

___ __ **"IN THE FREY,"** PHOTO MARCUS MÅM, STYLING ELISABETH STEWART. PAGES FROM *FASHIONS OF THE TIMES - THE NEW YORK TIMES MAGAZINE*, PART 2, SPRING 2001

A DRIVE THROUGH ALBERT FREY'S Palm Springs

ILLUSTRATION BY BILL BROWN

Of the 200 projects that Frey designed in Palm Springs between 1934 and 1988, these are the most intact and notable.

1. **Tramway Gas Station** (now Montana St. Martin Gallery), 2901 North Palm Canyon Drive.
2. **Tramway Valley Station,** Tramway Road.
3. **Carey-Pirozzi House,** 651 West Via Escuela.
4. **Loewy House,** 600 West Panorama Drive.
5. **Villa Hermosa,** 155 Hermosa Place.
6. **Nichols Building,** 891-899 North Palm Canyon.
7. **Clark & Frey Office Building,** 879 North Palm Canyon.
8. **Kocher-Samson Building,** 766 North Palm Canyon.
9. **Swanson Office Building,** 740 North Palm Canyon.
10. **Frey House II,** 686 West Palisades Drive.

11. **Premiere Apartments,** (at the Orchid Tree Inn), 261 South Belardo Road.
12. **First Church of Christ Scientist,** Riverside Drive at Random Road.
13. **Cree House II,** Raymond Drive, Cathedral City.
14. **Ralph's Supermarket,** Ramon Road at Sunrise Way.
15. **City Hall,** 3200 East Tahquitz Canyon Way.
16. **Fire Station I,** 277 North Indian Canyon Drive.
17. **Ballentine Movie Colony Inn,** 726 North Indian Canyon Drive.
18. **Katherine Finchy School,** 777 East Tachevah Road.
19. **Sieroty House,** 695 East Vereda Sur.
20. **Albert Frey House** (at the Palm Springs Racquet Club), 2743 North Indian Canyon Drive.

Photographs by Koto Bolofo

Esquire heads to the Frey House, where, with the help of a few of today's most interesting young actors, we re-create scenes from Godard's stylish 1963 classic, *Contempt.* What better way to demonstrate the timeless elegance of the latest look in men's fashion: the crisp silhouette of midcentury suits and sport coats in graphic black and white.

ESQUIRE 151

__ __ CINDY SHERMAN, *UNTITLED FILM STILL # 50*, 1979, GELATIN SILVER PHOTOGRAPH, 20.5 X 25.5 CM. COURTESY THE ARTIST AND METRO PICTURES, NEW YORK

a perfect world

Every character in a perfect world travel studies...and like full designs to are willing to accommodate the most heightened of realities.

PHOTOGRAPHED BY PHILIP-LORCA DICORCIA

[from left] **Daryl K.** stretch wool jersey top and wool flannel pants, at Barneys New York and Daryl K, New York. On her **Gap's** cotton shirt and cotton pants, from Gap, nationwide. **Missoni** wool cardigan, wool turtleneck and wool skirt. At Missoni, New York, Marida Bührk, shoes.

[from left]
Calvin Klein's wool and cashmere
shell and skirt, at Bloomingdale's,
New York and Calvin Klein, New York.
Chanel shoes.
On him: **Polo Ralph Lauren**'s wool suit,
cotton shirt and tie, at Polo Ralph Lauren,
New York.
On little boy: **Gap**'s cotton shirt and cot-
ton pants, at Gap, nationwide.
On her: **Lucien Pellat-Finet**'s cashmere
sweater, at Lucien Pellat-Finet New York,
with **Narciso Rodriguez**'s wool skirt, at
Bergdorf Goodman. Tretorn shoes.

Styled by Michel Botbol. Production by
Shaheen Knox/Nice Productions; casting
by Andrea Kurzman, Inc.; hair by Steven
Ward for Garren New York; makeup by
Mark Carrasquillo for Atlantis New York;
models: Lynn Howland/Ford, Lisa
Parker/Ford, Ryan Denver/CED, Sheena
McGalan/Margaret & Schuller and Peter
Hudson/GMT. Fashion assistants: Matthew
Edelstein and Sage Hunihan.

Opening cityscape shot from Hugo Boss
Showroom, New York.

[from left]
On him: **Paul Smith**'s wool
sweater and cotton pants, at select
Barneys New York; with **Gap**'s
cotton shirt, at Gap, nationwide.
Michael Kors' cashmere
turtleneck, cashmere cardigan
and leather skirt at Neiman
Marcus, Beverly Hills and Jeffrey,
New York. Chanel shoes.
Prada's wool coat with appliqué
leather leaves, at Prada, Chicago
and New York.

)
wool melton peacoat by
..rdert, at Saks Fifth Avenue,
York; Eric Bergère's cotton
..ra spandex pants, at Marly
...erry Hill, NJ. Hermès bag,
...Vuitton shoes.
..., **Paul Smith**'s wool/
..., at select Barney's stores.
...ap's cotton chino and
...shirts at Gap, nationwide.

Hermès' wool shirt and wool
and cotton pants, by Martin
Margiela, at Hermès, nationwide.

LESS IS MORE __ In 1922, when he was young and working in Berlin, the architect Ludwig Mies van der Rohe, apropos his very theoretical project for an Office Building, wrote, in German: "Maximum effect, with the least wastage of means." Already the expression hinted at the "personal" motto that, much later at his retrospective at MoMA in New York, the Mephistophelean curator Philip Johnson, was to attribute to him. Even after that there were times when Mies would repeat the words "Less is more" in English. Without elaborating on his spiritual, tectonic, elegant, perfect works. And without imagining that by that same slogan, he would point the way for artists toward a splendid aesthetic horizon. In their efforts to reach that horizon, unattainable anyway, tomorrow's artists will work on the materiality of pure, crude or polished material; the only development in the early and absolutely immaterial years of the twenty-first century. **VS**

PHILIP JOHNSON IN THE GLASS HOUSE. PHOTO © INGE SCHOENTHAL FELTRINELLI/GRAZIA NERI

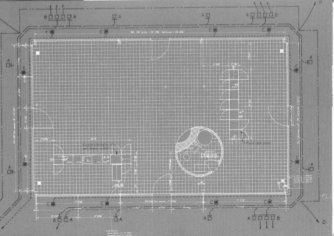

A new romanticism characterizes the glass house built by Philip Johnson on a wooded hill in New Canaan, Connecticut. This is especially apparent at night when the candles and fireplace, reflected repeatedly in the glass walls, seem to have escaped out of doors to float in the air among the trees. Except for bed, bath and kitchen-unit lights, this one-room house is illuminated by carefully planned indirect lighting from outside sources. Above: the room lighted by candles and fireplace. Left: the room lighted indirectly from the exterior of the house. Below: architect's blueprint presents a detailed analysis of lighting scheme.

D. Light is shot up at the ceiling inside, from floodlights buried in a ground trench just outside the plate-glass walls, to be diffused over the room. This provides the principal lighting of the interior.
The light is voice-controlled—a microphone picks up the magic syllables, known only to the owner, that start the motor-operated regulator.

C. At night, spotlights located on the roof of the house pick out the surrounding trees to form a luminous backdrop.

...o the lawn ...iving ...thin, ...end-...und.

B. A mixture of spots and floodlights placed at the foot of trees, in the near and far background, light the landscape and give further perspective to the tree backdrop mentioned in C.

The architect's schedule for the lighting of the house and its surrounding areas.

Romantic Lighting for a Glass House

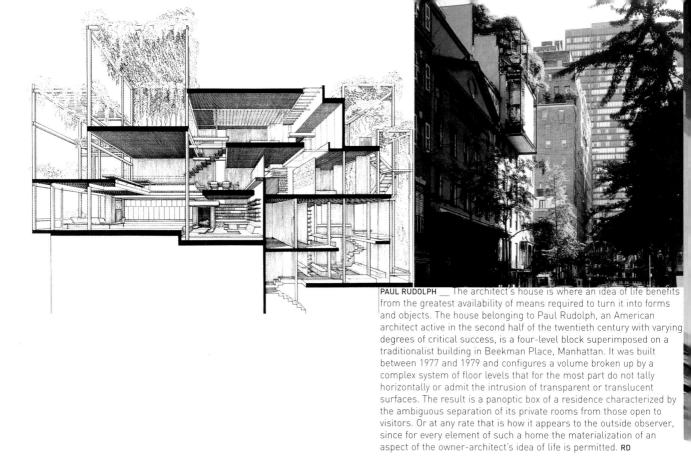

PAUL RUDOLPH __ The architect's house is where an idea of life benefits from the greatest availability of means required to turn it into forms and objects. The house belonging to Paul Rudolph, an American architect active in the second half of the twentieth century with varying degrees of critical success, is a four-level block superimposed on a traditionalist building in Beekman Place, Manhattan. It was built between 1977 and 1979 and configures a volume broken up by a complex system of floor levels that for the most part do not tally horizontally or admit the intrusion of transparent or translucent surfaces. The result is a panoptic box of a residence characterized by the ambiguous separation of its private rooms from those open to visitors. Or at any rate that is how it appears to the outside observer, since for every element of such a home the materialization of an aspect of the owner-architect's idea of life is permitted. **RD**

___ __ **RUDOLPH HOUSE**: CROSS-SECTION, EXTERIOR ON BEEKMAN PLACE, LIVING ROOM WITH VIEW OF DINING ROOM AND GLIMPSE OF BEDROOM, NEW YORK, 1977-1979 AND SUCCESSIVE RENOVATIONS, DESIGN PAUL RUDOLPH. PHOTO PETER AARON/ESTO

___ **BEDROOM IN PAUL RUDOLPH'S FIRST APARTMENT ON BEEKMAN PLACE**, NEW YORK, 1967, DESIGN PAUL RUDOLPH. PHOTO PRINTS AND PHOTOGRAPH DIVISION, LIBRARY OF CONGRESS

___ JILL ST. JOHN AND SEAN CONNERY IN *DIAMONDS ARE FOREVER*, 1971, DIRECTOR GUY HAMILTON

__ __ **HALSTON IN HIS NEW YORK HOUSE, DESIGNED BY PAUL RUDOLPH,** 1978. PHOTO HARRY BENSON © GRAZIA NERI

HALSTON __ I was fortunate to have been in the townhouse in the early eighties, when I first arrived in New York, and I remember being stunned by the beauty of it. Clean, simple, streamlined. You walked down into this huge sunken living room; the furniture and the color of the rooms were this perfect shade of gray. It really had an effect on me. In many ways I have integrated this design philosophy into my life. **Tom Ford**

Halston, born Roy Frowick Halston in 1932 in Des Moines, Iowa, was the first fashion superstar. A fashion designer with an aesthetic vision expressed in hundreds of products and over thirty licenses – from accessories to linens, carpets and wigs. He succeeded in dressing the international jet set as well as the Braniff airline hostesses, the Boy Scouts of America and the athletes at the 1976 Olympics. Like his friend Andy Warhol, he understood immediately the cult of celebrity and declared that he was good at his job only in proportion to the famous people he dressed: Jackie Kennedy and Martha Graham, Elizabeth Taylor and Liza Minelli, Bianca Jagger and Bebe Paley – none of the female icons of the seventies escaped his charm. Ironically, Halston was the first fashion designer to become almost more famous than the women he dressed.

He created a lifestyle where every detail was double-checked, from dresses to music, lights and fragrances, from interior designs in a thousands shades of gray to orchids scattered about his mirrored rooms. His minimalist aesthetic blended the glamour of art deco and haute couture traditional luxury with an uninhibited vision of the modern world and its infatuation with freedom and comfort. He defined the taste of an epoch, the sexy seventies of Studio 54, dressing them with cashmere drapery, silk caftans and ultra-suede jackets, and suffusing them with the decadent, nauseating scent of his perfume. For the bottle – a giant tear in black glass with a dimpled surface, created in collaboration with designer Elsa Peretti – Halston requested and got permission for the logo to be omitted from it. **ST**

TOM FORD ON *LA CHAISE* **BY CHARLES EAMES**, PHOTO SANTI CALECA. PAGE FROM *INTERNI*, NO. 485, NOVEMBER 1998

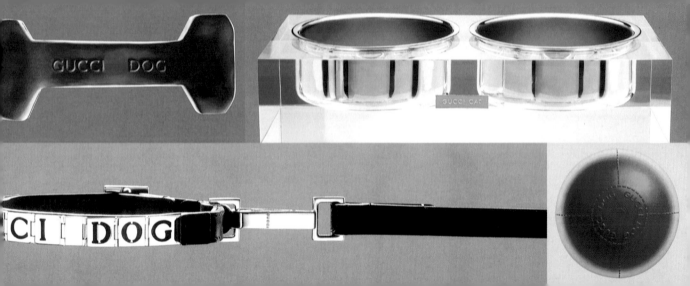

___ __ **GUCCI HANDCUFFS**, USED BY SYLVIE FLEURY FOR THE INVITATION TO HER SOLO SHOW AT GALERIE THADDAEUS ROPAC, PARIS, JANUARY 2002. PHOTO © CHARLES DUPRAT, COURTESY GALERIE THADDAEUS ROPAC, PARIS

___ __ **MARCELLO MASTROIANNI AND URSULA ANDRESS** IN *LA DECIMA VITTIMA*, 1965, DIRECTOR ELIO PETRI. PHOTO © FARABOLAPHOTO

___ __ **FURNITURE DESIGNED BY EILEEN GRAY IN MADAME MATHIEU LÉVY'S APARTMENT ON RUE DE LOTA**, PARIS, 1933. FROM PHILIPPE GARNER, *EILEEN GRAY: DESIGNER AND ARCHITECT*, COLOGNE: BENEDIKT TASCHEN VERLAG, 1993

___ ___ **COSTUME NATIONAL STORE, TOKYO,** 1996, DESIGN ENNIO CAPASA IN COLLABORATION WITH COSIMO ANTONACI ___ ___ **COSTUME NATIONAL STORE, NEW YORK,** 2001, DESIGN ENNIO CAPASA IN COLLABORATION WITH MARMOL & RADZINER**.** PHOTO DAVID JOSEPH

GLASSHOUSE, COSTUME NATIONAL HEADQUARTERS, MILAN, 2001, DESIGN ENNIO CAPASA IN COLLABORATION WITH VUDAFIERI PARTNERS. PHOTO SANTI CALECA

0 8 5

__ __ EXTERIOR VIEW OF **VILLA NOAILLES**, HYÈRES, 1923, DESIGN ROBERT MALLET-STEVENS. FROM FRANÇOIS CARRASSAN, ED., *LA VILLA NOAILLES: UNE AVENTURE MODERNE*, PARIS: FLAMMARION, 2001

MODERN CÔTE D'AZUR __ Patronage of avant-garde and, in particular, of surrealist artists, combined with modern body care, were what distinguished the life of Charles and Marie Laure de Noailles at their villa at Hyères on the French Riviera, which was originally designed for them by Robert Mallet-Stevens in 1923 and enlarged and modified by Stevens and other architects in subsequent years. One of these interventions was the installation of the covered pool. That event, extraordinary for the period, prompted Charles to commission from Jacques Manuel a film, entitled *Biceps et Bijoux* (1928). "Young, fond of sport and the outdoor life, and friendly toward any novelties expressing the desires of a generation, they belong and wish to belong to their time was how Charles and his circle were described. Diving, gym equipment, a bar, changing room and sauna – once again everything had been thought of for the comfort of their guests. Whilst on the walls, large mirrors multiplied reflections of the pool, a solarium provided an extension of the south beach, where four armchairs in green lacquered wood and assorted shades of canvas were set out for sunbathing and for the unprecedented pleasures of relaxation. Since Madame Récamier, never had women bared so much leg. With dark and short hair, the new "sweater ladies" were initiated into the joys of swimming. Like dance steps, all the strokes were new: the overarm stroke, the crawl, the trudgen. And the aquatic sports were now countered by a new allure, an informal style of dress consisting of open-necked supple blouses, pure tussah-silk and generously open sandals." (Laurence Benaïm, "La vie de château selon Marie Laure," in *La villa Noailles. Une aventure moderne*, Paris: Flammarion, 2001). **RD**

__ __ STILLS FROM *BICEPS ET BIJOUX*, FILMED IN 1928 BY JACQUES MANUEL AT VILLA NOAILLES, HYÈRES __ __ INTERIOR OF **VILLA NOAILLES**, HYÈRES, 1923, DESIGN ROBERT MALLET-STEVENS. PHOTO JEAN-MARIE DEL MORAL. FROM FRANÇOIS CARRASSAN, ED., *LA VILLA NOAILLES: UNE AVENTURE MODERNE*, PARIS: FLAMMARION, 2001

LIVING ROOM OF YVES SAINT LAURENT'S PARIS HOUSE, PHOTO HORST P. HORST. FROM BARBARA PLUMB, *HORST: INTERIORS*, BOSTON: BULFINCH PRESS, 1993. PHOTO © THE CONDÉ NAST PUBLICATIONS, INC.

___ YVES SAINT LAURENT PHOTOGRAPHED FROM BEHIND DURING ONE OF HIS FASHION SHOWS, PARIS, 29 JANUARY 1962, PHOTO © PIERRE BOULAT/GRAZIA NERI

DAS AN

EIN BLATT ZUR E
ABENDLAENDISC
IN OESTERREICH:
VON ADOLF LOOS

TAILORS AND OUTFITTERS
GOLDMAN & SALATSCH

K. U. K. HOF-
LIEFERANTEN
K. BAYER. HOF-
LIEFERANTEN

KAMMER-
LIEFERANTEN
Sr. k. u. k. Hoheit des
Herrn Erzherzog Josef
etc. etc.

WIEN, I. GRABEN 20.

H
A
f
V

Gr

Ei

An

Üt

C
be

CO
er

____ ADOLF LOOS, RIGHT, IN THE KNIZE PARIS HEADQUARTERS, DESIGNED BY HIM IN 1927-1928. LEFT, PROBABLY FRITZ WOLFF, OWNER OF THE VIENNESE FASHION HOUSE
____ A HOUSE FOR JOSEPHINE BAKER IN PARIS, VIEW OF THE RELIEF MODEL, 1928, DESIGN ADOLF LOOS

Preis 20 h   Nr. 2   WIEN, 15. OKTOBER 1903   Preis 20 h

ERE

DAS ANDERE

UEHRUNG
R KULTUR
CHRIEBEN
I. JAHR

EIN BLATT ZUR EINFUEHRUNG
ABENDLAENDISCHER KULTUR
IN OESTERREICH: GESCHRIEBEN
VON ADOLF LOOS   I. JAHR

ADOLF LOOS ___ Only two issues of *Das Andere*, or *The Other. Journal for the Introduction of Western Civilization in Austria*, came out, in October 1903. The publication was entirely edited by Adolf Loos, who threw himself into the task by focusing on news and on Viennese products or on readers' questions about manners, apparel or home furnishing. Among the few Viennese esteemed by Loos and for whom *Das Andere* was not therefore required reading, were the tailors Goldman & Salatsch, who placed an advertisement on the cover of both issues. Loos was naturally an assiduous customer of theirs, and was also the architect of the building in downtown Vienna in which their shop and atelier were later located. One of the Viennese fashion houses with which Loos was also closely associated was Knize. He designed their store on the Graben and subsequently their shop in Berlin. During his years in Paris he furthermore induced them to create a branch in the French capital, too. The store designed by Loos for the Avenue des Champs-Elysées (1927-1928) occupied premises that he himself had chosen and the purchase of which he subsequently negotiated in person. Fritz Wolff, the owner of that fashion house, possesses a portrait of the architect, a cubist sculpture displayed on the mantelpiece of the atelier. Naturally this portrait might in the same way be found in the Vienna or Berlin stores, or in the places Loos might equally be observed comfortably passing his time. RD

__ __ **"AUSTRO TURF,"** PHOTO ELFIE SEMOTAN, TEXT HERBERT MUSCHAMP, STYLING ROBERT E. BRYAN. PAGES FROM *MEN'S FASHIONS OF THE TIMES - THE NEW YORK TIMES MAGAZINE*, PART 2, FALL 2001. LOCATION **ARCHITECTURE BY ADOLF LOOS**: MÖLLER HOUSE, VIENNA, 1927-1928; GOLDMAN & SALATSCH BUILDING, VIENNA, 1909-1911; ANGLO-ÖSTERREICHISCHE BANK BUILDING, VIENNA, 1914; KÄRNTNER BAR, VIENNA, 1908

Inside Loinhaus, built in 1910 for a top tailoring firm in Vienna and now a bank.

Austro turf

WELCOME TO THE LUXE AUSTERITY OF ADOLF LOOS, THE TURN-OF-THE-CENTURY VIENNESE ARCHITECT, WHOM HERBERT MUSCHAMP WOULD CHOOSE — ABOVE ALL OTHERS — TO BUILD HIS DREAM HOUSE.

Photographs by Elfie Semotan. Styled by Robert E. Bryan.

GIORGIO ARMANI

_ _ **BOUTIQUE GIORGIO ARMANI, MILAN**, 2000, CREATIVE DIRECTOR GIORGIO ARMANI, DESIGN CLAUDIO SILVESTRIN

__ __ **BOUTIQUE GIORGIO ARMANI, SAO PAOLO**, BRAZIL, 2001, CREATIVE DIRECTOR GIORGIO ARMANI, DESIGN CLAUDIO SILVESTRIN

___ **PITTI IMMAGINE DISCOVERY**, EXHIBITION SPACE, FLORENCE, 1999, DESIGN CLAUDIO SILVESTRIN

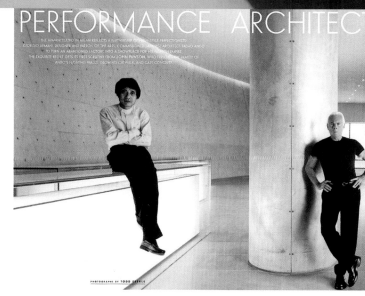

PERFORMANCE ARCHITECT

THE ARMANI TEATRO IN MILAN REFLECTS A PARTNERSHIP OF TWO-STYLE PERFECTIONISTS.
GIORGIO ARMANI, DESIGNER AND PATRON OF THE ARTS, COMMISSIONED JAPANESE ARCHITECT TADAO ANDO
TO TURN AN ABANDONED FACTORY INTO A SHOWPLACE FOR HIS FASHION EMPIRE.
THE EXQUISITE RESULT GETS ITS FIRST SCRUTINY FROM JOHN PAWSON, WHO EVOKES THE BEAUTY OF
ANDO'S FLOATING WALLS, GLOWING CATWALK, AND CAST CONCRETE.

PHOTOGRAPHS BY TODD EBERLE

___ **ARMANI/TEATRO,** MILAN, 2001, DESIGN TADAO ANDO __ __ **TADAO ANDO AND GIORGIO ARMANI IN THE FOYER OF THE ARMANI/TEATRO,** PHOTO TODD EBERLE. PAGES FROM "PERFORMANCE ARCHITECTURE," *VANITY FAIR,* OCTOBER 2001

___ ___ → (PP. 104-106, P. 109) **MANI ADVERTISING CAMPAIGN**, SPRING/SUMMER 2000, PHOTO PHILIP-LORCA DICORCIA ___ ___ → (PP. 107-108) **ARMANI/VIA MANZONI 31, MILAN**, 2000, CREATIVE DIRECTOR GIORGIO ARMANI, DESIGN MICHAEL GABELLINI

___ JIL SANDER SHOWROOM, HAMBURG, 1996, DESIGN MICHAEL GABELLINI. PHOTO © PAUL WARCHOL

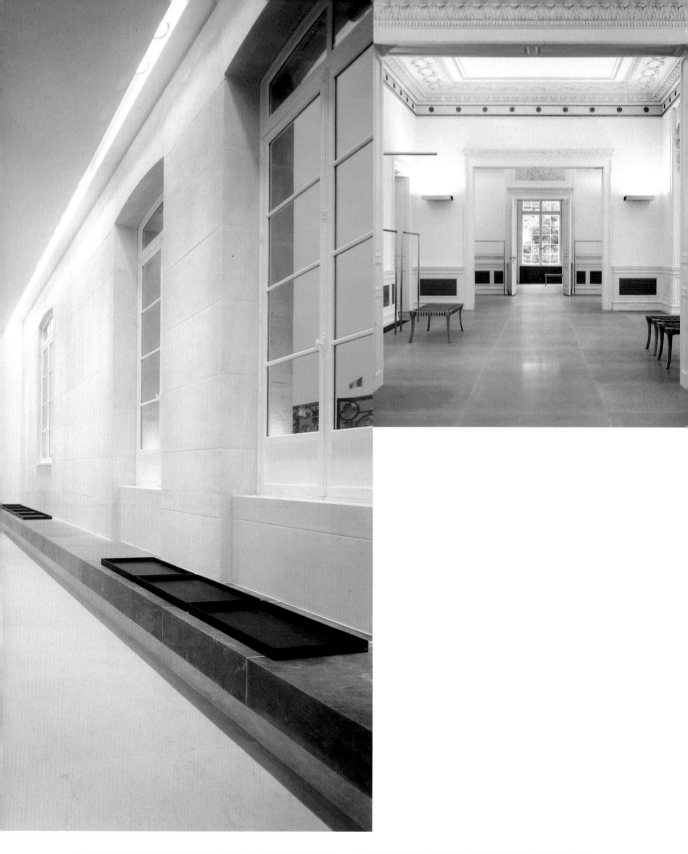

LINDA DRESNER STORE, NEW YORK, 1984, DESIGN J.W. FRED SMITH. PHOTO © 1984 PAUL WARCHOL

_ _ → NICOLA PELLEGRINI, *LA MIA STANZA DIVISA IN DUE*, INSTALLATION AND PERFORMANCE, *BOOM!*, MANIFATTURA TABACCHI, FLORENCE, JUNE-JULY 2001. COURTESY LUIGI FRANCO ARTE CONTEMPORANEA, TURIN

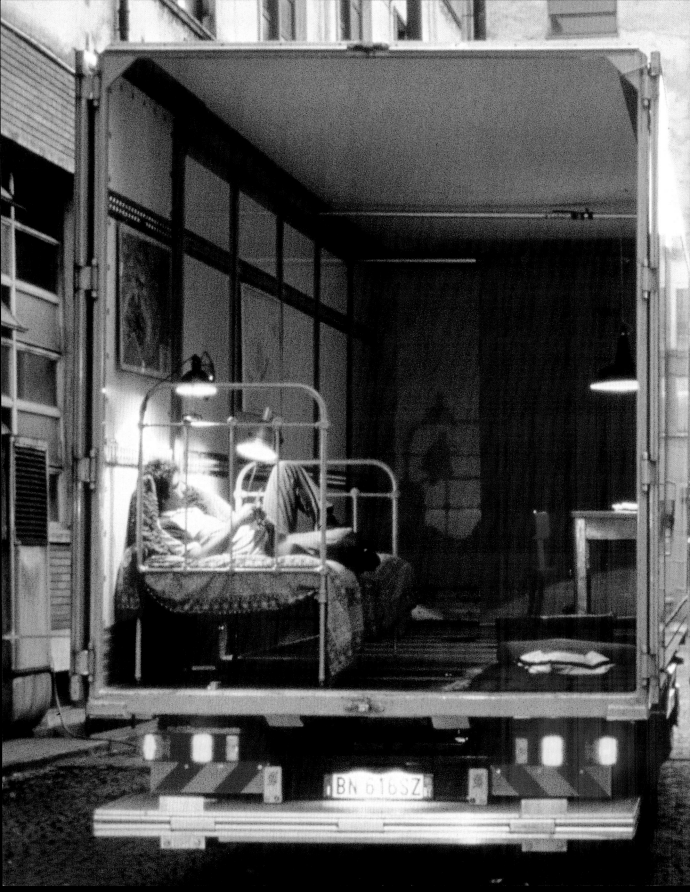

CROSS VIEW   PHOTOGRAPHED BY STEVEN MEISEL

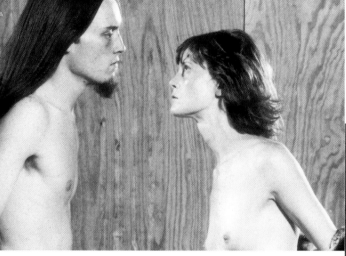

"CROSS VIEW," PHOTO STEVEN MEISEL. PAGES FROM *VOGUE ITALIA*, NO. 579, NOVEMBER 1998

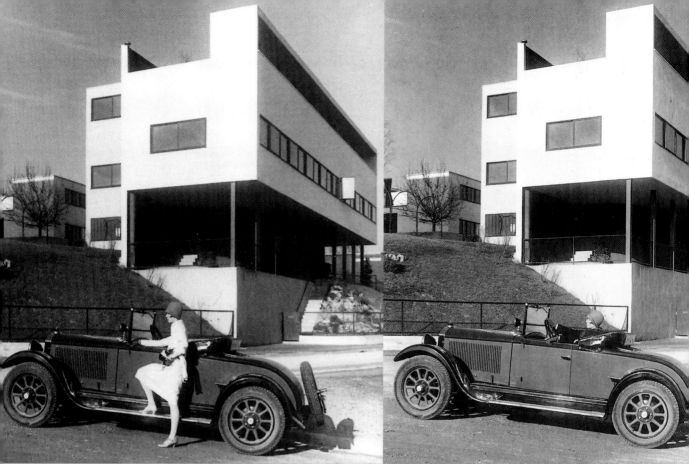

THE ARCHITECTURE OF THE MODERN MOVEMENT AS AN ADVERTISING SET ___ For the *Deutscher Werkbund* exhibition in 1927, the Weissenhofsiedlung, an estate composed of houses based on a model of white parallelepipeds, was built in Stuttgart. Its architects included all those subsequently hailed as the greatest masters of that architecture, including Le Corbusier, who contributed two houses. According to the American critic Mark Wigley, the photographs taken there for a Mercedes-Benz advertising campaign are clearly fashion images. And Le Corbusier's building, which appears in those photographs, "is understood as a fashion statement, despite his insistent protestations to the contrary," for example by emphatically rejecting any connection with fashion when explaining the thinking behind those same houses designed by him in Stuttgart. **RD**

____ **AD FOR MERCEDES-BENZ**, IN THE BACKGROUND LE CORBUSIER AND PIERRE JEANNERET'S DOUBLE 14/15 HOUSE IN WEISSENHOF, STUTTGART, 1927. COURTESY MERCEDES-BENZ HISTORIC ARCHIVES, STUTTGART

___ STILLS FROM THE FILM **ARCHITECTURE D'AUJOURD'HUI**, DIRECTOR PIERRE CHENAL IN COLLABORATION WITH LE CORBUSIER, FILMED AT VILLA STEIN, GARCHES (FIRST COLUMN) AND VILLA SAVOYE, POISSY (SECOND COLUMN), DESIGNS BY LE CORBUSIER, RESPECTIVELY 1926-1928 AND 1929. FROM "UN MODERNO MASS-MEDIA," *DOMUS*, NO. 687, OCTOBER 1987 ___ ___ → KRZYSZTOF WODICZKO, **HOMELESS VEHICLE IN NEW YORK CITY**, 1988-1989, GALERIE LELONG, NEW YORK. COURTESY THE ARTIST AND GALERIE LELONG, NEW YORK

MINIMALISM __ The reader is referred to the entries found in the most discerning and recent art dictionaries for a concise history, dating from the seventh to the eighth decades of the twentieth century, of this art movement, also known by other names – among the more indicative being Primary Structures or ABC Art. There you will find the North American artists (chiefly Donald Judd), and maybe also the equally great authors of international literature, Samuel Beckett and Ernest Hemingway (though Hemingway actually died in 1961), and in international design Max Bill, Ludwig Mies van der Rohe, Louis Kahn. . . . None of them would have accepted the "minimalist" label, and it would be worthwhile explaining why. And a note will be devoted to the phenomenon that spread from East to West, neominimalism in the visual and other arts, always sober, elegant, picturesque, almost never sublime. Continuation is not expected, nor hoped for. In fact, it is not the tendential minimalism that will remain, but the categorical one. Will a category remain? Yes it will, precisely a category, working and analytical, the one whose manifesto could still be the motto "less is more." **VS**

__ __**PAWSON HOUSE, STAIRS**, LONDON, 1994, DESIGN JOHN PAWSON PHOTO © JONATHAN PLAYER/CAMERAPRESS/GRAZIA NERI

___ **PAWSON HOUSE, INTERIORS**, LONDON, 1994, DESIGN JOHN PAWSON. PHOTO © JONATHAN PLAYER/CAMERAPRESS/GRAZIA NERI

CALVIN KLEIN STORE, SEOUL, 1996, DESIGN JOHN PAWSON, PHOTO NAKASA AND PARTNERS. FROM DEJAN SUDJIC, *JOHN PAWSON WORKS*, LONDON: PHAIDON, 2000

___ ___ **CALVIN KLEIN STORE, MADISON AVENUE, NEW YORK**, 1995, DESIGN JOHN PAWSON. LEFT IMAGE: PHOTO TODD EBERLE, FROM DEJAN SUDJIC, *JOHN PAWSON WORKS*, LONDON: PHAIDON, 2000

Calvin Klein
men, women, home

Donald Judd Furniture

__ __**DONALD JUDD FURNITURE**, FOLDING CATALOGUE. PHOTO TODD EBERLE/1996 © DONALD JUDD ESTATE LICENSED BY VAGA, NY

84

___ **DONALD JUDD'S HOUSE**, 101 SPRING STREET, NEW YORK, PHOTO TODD EBERLE. FROM *DONALD JUDD: RÄUME SPACES*, OSTFILDERN: CANTZ, 1993

1 3 3

John Pawson and Annie Bell   Living and Eating

     _ _ _ JOHN PAWSON AND ANNIE BELL, *LIVING AND EATING*, NEW YORK: CLARKSON POTTER, 2001

__ __ RIRKRIT TIRAVANIJA, *PAD THAI*, 1990, PERFORMANCE, PAULA ALLEN GALLERY, NEW YORK. COURTESY THE ARTIST

MARTHA STEWART __ Martha Stewart is a prophet of lifestyle and total living. Perfectly attuned to American upper class custom, she indicates how every detail is an integral part of everybody's quality of life. Her advice on cooking, where to vacation and what to put in your home are a precious guide to her devoted audiences, and have become a huge publishing success, thanks to the numerous books dedicated to her, to the magazine *Martha Stewart Living*, and to the Web site and TV program directed by her.

Martha Stewart has even stepped into the temple of contemporary art with the Chinati Foundation, created by sculptor Donald Judd in 1979, at Marfa, Texas. Also present at Marfa, in addition to Judd's own works, are permanent installations by Ilya Kabakov, Claes Oldenburg, Dan Flavin and Carl Andre (to mention just a few), plus temporary exhibitions. Meanwhile Stewart did a program on Texan cooking, instantly dubbed "Martha on Marfa," with a photographic report by Todd Eberle. **LP**

The barbecue and mariachis were Texas traditional: the museum setting wasn't

Martha in MARFA

THIS PAGE: A former horse arena at the Chinati Foundation in Marfa, Texas, was the setting for a West Texas-style barbecue. The late artist Donald Judd used the renovated arena for dinner parties. OPPOSITE: Martha Stewart, who has long admired Judd's work, meets Texas chefs Louis Lambert, left, and Grady Spears.

"Texas barbecue," said Lambert, left, "is about process: a hot fire and a good piece of meat." He grilled the meats at this Judd-designed barbecue pit working with Spears and Kate Shepherd, a Chinati resident artist. OPPOSITE: On the buffet, dinner was served in copper-glazed, clay, and volcanic-stone bowls.

BEECROFT WEDDING PROJECT __ "To accept the prospect of marriage may also however mean to test one's talents as an artist, and to transform that decision into an artwork. In this way the demarcation line between true and not true, life and art, will be abolished. So that the various stages of preparation for the event can be faced as if it were a new performance." On 31 July, I got an email from Vanessa, the first on what for the sake of convenience she was to refer thenceforth as her Wedding Project. She wrote: "I am getting married 14 September in the little church on the hill at Portofino. I am trying to dress all the guests in white and, if I can, to have a photograph taken." So began, almost without my realizing, an "epic" experience, the achievement of a work that was going to be very ambitious considering the race against time, its major production requirements and the necessity to work out a viable interaction between Vanessa and *Vogue*, art and fashion. On 1 August another message followed: "The guests, a few friends and close family (very few), are becoming the subject of a shoot. All in white – priest included – in the little white church, in front of the statue of St. Sebastian. Todd Eberle will take the photo, a group portrait. Do you think we could get the help of a designer or someone else to dress the company? Could you advise me? The idea is to create a work, a statement. My guests will represent the liberal arts, the law, the family, the art market and that of the production of exhibitions and events. . . ." The project, as far as the production of clothes and accessories was concerned, was to be handled by four different names in Italian fashion. Trussardi would do the men's cotton suits, complete with shirts and shoes. Alberta Ferretti the cotton skirts with transparent silk pleated blouses for some of the lady guests, plus the Empire-style dress for Colleen, the groom's sister. Prada was making the two page-suits for the teenagers Rachel Polla and Jennifer Beecroft, together with the high-waist, off-the-shoulder dresses for the bridesmaids. Finally, Alessandro Dell'Acqua designed Vanessa's coat-and-skirt, and the suits with tuxedo sateen finishes for Greg, Alexander Beecroft (best man) and Ettore Bertolotti (the bride's grandfather). The guests gathered at a hotel in Rapallo on 13 September, to get through an extremely busy schedule and a highly organized dress rehearsal. **Mariuccia Casadio**, *Vogue Italia*, no. 604, December 2000

___ **BISTROT IN THE COLETTE STORE**, PARIS. © SIDALI-DJENIDI

___ "ONE BLIN... TWO BLINIS... THREE BLINCHIKS...," PHOTO YUTAKA YAMAMOTO. PAGES FROM *INVIEW*, NO. 17, JANUARY 2001 __ __ → OTTONELLA MOCELLIN, *ALL THAT SHE MEANT WAS GOOD*, 1996-1997, CIBACHROME, 34 X 74 CM. COURTESY LUIGI FRANCO ARTE CONTEMPORANEA, TURIN

As the legendary Four Seasons restaurant turns 40, MIMI SHERATON returns to early 1959, when Joseph Baum and Jerome Brody assembled a perfectionist presidium—including chefs Albert Stöckli and Albert Kumin—to create the first truly contemporary American restaurant, in New York's Seagram Building, designed by Mies van der Rohe and Philip Johnson. For Alex von Bidder and Julian Niccolini, who now preside over this ground zero of power lunching, the divinity is still in the details, from Michael Eisner's post-coronary-bypass diet to the bison fillet from Edgar M. Bronfman's ranch to the status seating of such regulars as Barbara Walters, Barry Diller, and Sanford Weill

SEAS
IN T

PHOTOGRAPH BY

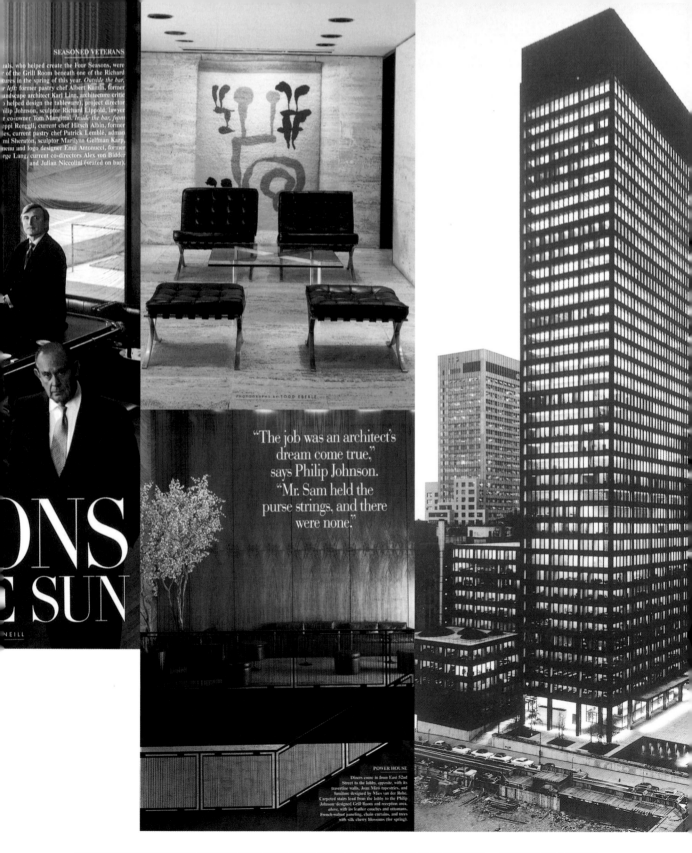

PHOTOGRAPHS by TODD EBERLE

"The job was an architect's
dream come true,"
says Philip Johnson.
"Mr. Sam held the
purse strings, and there
were none."

ONS
E SUN

NEILL

POWER HOUSE
Diners come in from East 52nd
Street to the lobby, *opposite*, with its
travertine walls, Joan Miró tapestries, and
furniture designed by Mies van der Rohe.
Carpeted stairs lead from the lobby to the Philip
Johnson–designed Grill Room and reception area,
above, with its leather couches and ottomans,
French-walnut paneling, chain curtains, and trees
with silk cherry blossoms (for spring).

__ __ THE BRASSERIE, IN THE BASEMENT OF THE SEAGRAM BUILDING, NEW YORK, 2000, DESIGN DILLER + SCOFIDIO, PHOTO MICHAEL MORAN

1 4 9

___ **DEGUSTATION ROOM AT THE DOMINUS WINERY**, YOUNTVILLE, NAPA VALLEY, CALIFORNIA, 1995-1997, DESIGN HERZOG & DE MEURON, PHOTO TIMOTHY HURSLEY

Thierry Mugler's black
rubberized silk toile jacket, at
Bergdorf Goodman, New York.
Martin Katz earrings.

JORGE PARDO __ The tables, chairs, lamps and interiors designed by Jorge Pardo remind us of modern architectural classics, from Alvar Aalto to Le Corbusier. In all his work, the artist deliberately confuses the boundaries between design, art and architecture so as to put the spectator into a state of growing cognitive uncertainty. In recent years Pardo designed a wooden landing-stage at Münster for the 1997 edition of the *Sculpture Project* exhibition, which later became a permanent installation. He designed a café for the Leipzig Fair, a reading room at the Boijmans Van Beuningen Museum in Rotterdam, the reception area for the Fabric Workshop and Museum in Philadelphia, and his own residence in Los Angeles by commission of the Museum of Contemporary Art. In 2000 Pardo converted the ground floor of the Dia Center for the Arts in New York and designed a café for the Glasgow Contemporary Art Center. In an interview released on that occasion, Pardo had this to say about his spectator strategy: "I don't care for this term since the strategy is carried out at the expense of the process, which is the phase closest to my heart. I like to speculate on the differences between an artist's café, an artistic café, a café that would like to look like an artistic café, and a café designed by an artist, or perhaps a work of art. In what way does my practice as a painter and sculptor look to architecture? I don't know, but I hope to find out where this thought will lead me." **EDC**

BALLY

COVER OF *VOGUE ITALIA*, NO. 583, MARCH 1999, PHOTO STEVEN MEISEL, FASHION EDITOR KARL TEMPLER

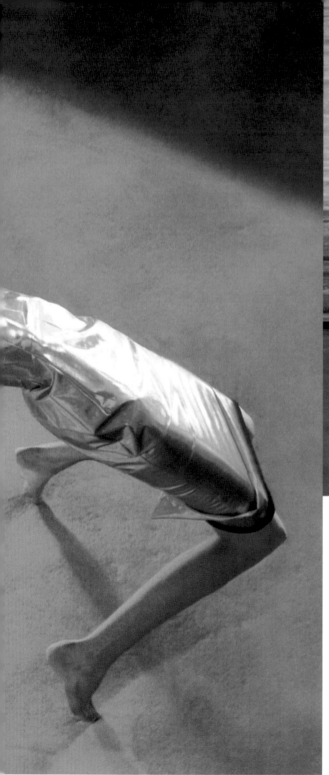

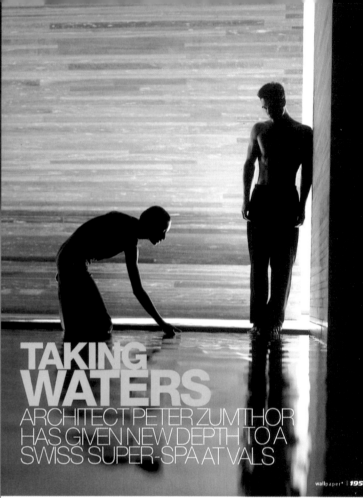

TAKING
WATERS
ARCHITECT PETER ZUMTHOR
HAS GIVEN NEW DEPTH TO A
SWISS SUPER-SPA AT VALS

THIS IS THE LANDSCAPE OF THE COMPUTER GAME 'DOOM II' –
THE SHEER WALLS, THE LABYRINTHINE CORRIDORS, THE STAIRS LEADING THROUGH,
LEADING TO MORE STAIRS, MORE CORRIDORS

Massage

202 | wallpaper

STONE AND WATER __ Mountain, stone, water, building in stone, building with stone, building into the mountain, building out of the mountain – our attempts to give this chain of words an architectural interpretation, to translate into architecture its meanings and sensuousness, guided our design for the building and step by step gave it form.
Consequently the design process was a playful but patient process of exploration independent of rigid formal models. Right from the start, there was a feeling for the mystical nature of a world of stone inside the mountain, for darkness and light, for the reflection of light upon water, for the diffusion of light through steam-filled air, for the different sounds that water makes in stone surroundings, for warm stone and naked skin, for the ritual of bathing. From the start, there was the pleasure of working with these things, of consciously bringing them into play. Only much later, when the design was almost complete, did I visit the old baths in Budapest, Istanbul and Bursa, and understand more fully not only the sources of these seemingly universal images, but their truly archaic nature.
So our bath is not a showcase for the latest aqua-gadgetry, water jets, nozzles or chutes. It relies instead on the silent, primary experiences of bathing, cleansing oneself, relaxing in the water; on the body's contact with water at different temperatures and in different kinds of spaces; on touching stone. **Peter Zumthor**, *A + U Architecture and Urbanism*, no. 2, 1998

_____ VALS BATHS, THE SPACE AROUND THE CENTRAL BASIN, 1990-1996, DESIGN PETER ZUMTHOR. PHOTO MICHAEL BÜHLER _____ PETER ZUMTHOR AT THE VALS BATHS, PHOTO TODD
EBERLE. PAGE FROM "SWISS MYSTIQUE," *VANITY FAIR*, JULY 2001 _____ **VALS BATHS, EAST FACADE**, 1990-1996, DESIGN PETER ZUMTHOR. PHOTO THIBAUT CUISSET/METIS/GRAZIA NERI

NEW NOMADS __ How do we imagine the clothes of the future? With minimal forms in close-fitting synthetic fabrics? Star Trek scenarios? No, maybe it isn't so simple. It is, in fact, not necessary anymore to project ourselves onto distant planets to outline the near future. Gibson and the cyberpunk writers have shown how it is already in our midst and how cyberspace has redefined our perception of reality.

Well-being likewise fits into this scenario now being defined. A new form of technological mysticism is, in fact, taking shape, made possible by the designing of wearable technologies. New Nomads is an Eastern-shaped dress, which creates both a space-time short circuit between past and future, between asceticism and hi-tech sophistication, and new sensations of contentment for their wearers – thanks to conductive fabrics, cabled cloths and sensor-embroideries. **LP**

_ _ **TIANJIN GREAT MUSEUM**, CHINA, 2000, DESIGN SHIN TAKAMATSU AND MAMORU KAWAGUCHI. FROM *GA DOCUMENT*, NO. 65, MAY 2001

1 6 3

__ __ THOMAS RUFF, *H.T.B. 01.*, 1999, COLOR PHOTOGRAPH, 130 X 155 CM, EDITION OF 5. COURTESY THE ARTIST AND ZWIRNER & WIRTH, NEW YORK

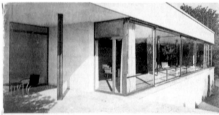

RUFF+MIES __ . . . When I did my first architectural series, in 1987-1991, I chose the typical, undistinguished buildings my generation grew up surrounded by. I thought that high architecture might overshadow the image itself, that a Mies building would be too beautiful. I was worried that there would be too much Mies and too little Ruff. But after gaining experience making various series in the meantime, I thought I could transform even Mies architecture into a Ruff image. When Julian proposed the project in 1999, I realized I was ready for Mies – that I could make his architecture look different from the way it had appeared in previous photographs.

. . . My idea now was to work in several modes: straight architectural shots, interior photographs like the ones I was making twenty years ago, stereoscopic photographs, and computer-manipulated images. Some of the computer alterations were done to create the impression of speed – something modernity has always been closely associated with. When Mies's German Pavilion was built for the 1929 International Exhibition, it must have looked like a UFO had landed in Barcelona. Speed in photography is always blurry, and my picture of the German Pavilion looks like a high-speed locomotive – modernity arriving at the train station of the present (albeit the present of 1929). **Thomas Ruff**, *Artforum*, summer 2001

MODERN ARCHITECTURE

MUSEUM OF MODERN ART

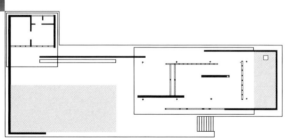

__ __ PLAN OF THE **GERMAN PAVILION**, INTERNATIONAL EXHIBITION, BARCELONA, 1928-1929, DESIGN LUDWIG MIES VAN DER ROHE. FROM HENRY-RUSSELL HITCHCOCK AND PHILIP JOHNSON, *THE INTERNATIONAL STYLE*, NEW YORK: W. W. NORTON & COMPANY, 1932 __ __ *MODERN ARCHITECTURE: INTERNATIONAL EXHIBITION*, EXHIBITION CATALOGUE, NEW YORK: MUSEUM OF MODERN ART, 1932. COVER: **TUGENDHAT HOUSE**, BRNO, 1928-1930, DESIGN LUDWIG MIES VAN DER ROHE __ __ → JENNY HOLZER, **INSTALLATION AT NEUE NATIONALGALERIE, BERLIN**, FEBRUARY-APRIL 2001. PHOTO © JENNY HOLZER

1 6 5

___ **PARFUMERIE HELMUT LANG, NEW YORK,** 1998, DESIGN GLUCKMAN MAYNER ARCHITECTS, INSTALLATION JENNY HOLZER. PHOTO ELFIE SEMOTAN

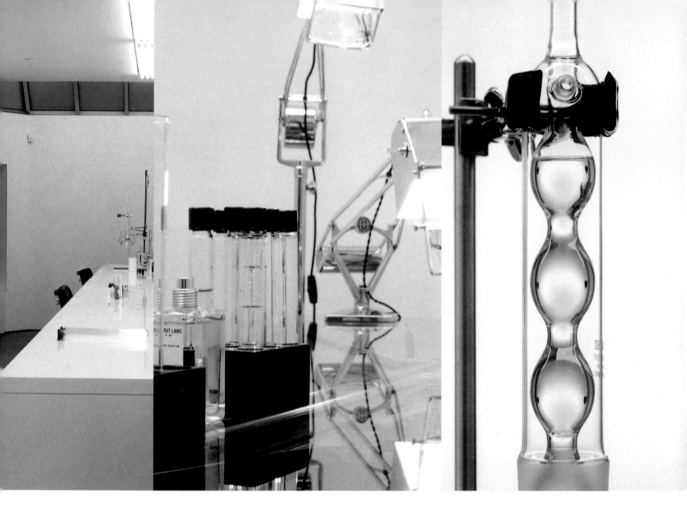

BOUTIQUE HELMUT LANG, 80 GREENE STREET, NEW YORK, 1997, DESIGN RICHARD GLUCKMAN ARCHITECTS, INSTALLATION JENNY HOLZER. GELATIN SILVER PHOTOGRAPHS ELFIE SEMOTAN, COLOR PHOTOGRAPH FROM *SPACE FRAMED: RICHARD GLUCKMAN ARCHITECT*, NEW YORK: THE MONACELLI PRESS, 2000

__ __ **GAGOSIAN GALLERY**, NEW YORK, 1991, DESIGN RICHARD GLUCKMAN ARCHITECTS, PHOTO EDWARD HUEBER. FROM *SPACE FRAMED: RICHARD GLUCKMAN ARCHITECT*, NEW YORK: THE MONACELLI PRESS, 2000

_____ **DIA CENTER FOR THE ARTS**, NEW YORK, 1987, DESIGN RICHARD GLUCKMAN ARCHITECTS, PHOTO NOEL ALLUM/DAN CORNISH. FROM *SPACE FRAMED: RICHARD GLUCKMAN ARCHITECT*, NEW YORK: THE MONACELLI PRESS, 2000

TOKYO-GO __ After five days of free entry (22-26 January, during fashion week), the Site de création contemporaine at the Palais de Tokyo is open from midday to midnight. You pay (5.30 Euro, admission free for under-eighteens and the disabled) as if for a museum. But is it a museum? Hard to say. A sponsored social center (and what a sponsor: in addition to the Ministère de la Culture et de la Communication, Pioneer, Bloomberg – the new mayor of New York's corporation), a new Beaubourg that does its utmost not to look like one, a workshop for young artists over twenty-five. During the opening days it was a delightfully chaotic sight. The interior of the monumental thirties exhibition hall resembles a building site (and as a matter of fact it is, because the money has momentarily dried up); the installations succeed one another without too many explanations and merge with the deliberate poverty of the place. Artists' writings on the plaster next to the notice saying NO WRITING ON THE WALL, notices with enigmatic phrases (Monica Bonvicini), bits of broken mortar from a destroyed prison (Elmgreen & Dragset), silicone corpses (Virginie Barré), gray rubber hydrants and electric plugs (Loris Cecchini), dirt from a South African shanty town (Kay Hassan), the art market (Navin Rawanchaikul) or the minimal objects market (Surasi Kusolwong), where you expect a salesman to appear. Not by chance the architects Anne Lacaton and Jean-Philippe Vassal, who specialize in low budget architecture, drew their inspiration from Djemaa El-Fna Square at Marrakech, a market, meeting place and free space. A space occupied, this time, by artists, unlike the architect museums. See the Web site www.palaisdetokyo.com. Among other things, under the heading *Actualités*, they are looking for a lighting and sound director for concerts, performances and showcases: an artist. **RM**

__ __ LORIS CECCHINI, *STAGE EVIDENCE*, INSTALLATION AT PALAIS DE TOKYO, PARIS, JANUARY-MARCH 2002, VARIOUS ELEMENTS IN RUBBER URETHANE. PHOTO M. DOMAGE, COURTESY GALLERIA CONTINUA, SAN GIMIGNANO

1 7 5

___INTERVENTION BY PIERRE HUYGHE FOR THE **CHANGING ROOM IN THE DIOR HOMME STORE, VIA MONTENAPOLEONE 14, MILAN**, 2002 __ __ PIERRE HUYGHE, *ATARY LIGHT*, 1999, PROGRAM FOR VIDEOGAME, 49. ESPOSIZIONE INTERNAZIONALE D'ARTE, LA BIENNALE DI VENEZIA, VENICE, 2001. COURTESY MARIAN GOODMAN GALLERY, NEW YORK

DIOR HOMME __ Every design is specific. Artistic additions create an initiatory course into spaces in transformation. The artistic contributions are associated specifically with each place and assume the appearance of architectural features. The artistic devices make it possible to adapt each space interactively.

In Milan Pierre Huyghe intervened on the fitting room. The elongated space suggests movement. The space is dynamic and induces immediate use: a clearing. An intimate space where a transformation, a brief moment in which to rediscover one's image, is experienced. As you go in, the length of the left wall is covered with lamps from top to bottom. This wall of lamps is in turn covered with frosted glass. The right wall is equipped with sensors and faced in the same homogeneous surface as the left wall. The ceiling is well lit and fixed. As the visitor moves inside the room, he cuts a series of invisible beams corresponding to the position of his body. At the same time the lamps produce his illuminated double.

Suddenly this illuminated double appears and accompanies the visitor as he moves about, always slightly out of sync.

It is the manifestation of movement inhabiting space.

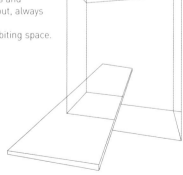

____DIOR HOMME STORE, VIA MONTENAPOLEONE 14, MILAN, 2002, DESIGN HEDI SLIMANE WITH ARCHITECTURE & ASSOCIÉS, WITH INTERVENTIONS BY PIERRE HUYGHE AND PIERRE CHARPIN

1 7 7

_____ SALON DIOR HOMME, 40 RUE FRANÇOIS 1ᵉʳ, PARIS, 2001, DESIGN HEDI SLIMANE _____ STAGE SET FOR THE DIOR HOMME FASHION SHOW - BOYS DON'T CRY, SPRING/SUMMER 2002, CARREAU DU TEMPLE, PARIS

____ **"PARIS VIII,"** PHOTO ANUSCHKA BLOMMERS & NIELS SCHUMM. LOCATION **COMME DES GARÇONS STORE**, RUE DU FAUBOURG SAINT-HONORÉ, PARIS, DESIGN ARCHITECTURE & ASSOCIÉS. PAGES FROM *BIG PARIS*, NO. 38

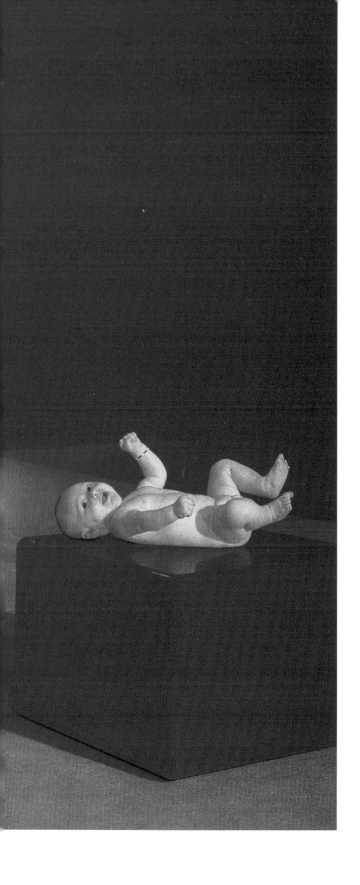

PRADA

__ __ ANDREAS GURSKY, *PRADA II*, 1997, COLOR PHOTOGRAPH, 166 X 316 CM. © ANDREAS GURSKY

_____ **PRADA WOMEN'S STORE, VIA MONTENAPOLEONE, MILAN,** 2001, DESIGN STUDIO BACIOCCHI _____ → **AD FOR THE EXHIBITION** *MARC QUINN* **AT FONDAZIONE PRADA**, MILAN, 5 MAY-10 JUNE 2000 _____ → MARC QUINN, *GARDEN*, 2000, INSTALLATION AT FONDAZIONE PRADA, MILAN, COLD ROOM (1270 X 543 X 320 CM), POOL (685 X 215 X 255 CM), GARDEN WITH MORE THAN 1000 PLANTS, 25 TONS OF SILICONE OIL. PHOTO ATTILIO MARANZANO, COURTESY FONDAZIONE PRADA, MILAN

Fondazione Prada Marc Quinn

May/June 2000

Fondazione Prada

20135 Milan via Spartaco 8
Ph. +39.02.54670216/0202
Fax +39.02.54670258
www.fondazioneprada.org

__ __ LOUISE BOURGEOIS, *SPIDER*, 1997, INSTALLATION AT FONDAZIONE PRADA, MILAN. PHOTO ATTILIO MARANZANO, COURTESY FONDAZIONE PRADA, MILAN

Tickets ↙

Galleries ↘

INSTALLATION BY LOUISE BOURGEOIS IN THE ATRIUM OF THE TATE MODERN, LONDON, 2000. PHOTO © JEAN-CLAUDE N'DIAYE/IMAPRESS/GRAZIA NERI

__ __**TATE MODERN, THE LARGE ENTRANCE HALL**, LONDON, 1995-2000, DESIGN HERZOG & DE MEURON. PHOTO © ST. JOHN POPE/LEVERTON IPS/GRAZIA NERI

_____ **PRADA STORE, TOKYO. VIEW OF THE RELIEF MODEL,** 2001, DESIGN HERZOG & DE MEURON __ __ **PRADA STORE, LOS ANGELES. VIEW OF THE RELIEF MODEL,** 2001, DESIGN REM KOOLHAAS/OMA

THE REBEL IN PRADA

WHEN THE GOING GETS TOUGH, THE TOUGH—IN THIS CASE,
ITALIAN DESIGNER MIUCCIA PRADA AND DUTCH ARCHITECT
REM KOOLHAAS—RE-INVENT SHOPPING. FORGET THE DIRE ECONOMIC CLIMATE AND
DELAYED F.O.: PRADA HAS JUST OPENED A $50 MILLION NEW STORE IN NEW YORK'S SOHO, EXPLORING KOOLHAAS'S
BOLDLY EXPERIMENTAL DESIGN, WITH ITS HIGH-TECH DRESSING ROOMS,
THEATRICAL PERFORMANCE SPACE, AND BLEND OF 21ST-CENTURY FUTURISM AND TIMELESS EROTICISM,
INGRID SISCHY REPORTS ON A COLLABORATION BETWEEN
RENEGADES TO TEST THE BOUNDARIES OF FASHION

HE CAN GET IT FOR YOU RETAIL
Shortly before the opening of Prada's
new store in SoHo, architect Rem Koolhaas stands
on steps which will be used for displaying shoes.
Lose the shoes and you've got theater-style
seating for performances and movie screenings.
Photographed on December 9, 2001.

PHOTOGRAPHS BY TODD EBERLE

_____ **PRADA STORE, BROADWAY, NEW YORK,** 2002, DESIGN REM KOOLHAAS/OMA. PHOTO © FRANCO ROSSI _____ **REM KOOLHAAS IN THE PRADA STORE, BROADWAY, NEW YORK.**
PAGES FROM "THE REBEL IN PRADA," TEXT INGRID SISCHY, PHOTO TODD EBERLE, *VANITY FAIR*, NO. 498, FEBRUARY 2002

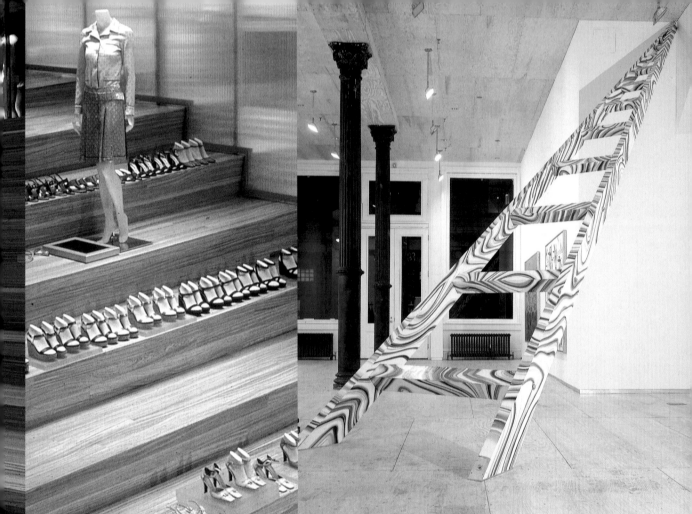

PRADA __ The Prada's call it an "epicentre", not a shop. It claims both the future and the past. Sophisticated technology, at the time of writing not fully functioning, links the virtual, material and human worlds, product, shopper and salesperson. A chequered marble floor alludes to the very first Prada store, in the Galleria in Milan, as baroque churches allude to Solomon's Temple. It claims the world with a map showing Prada's global reach by creating a self-sufficient internal landscape, a zebra-wood valley under a polycarbonate sky. It claims public life, as the intention is to create the sort of intense public space that, according to Koolhaas, shopping has put out of business. The theatre, by day used for displaying shoes, is used outside shopping hours for public performances. Prada, a retail chain with ambitions to be a cultural centre, has taken the place of the Guggenheim, a cultural body that mimics a retail chain. Koolhaas, of course, works for both. **Deyan Sudjic**, *Domus*, no. 845, February 2002

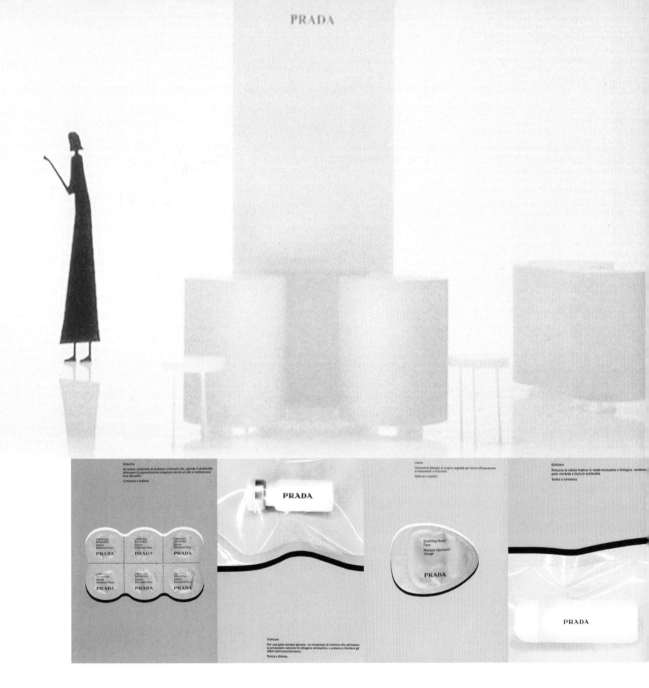

DAMIEN HIRST, PHARMACY __ *Naturally art is very closely tied up with all the communication systems; art is a synthetic dimension of communication and this can cause rapid changes.*
First of all, art is about life and always has been, whereas the art world is about money, and always has been. I believe that in the 1960s the problem was not art but the art world, and I find it much easier to ignore the art world and to achieve my aims through art. I think that if you concentrate on the future, as I do, you can do anything. If you start doing a certain thing, it is not difficult to think of opening a restaurant, designing disc sleeves or the image of a recording studio, or creating fashion. I mean, art can be anything and go anywhere. **Pierre Restany**, "Back into the Pop Era: Pierre Restany Interviews Damien Hirst," *Domus*, no. 806, July-August 1998

____ **PHARMACY, RESTAURANT AND BAR**, LONDON, 1998, DESIGN DAMIEN HIRST, JONATHAN BARNBROOK AND JASPER MORRISON, PHOTO ANNABEL ELSTON. FROM "GOOD CHEMISTRY," *I.D. MAGAZINE*, MARCH-APRIL 1998

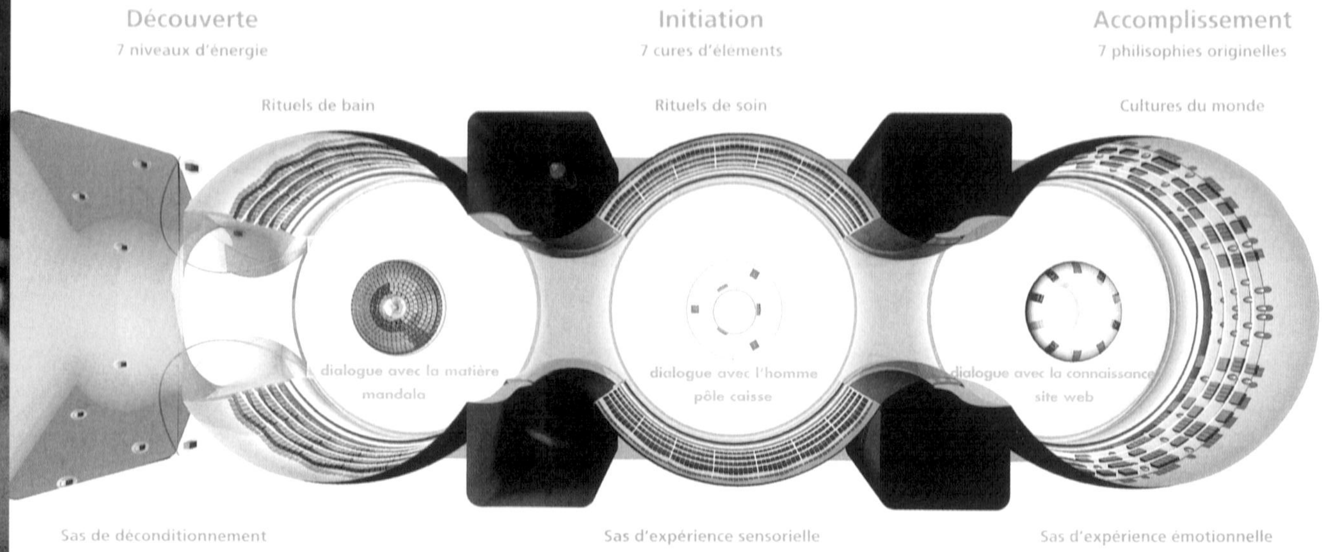

Découverte
7 niveaux d'énergie

Initiation
7 cures d'élements

Accomplissement
7 philisophies originelles

Rituels de bain

Rituels de soin

Cultures du monde

dialogue avec la matière
mandala

dialogue avec l'homme
pôle caisse

dialogue avec la connaissance
site web

Sas de déconditionnement

Sas d'expérience sensorielle

Sas d'expérience émotionnelle

__ __ **MAGASIN SEPHORA BLANC**, PARIS BERCY, 2000, DESIGN CHAFIK GASMI. FROM *ARCHITECTURE INTÉRIEURE CRÉÉ*, NO. 299, 2ND QUARTER 2001

2 0 3

__ __ **CROSS CONTAINER, 1992, PROGETTO OGGETTO LINE BY CAPPELLINI**, DESIGN THOMAS ERIKSSON

__ __ **DIESEL SAVE YOURSELF ADVERTISING CAMPAIGN**, 2001, PHOTO JEAN-PIERRE KHAZEM __ __ → YAYOI KUSAMA, *I'M HERE BUT NOTHING*, 2000, INSTALLATION, LE CONSORTIUM, DIJON. FROM *YAYOI KUSAMA*, DIJON: LES PRESSES DU RÉEL, 2001

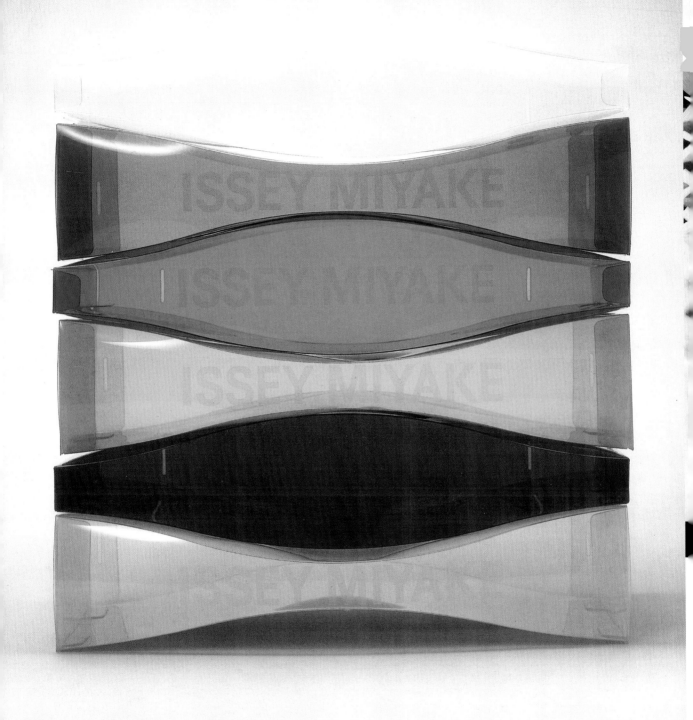

__ __ **BOW AND TUMMY**, HOLIDAY BAGS FOR ISSEY MIYAKE, 1997, DESIGN KARIM RASHID. FROM *KARIM RASHID: I WANT TO CHANGE THE WORLD*, LONDON: THAMES & HUDSON, 2001
__ __ ISSEY MIYAKE, **FLYING SAUCER**, SPRING/SUMMER 1994 COLLECTION, PHOTO RAYMOND MEIER. FROM *ISSEY MIYAKE: MAKING THINGS*, EXHIBITION CATALOGUE, PARIS:
FONDATION CARTIER POUR L'ART CONTEMPORAIN, 1998

___ A-POC/ISSEY MIYAKE STORE, PARIS, 2000, DESIGN ERWAN AND RONAN BOUROULLEC. PHOTO MORGANE LE GALLE

__ __ **PLEATS PLEASE/ISSEY MIYAKE, SOHO, NEW YORK STORE**, 1998, DESIGN TOSHIKO MORI WITH GWENAËL NICOLAS. PHOTO © PAUL WARCHOL __ __ **ISSEY MIYAKE MEN, SEIBU STORE, TOKYO**, 1988, DESIGN SHIRO KURAMATA. PHOTO MIKIO SEKITA

_____ ISSEY MIYAKE, ***STARBURST***, FALL/WINTER 1998 COLLECTION, PHOTO RAYMOND MEIER. FROM *ISSEY MIYAKE: MAKING THINGS*, EXHIBITION CATALOGUE, PARIS: FONDATION CARTIER POUR L'ART CONTEMPORAIN, 1998

___ **TRIBECA ISSEY MIYAKE STORE, HUDSON STREET, NEW YORK**, 2001, DESIGN FRANK O. GEHRY AND GORDON KIPPING. PHOTO © PAUL WARCHOL

at long last, lunch

And breakfast, too, reports Jeffrey Steingarten. But the architectural genius of Frank Gehry's Condé Nast cafeteria, writes Rowan Moore, offers much more than just food for thought. Photographed by Raymond Meier.

DANGEROUS CURVES
Gehry's undulating titanium walls playfully reflect light, evoking a sense of movement on a powerful landscape.
Fashion Editor: Elissa Santisi

"AT LONG LAST, LUNCH," PHOTO RAYMOND MEIER; PAGES FROM *VOGUE*, JUNE 2000. LOCATION **CONDÉ NAST CAFETERIA**, NEW YORK, 2000, DESIGN FRANK O. GEHRY

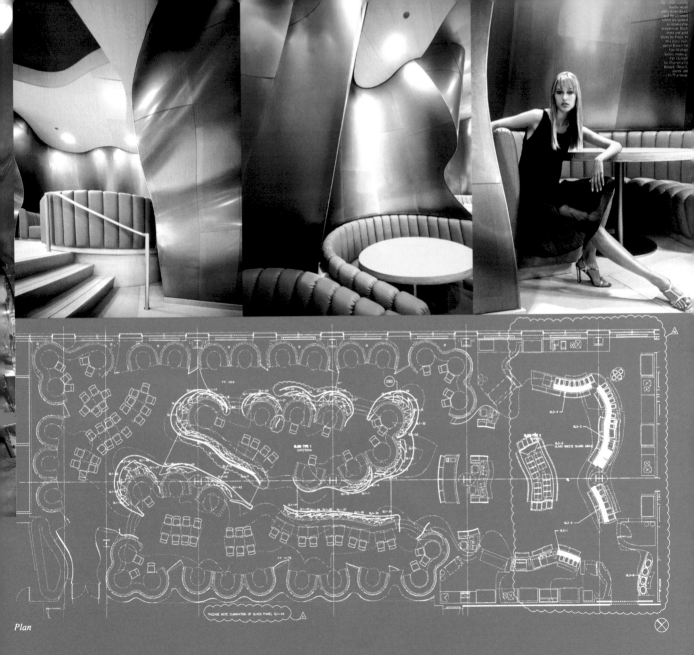

Plan

_____ **CONDÉ NAST CAFETERIA AND PLAN,** NEW YORK, 2000, DESIGN FRANK O. GEHRY

GUGGENHEIM MUSEUM, BILBAO, 1997. DESIGN FRANK O. GEHRY. PHOTO © ERIK SAMPERS/GRAZIA NERI

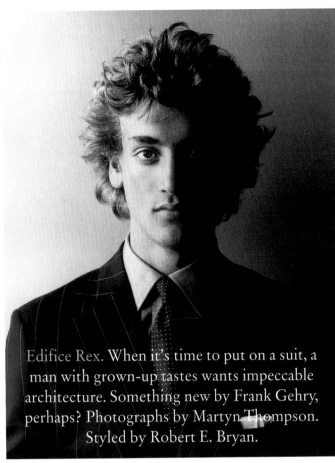

Edifice Rex. When it's time to put on a suit, a man with grown-up tastes wants impeccable architecture. Something new by Frank Gehry, perhaps? Photographs by Martyn Thompson. Styled by Robert E. Bryan.

Frank Gehry's Experience Music Project in Seattle.

Opposite: Single-breasted bead-striped wool suit $1,184, and glen-plaid cotton dress shirt, $148.50, Paul Stuart. At Paul Stuart, Madison Avenue at 45th Street and Chicago. Tie, Paul Stuart.

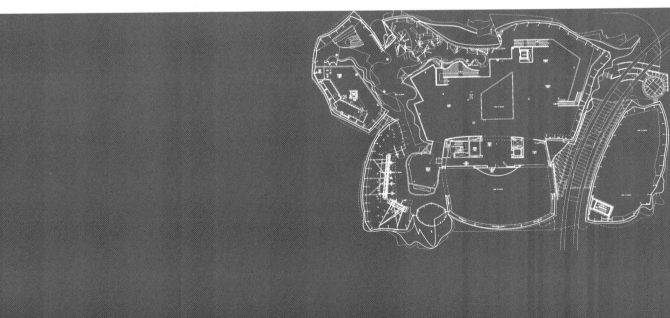

"EDIFICE REX," PHOTO MARTIN THOMPSON, STYLING ROBERT E. BRYAN. PAGES FROM *MEN'S FASHIONS OF THE TIMES - THE NEW YORK TIMES MAGAZINE*, PART 2, FALL, 2000. LOCATION **EXPERIENCE MUSIC PROJECT**, SEATTLE, 2000, DESIGN FRANK O. GEHRY _____ **EXPERIENCE MUSIC PROJECT**, PLAN OF THE MEZZANINE AND THE ROOF, SEATTLE, 2000, DESIGN FRANK O. GEHRY

e towering walls
oove the entrance to
e museum.

pposite: Pinstriped
ool suit, $495, Perry
lis Portfolio. At
oomingdale's or
ww.perryellis.com.
otton dress shirt, $125,
homas Pink. At Thomas
nk stores. Tie, Savoia
othiers. All pocket
uares, Robert Talbott.

ooming by Tommy
ascia for Link, Fashion
sistant: Alvaro Salazar.
dels: Matthew
edon, Gerard Smith
d Eric Werner.

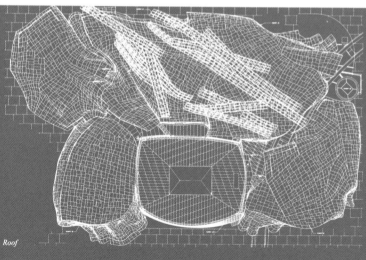

Roof

The tour complete, our guide leaves through the pivoting glass door in an aluminum tunnel designed by Future Systems (see **nest**'s winter 1998-1999 issue, pages 136–45, for the home of Future Systems' Amanda Levete and Jan Kaplicky). The shape of the tunnel resembles the inverted hull of a boat and was constructed in a shipyard in Cornwall, England.

____ **COMME DES GARÇONS STORE, CHELSEA, NEW YORK**, 1999, DESIGN FUTURE SYSTEMS, TAKAO KAWASAKI AND STUDIO MORSA, PHOTO ANTOINE BOOTZ. PAGE FROM "SCENTS OR SENSIBILITY," *NEST*, NO. 6, FALL 1999

255 COMME DES GARÇONS, NYC 1998

Rei Kawakubo, the Japanese fashion designer who launched the famous Comme des Garçons label in 1973, is celebrated for her innovative approach to the materials and structure of clothes. Such sophisticated garments demand retail environments to match and so Comme des Garçons formed a natural alliance with Future Systems as collaborators and architects for its three most recent shops.

The first, completed in the spring of 1999, is a flagship shop in New York. The site chosen for the project is a run-down looking nineteenth-century industrial building in West Chelsea, an area more associated with contemporary art galleries than fashion shops (the store has relocated from the increasingly commercial SoHo area). Rather than refurbish the entire structure, the approach has been to retain the original exterior – complete with existing fire escapes and signage – and simply to insert a new and intriguing shop behind.

To transport the shopper from the gritty life of the street to the serene and contemplative environment of the interior, Future Systems has devised a shapely 'link' structure which is as innovative in form and materials as Kawakubo's clothes. 'This is a real monocoque structure,' explains Kaplicky, describing how – just like an egg shell – the skin and structure of the tunnel are one. 'There are no ribs or spars and so it is a first in architecture.' The tunnel is made from 6 mm aluminium sheets, cut and assembled to the architect's computer drawings, in the Pendennis boatyard in Cornwall. The hand-sanded finish gives it a crafted appearance, which contrasts with its machine-made aesthetic.

For Future Systems this modest project represents another milestone in the history of the practice. As with the Media Centre at Lords, the structure has been prefabricated in a workshop environment and finished to a high standard before being packed and transported to site. Once there, it was 'grafted' behind the existing brick structure, complete with a pivoting glass door and a row of glowing red light fittings set into the floor.

For Kawakubo meanwhile, the tunnel provides a dramatic interface between her work and the city. 'The concept was to create something hidden, something private,' she says. 'To give the sensation of exploration. A tunnel to take you from one world into the next.'

monocoque tunnel

translucency

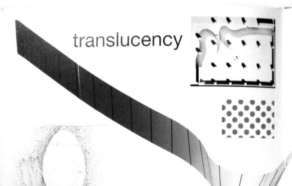

257 COMME DES GARÇONS, TOKYO 1998

curved

glass wall

As part of an ongoing collaboration between Comme des Garçons and Future Systems, the architects were commissioned to remodel the exterior of their flagship Tokyo store.

To counter the banal building which plays host to the shop, Future Systems developed a scheme for a dramatic glazed facade which lends a softer and unexpectedly organic line to the street corner. Replacing the conventional shop window, this new facade consists of a series of large panels of glass covered with spotted film. These are not only set at a dramatic angle of 18 degrees but many of the panels are also curved. The sensuous snaking line of this window recalls the elegant curved shopfronts of the Modern Movement, both in Kaplicky's home city of Prague and elsewhere. In this updated version however, the brightly coloured film on the glass reflects the rapid movement of the contemporary city. At the same time it challenges the tasteful, but dull, minimalism which has become the clichéd style of high fashion stores the world over.

__ __ **MARNI STORE, MILAN,** 2000, DESIGN FUTURE SYSTEMS. PHOTO © FRANCO ROSSI __ __ **MARNI STORE, LONDON,** 2000, DESIGN FUTURE SYSTEMS. PHOTO RICHARD DAVIES

DA SINISTRA. ABITO DI JERSEY E PELLE; TUBINO DI CRÊPE DI SETA SENZA MANICHE; PULL DI LANA ASIMMETRICO E GONNA; TOP CON MANICHE A FENDITURA E SHORTS. TUTTO MASKA. STIVALI, DA SINISTRA: ROBERTO CAVALLI, COSTUME NATIONAL, KALLISTÉ, GUCCI.

THINK
GRAPHIC
by ellen
von unwerth

THE CIRCLE AND THE CUPOLA __ The starting point is the circle, the geometric figure that structures our behavior. . . . Our visual field is circular, and so is that of our hearing, which cannot exceed three and a half meters between mouth and ears, otherwise we have to raise our voice and communication becomes aggressive. . . so my circular forms are the result of evidence. The orthogonal system is superseded, circular elements are much simpler. They existed even before architecture: as in certain huts, *trulli*, igloos, all self-bearing. . . . I, for example, can build cupolas with a diameter of 15 meters and a thickness of only 5 centimeters. . . . Furthermore, the circle is the simplest geometric construction: it has just one dimension, its radius. The hemisphere is by its nature self-bearing and non-deformable: no wall, no roof, a homogeneous whole. It is a construction within everybody's reach. **Antti Lovag**, 1986

Begun in 1975 – without a building license – the "palais des bulles," designed and built by Antti Lovag, spreads like a bunch of cupolas of varying dimensions. Resting on the Esquillon site at Théoule, it catches the eye of those passing along the seashore. This paradise-home displays an uncertain identity: it seems to be the product of a wild architect, or the fruit of some kind of hippy ideology searching for a spontaneous harmony with the natural landscape. Put up for sale by Sotheby's in 1989 for 50 million francs, it was bought by Pierre Cardin. The house offers its owner 1,200 habitable square meters. They include two reception halls, eight bedrooms, a library, a conference room, a cinema, a playroom, and 8,500 meters of land with swimming pool, terraces, palm grove, pond, amphitheater . . . Pierre Cardin – who was in his time the creator of "robes-bulles" – has added to Antti Lovag's masterpiece his own collection of objects from the seventies, thus interpreting the house in a new and very apt way.

__ __ "THINK GRAPHIC," PHOTO ELLEN VON UNWERTH, FASHION EDITOR ALICE GENTILUCCI. PAGES FROM *VOGUE ITALIA*, NO. 613, SEPTEMBER 2001. LOCATION **PIERRE CARDIN'S PALAIS DES BULLES**, ESQUILLON, CÔTES D'AZUR, 1975-1989, DESIGN ANTTI LOVAG

_ _ **PIERRE CARDIN'S PALAIS DES BULLES, BEDROOM,** ESQUILLON, CÔTES D'AZUR. PHOTO © SYLVIE RUAU/SAOLA FRANCE/GRAZIA NERI

CLOTHES BY PIERRE CARDIN, WITH *SUPERONDA* (DESIGN ARCHIZOOM, 1967). PHOTO © SNOWDON/CAMERA PRESS/GRAZIA NERI __ __ **PIERRE CARDIN,** PHOTO LIDO. FROM *L'OFFICIEL,* NO. 583, MARCH 1971

_____ **COVERED STRUCTURES, DESIGN VERNER PANTON,** FOR STORZ & PALMER, GERMANY, 1967. FROM *MOBILIA*, NO. 141, APRIL 1967 __ __⟶ ANGELA BULLOCH, ***SUPERSTRUCTURE***
WITH SATELLITES, 1997. COURTESY FONDAZIONE SANDRETTO RE REBAUDENGO PER L'ARTE, TURIN

Disegnato per Moderno da Carlo Colombo divano Mono con pouf, su ruote, con struttura in metallo e imbottitura in poliuretano, rivestito in tessuto sfoderabile; è dotato di due ruote posteriori.

Designed for Moderno by Carlo Colombo, Mono the divan with pouf on wheels, with structure in metal and polyurethane filler, and removable fabric cover; the divan is fitted with two rear wheels.

Disegnato da Rodolfo Dordoni per Minotti, Pollock ha struttura in legno massello e metallo, imbottitura in poliuretano, cuscini in piuma d'oca e rivestimento in tessuto sfoderabile o pelle.

Designed by Rodolfo Dordoni for Minotti, Pollock has a structure in solid wood and metal, polyurethane filler, goosedown cushions and covering in removable fabric or leather.

Disegnato da Piero Lissoni per Living, divano Metro Quadro ha struttura in tubolare metallico e scocche -per schienali e braccioli- in tamburato di pioppo e abete; l'imbottitura è in espanso e il rivestimento in tessuto sfoderabile o pelle.

"SOFT LIVING," PHOTO GIONATA XERRA, EDITOR NADIA LIONELLO. PAGES FROM *INTERNI*, NO. 497-498, JANUARY-FEBRUARY 2000

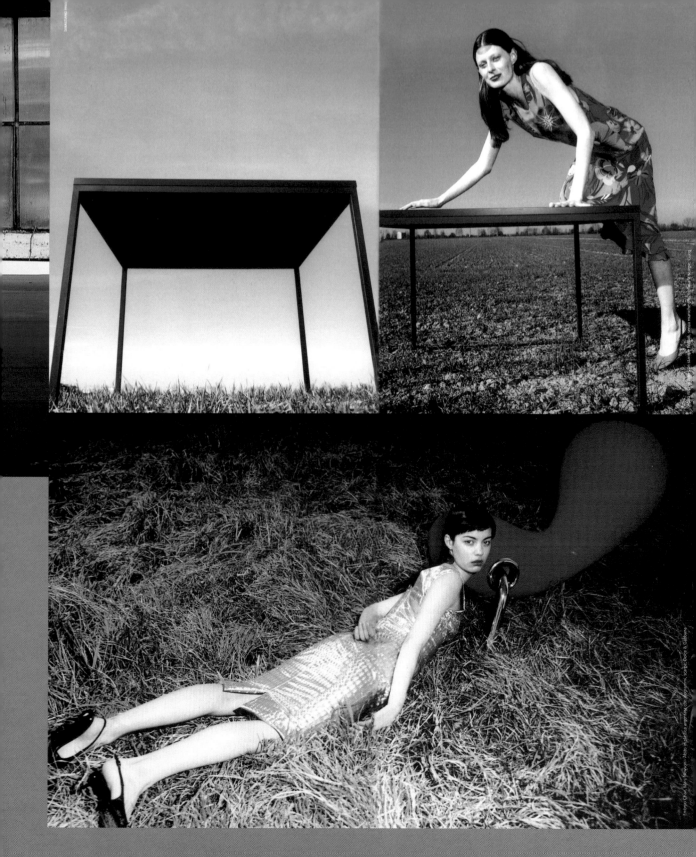

__ __ NINA SAUNDERS, *PURE THOUGHT 1*, 1995. COURTESY NOTE ARTECONTEMPORANEA, AREZZO

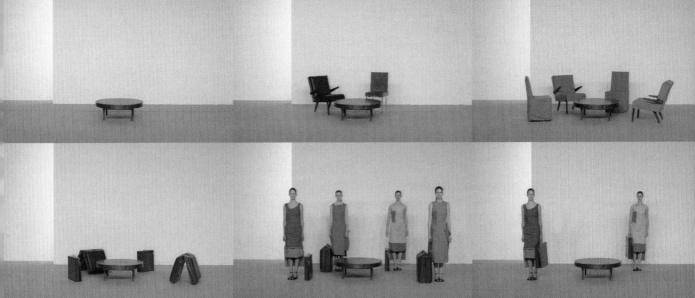

CHALAYAN __ For Chalayan the body has cultural connotations. Yet his clothes are not sexy, nor does he want them to be. "Sexiness doesn't come from what you wear." Often his clothes are thought provoking. For example, whereas many other designers create sexy corsets that evoke an idealised shape, Chalayan made a surgical corset that alludes to the idea of a body that is wounded and vulnerable. Another of his corsets was made of polished wood that bolted closed. Space is also central to his vision: clothing is an intimate zone around the body, architecture is a larger one. It also exists as territory, from which refugees can be expelled, taking with them only a few possessions. *After Words* (fall/winter 2000) opened on a set arranged to look like a living room, but the furniture covers became dresses, and the table was transformed into a skirt. Space also interacts with time, while culture and technology act on nature. A fibreglass dress opens electronically. Fascinated by flight, Chalayan's *Temporary Interference* (summer 1995) included prints based on the images on an air-traffic controller's screen. *Scenes of Tempest* (winter 1997) used patterning based on meteorological charts, reflecting Chalayan's vision of weather as a god or natural force. His collection *Airmail Clothing* (1999) was made from non-rip paper that could be folded into envelopes and sent through the mail. **Valery Steel**, in *Radical Fashion*, London: V & A Publications, 2001

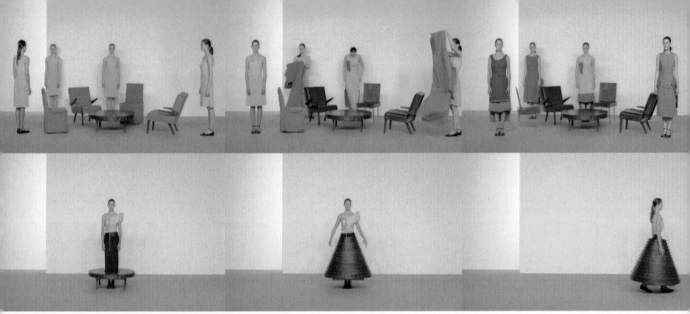

___ ___ **KARL LAGERFELD DRESS.** LOCATION **SATELLITE CITY TOWER**, MEXICO CITY, 1957, DESIGN LUIS BARRAGÁN AND MATHIAS GÖRITZ. FROM *VOGUE*, JANUARY 1966. COURTESY BARRAGÁN FOUNDATION, BIRSFELDEN, SWITZERLAND

MEN'S
FASHIONS OF THE TIMES

REVIVING THE LOOK OF THE FUTURE
BY ROBERT E. BRYAN

OPPOSITE. FROM LEFT: Nylon jacket, $220, knit viscose mock turtleneck, $180, canvas pants, $170, and Ultrasuede belt, $65. All by Austyn Zung. At Patricia Field, 10 East Eighth Street. Jacket also at Pavingas, Brooklyn, N.Y. (in black and white only). Loafers from To Boot New York Adam Derrick.

Nylon jacket, $260, and canvas pants, $130. At Laundry Industry, 122 Spring Street. Cashmere sweater from Cruciani, $495. At Bergdorf Goodman Men. Fred Hayman, Beverly Hills, Calif. T-shirt by Calvin Klein. Leather belt from De Vecchi. Loafers from To Boot New York Adam Derrick.

BELOW: White lamb jacket, $950, black sleeved shirt of lin cupro, $275, and b wool and rayon pa All by Calvin Klein and shirt at Calvin stores nationwide, at Macy's West. Bl shoes from To Boo Adam Derrick, $23 Bergdorf Goodman Louis, Boston.

BRASILIA __ Misled in part by the fact that most of the photographs in circulation date from the early years of its construction, contemporary architects tend to think of the inhabitants of Brasilia as characters in a novel by Ballard. As creatures moving about in empty, metaphysical spaces, forever poised between, as it were, a euphoria of modern living and the apocalypse of urban and apartment block conflict. In actual fact, Brasilia is today certainly a much less empty and metaphysical city, where the spaces between buildings have filled up with gardens and activities, and where – not counting all the satellite towns scattered around the monumental zone – over one million people live. The myth of Brasilia, like Esperanto and the conquest of the moon and many other symbols of late modernity, reached its peak and its first abrupt decline in the sixties. . . . Today, judged by a more disenchanted and different view of reality and of the history of architecture and of the city, Brasilia is perhaps on the way toward regaining a worthy place among the repertory of contemporary images and in the ideal museum of the twentieth century. Not as a perfect urban utopia anymore, nor as the image of life and the city of the future, but as one of the infinite conceptions of cities and metropolitan life, everywhere unfinished and inexact, everywhere chaotic, yet still necessary to the comparison and progress of ideas. **Pippo Ciorra**, "Brasilia, il mito della modernità," *Amica*, 9 October 1999

___ __ **"REVIVING THE LOOK OF THE FUTURE,"** BY ROBERT E. BRYAN, PHOTO PHILLIP DIXON. PAGES FROM *MEN'S FASHIONS OF THE TIMES - THE NEW YORK TIMES MAGAZINE*, PART 2, MARCH 1996. LOCATION **BRASILIA** WITH ARCHITECTURE BY OSCAR NIEMEYER: NATIONAL CONGRESS BUILDING, 1959; THREE POWERS PLAZA WITH PLANALTO BUILDING, 1958

COMBINING BLACK OR NAVY AND WHITE ENHANCES THE MODERN MINIMALIST SENSIBILITY.

THE SHORT, CROPPED JACKET, OR WINDBREAKER, IS THE FIRST CHOICE IN OUTERWEAR FOR THIS SPRING, WITH WHITE LEATHER THE NEWEST VERSION.

___ ___ "REVIVING THE LOOK OF THE FUTURE," PROJECT ROBERT E. BRYAN, PHOTO PHILLIP DIXON. PAGES FROM *MEN'S FASHIONS OF THE TIMES - THE NEW YORK TIMES MAGAZINE*, PART 2, MARCH 1996. LOCATION **BRASILIA** WITH ARCHITECTURE BY OSCAR NIEMEYER: CATHEDRAL, 1959; NATIONAL THEATER, 1958

_____ **NITERÓI MUSEUM OF CONTEMPORARY ART**, RIO DE JANEIRO, 1991-1996, DESIGN OSCAR NIEMEYER. PHOTO © RETO GUNTLI

SYLVIE FLEURY ___ It is certainly no coincidence that in the works, installations and environments of Sylvie Fleury the prevalent atmosphere smacks of pop. It was from the fifties, in fact, that in Western society forms of behavior that had previously been reserved to a privileged few became possible for many. Numerous hierarchies vanished and the borders between high culture and popular culture were abolished; mass movements and leisure pastimes came into being. Sylvie Fleury's work looks at this period in terms of style, too, exploring all the realms of added value and fetishistic production. In her works all the codes interact – fashion codes, art codes, high and low culture codes, but also male and female models – with an attitude that seems to encounter no resistance. Without any moralistic intent or desire to draw conclusions, she examines the world as a "shopping basket" and grabs its objects and contents. As Olu Oguibe writes: "Fleury can get us to question the illusory inspirations of the masses, whereby industrial production has made available objects hitherto accessible only to high society; and she knows how to draw our attention to the masquerade of consumerism as a form of democratized haute couture. But as she herself says, she loves shopping. She is not against this eccentric girl's vice; her criticism of taste is ambivalent and that is her strength." **EDC**

__ __ SYLVIE FLEURY, *8*, 2000, FIBERGLASS SPHERE, PAINTED GOLD; INSIDE: SWAROVSKI CRYSTALS ON BLACK FABRIC, DIAMETER 255 CM. COURTESY THE ARTIST, GALERIE HAUSER & WIRTH & PRESENHUBER, ZÜRICH__ __ → ATELIER VAN LIESHOUT, *LA BAIS-Ô-DRÔME*, 1995, VARIOUS MATERIALS, POLYESTER, 245 X 2113 X 670 CM. PHOTO ATELIER VAN LIESHOUT

Badeværelset er lavet som en stor vaskemaskine for mennesker.
The bathroom is arranged like a large man-washer.
Das badezimmer gleicht einer grossen waschmaschine für »den nackten affen«
La salle de bains est conçue comme une grande machine à laver les gens.

__ __ **INTERIORS OF THE FJOLLE HOUSE**, STOCKHOLM, 1969, DESIGN JOE COLOMBO, PHOTO ASGER SESSINGØ. FROM "COLOMBO, SPIES & FJOLLE," *MOBILIA*, NO. 169, AUGUST 1969

_ _ _ **DISPLAY FOR MANDARINA DUCK STORE, RUE SAINT HONORÉ, PARIS**, 2000, DESIGN NL ARCHITECTS FOR DROOG DESIGN _ _ _ *RAINBOW CHAIR*, 2000, DESIGN PATRICK NORGUET, BY CAPPELLINI

___ **CUSTOM-BUILT COOPER MINI,** "DRESSED" BY PAUL SMITH, 1998. PHOTO SANDRO SODANO

___ ___ **SET DESIGNS FOR PROGRAMS PRODUCED BY MTV ITALIA**, DESIGN STUDIO GIANFORMA FROM AN IDEA BY MAURIZIO VITALE, CREATIVE DIRECTOR MTV. FROM *INTERNI*, NO. 511, MAY 2001

__ __ **CHILDREN'S LIBRARY ON THE FIRST FLOOR OF THE SENDAI MÉDIATHÈQUE**, JAPAN, 2001, DESIGN TOYO ITO, FURNISHINGS KAZUYO SEJIMA

__ __ KRIS RUHS, VIEW OF THE EXHIBITION *INSTALLATION*, 2001, GALLERIA CARLA SOZZANI, MILAN. PHOTO LORENZO CAMOCARDI

__ __ **THE VERSATILITY OF FABRICS DESIGNED BY DAVID HICKS**. © DAVID HICKS AND NICOLAS JENKINS 1979

___ **HOMOSEXUAL HAPPENING AT THE KUSAMA STUDIO**, NEW YORK, 1968. FROM *YAYOI KUSAMA*, DIJON: LES PRESSES DU RÉEL, 2001

2 6 9

VANESSA BEECROFT ON GIO PONTI. **Interview by Giacinto Di Pietrantonio** __ *Ponti: Architect, designer . . . who made no distinction between writing, painting and designing.*

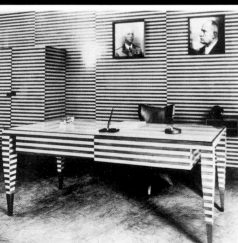

I pictured a striped room: the office of the Chairman of the Ferrania company in Rome, 1936, by Gio Ponti, and I decided to use it for a work.

Ponti: A contemporary neoclassic just like "Beecroft's Performances," especially the Sisters . . ."

The sister is neoclassical on one side, and on the other a doll like Lolita. Gio Ponti treats forms with ease, as if they were anthropomorphic. The octagonal villa, the elongated villa, could be moods, or a book of geometry.

Ponti: "I'm happy to talk with you, because I'm always alone and when I'm lying down I think that thoughts, too, lie down, whereas it's better if thoughts sit up for conversation."

Sister Ponti like Sister Jennifer is lying down and sitting up. She is in a classical posture in which I imagine all the Venuses and all the Mayas in the paintings and sculptures of my memory, and semi-reclining because she is posed, resting like an object on a base: inert.

Ponti: "I agree with Cocteau when he says that the new lies not in new forms expressing a thing, but in new ways of thinking of it."

Forms repeat themselves and grow old, whereas ideas are abstract and reinterpret themselves.

Ponti: A few favorite words: Invention, Expression, Academy, Machine, Interval, Experience. Perfect . . .

Marvelous! GDP in *Camera Italia*, catalogue of the exhibition curated by Giacinto Di Pietrantonio, Associazione Culturale VistaMare, Pescara, 2001

__ __ VANESSA BEECROFT, ***PONTI SISTER***, 2001, PERFORMANCE, *CAMERA ITALIA*, ASSOCIAZIONE CULTURALE VISTAMARE, PESCARA. PHOTO DUSAN RELJIN, © 2001 VANESSA BEECROFT. COURTESY DEITCH PROJECTS, NEW YORK __ __ **FERRANIA PRESIDENTIAL OFFICES, ROME**, 1936, DESIGN GIO PONTI

ENCHANTED ROOMS PROJECT CINZIA RUGGERI FOR *DOMUS* NO. 638, MAY 1982. PHOTO OCCHIOMAGICO. COORDINATION ALESSANDRO GUERRIERO

ORA-ÏTO __ Is it possible to simulate the language of big corporations without running into legal complications? Is it possible to operate on the global market with a virtual product? Yes, it is, if you happen to be Ora-ïto, the twenty-five-year-old multimedia idea man who deals in design, advertising, graphics, communications, video clips, architecture and web design. He is the man who seduced top names in the fashion system with projects as unlikely as they are irresistible. As in the case of the Vuitton knapsack presented on Ora-ito's Internet site, and immediately snapped up by potential buyers and journalists, who then discovered it was a virtual object that had never been in production and about which the French fashion house was completely in the dark. Since then Ora-ïto has been a unique case in the post-industrial design world. He has caught the eye of names like Adidas, Swatch, Issey Miyake and Kenzo, with whom his office is currently collaborating. Just as it is collaborating with Cappellini, who saw Ora-ito's dismantled and virtualized world and grabbed him to design its 2001 advertising campaign. Cappellini, described by the *Financial Times* as "the most prestigious Italian design company," could not have failed to notice the young designer's bizarre communications strategies. The company has, in fact, for years been fostering a global interpretation of life and living, combining a tendency to cosmopolitanism with its resolve to experiment constantly with new expressive and communicative forms. If Cappellini products are distinguished by their pluralism, Ora-ïto interpreted this multiplicity with advertising in a state of evolution. He designed a virtual house and put lamps, chairs, beds, tables and armchairs made by the company into it. For this advertisement, as with other designs, Ora-ïto didn't just create samplings or parodies and rearrangements of existing items: he operates on the borderline between the real and the artificial to redefine the rules of global communication. The web site features some of the many designs done by his Paris firm: the G-shaped house, in homage to the Gucci brand; the dystopian Paris 2010, where seven multinationals have bought some of Paris' most famous buildings, and the Arc de Triomphe is simply a big three-dimensional Nike poster; or the numerous virtual objects such as Cinderella 2001, an artificial shoe made in collaboration with Roger Vivier, inventor of the high heel. **LP**

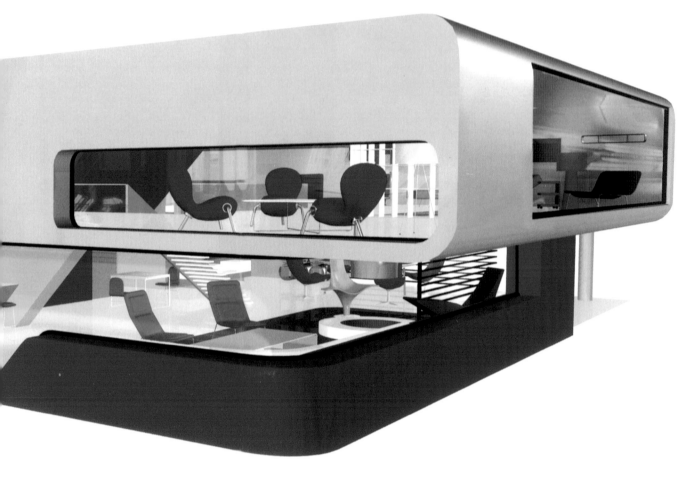

___ ___ *RIVE DROITE* ARMCHAIR, 2001, DESIGN PATRICK NORGUET WITH EMILIO PUCCI FABRICS, BY CAPPELLINI

___ **BOUTIQUE EMILIO PUCCI, MILAN**, 2001, DESIGN LENA PESSOA, MATHIEU PAILLARD AND VUDAFIERI PARTNERS. PHOTO SANTI CALECA

___ ___ LIMITED EDITION **FORD LINCOLN CONTINENTAL**, "DRESSED" BY EMILIO PUCCI, 1977. FROM SHIRLEY KENNEDY, *PUCCI: A RENAISSANCE IN FASHION*, NEW YORK: ABBEVILLE PRESS, 1991

180

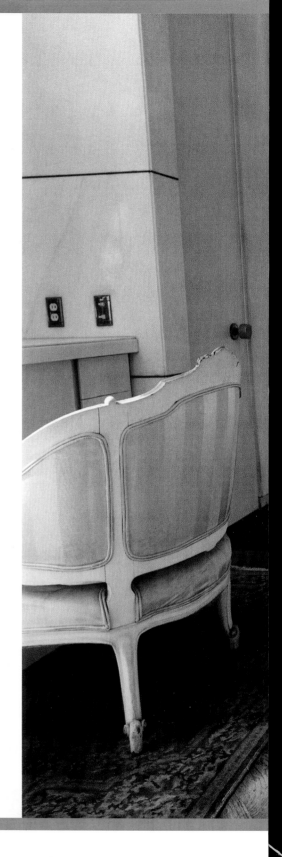

__ __ **"VERSACE,"** PHOTO STEVEN MEISEL, STYLING LORI GOLDSTEIN. PAGES FROM *VOGUE UNIQUE*, SUPPLEMENT TO *VOGUE ITALIA*, NO. 601, SEPTEMBER 2000

___ **A BEAUTIFUL LIFE**, PHOTO SLIM AARONS. THE DESERT HOUSE AT PALM SPRINGS, DESIGNED IN 1946-1947 BY RICHARD NEUTRA FOR EDGAR KAUFMANN. LIDA BARON MEETING NELDA LINSK, WIFE OF THE FAMOUS COLLECTOR FROM PALM SPRINGS, AND HER FRIEND HELEN DZO DZO. FROM SLIM AARONS, *A WONDERFUL TIME: AN INTIMATE PORTRAIT OF THE GOOD LIFE*, NEW YORK: HARPER & ROW, 1974. PHOTO © SLIM AARONS/HULTON GETTY/LAURA RONCHI

__ __ "VERSACE," PHOTO STEVEN MEISEL, STYLING LORI GOLDSTEIN. PAGES FROM *VOGUE UNIQUE*, SUPPLEMENT TO *VOGUE ITALIA*, NO. 601, SEPTEMBER 2000

These photographs were taken shortly after Liberace's death, before the contents of Las Vegas Villa were sent to auction. The Liberace compound in south Las Vegas, begun in 1976, was created from two adjoining tract houses. In time this establishment would boast 20 rooms, some of grand dimensions (save for the ceilings, which kept their original modest height). Las Vegas Villa was the entertainer's principal residence in his later years. Here in the living room and elsewhere glass and mirroring are indefatigable multipliers of stage-set glory; not even the fireplace (rear) is exempt from this all-important task. The mirror-clad grand piano is by Baldwin, with whom Liberace had a long-standing exclusive contract.

___ **LIVING ROOM IN LIBERACE'S LAS VEGAS HOUSE,** WITH MIRROR-CLAD BALDWIN PIANO. PAGES FROM **"LIBERACE'S TASTE,"** TEXT SUSAN YELAVICH, PHOTO GRANT MUDFORD, *NEST*, NO. 10, FALL 2000

___ ___ SHARON STONE DRESSED BY EMILIO PUCCI IN *CASINO*, DIRECTOR MARTIN SCORSESE, 1995. © UNIVERSAL STUDIOS

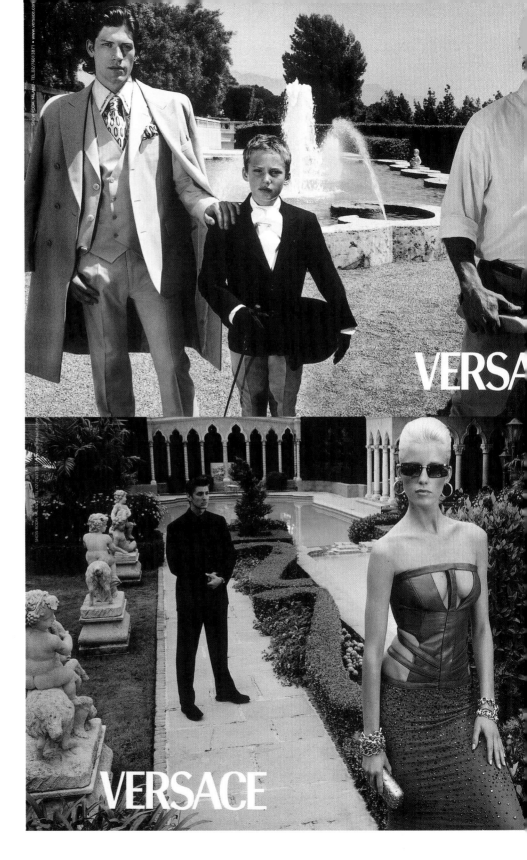

___ ___ **VERSACE ADVERTISING CAMPAIGN**, FALL/WINTER 2001, PHOTO STEVEN MEISEL

__ __ **DON JOHNSON AND PHILIP MICHAEL THOMAS,** IN *MIAMI VICE,* POLICE TELEVISION SERIES CREATED IN 1984. PHOTO © SHOOTING STAR/GRAZIA NERI __ __ FROM *MIAMI VICE.*
PHOTO © RAUL DE MOLINA/SHOOTING STAR/GRAZIA NERI

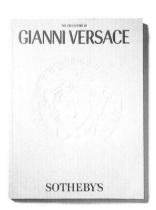

__ __ JOAN COLLINS IN **DYNASTY**, SOAP OPERA CREATED IN THE EIGHTIES. PHOTO © FABIAN W. WAINTAL/SHOOTING STAR/GRAZIA NERI

__ __ THE FLINTSTONE HOUSE, SET FOR THE FILM *THE FLINTSTONES*, 1994, DIRECTOR BRIAN LEVANT. PHOTO © SAMUELSON/SHOOTING STAR/GRAZIA NERI

_ _**DOLCE & GABBANA SHOWROOM, VIA SAN DAMIANO 7, MILAN,** 1995, DESIGN DOLCE & GABBANA. PHOTO SANTI CALECA

__ __ **WALTER ALBINI'S HOUSE IN MILAN**, BEDROOM PAPERED WITH PLASTIC PYTHON-STAMPED MATERIAL, AND **WALTER ALBINI'S HOUSE ON THE GRAND CANAL IN VENICE**, FOYER WITH BEADED CURTAINS AND FAUX MARBLE PLASTIC WALLS, PHOTO ALDO BALLO. FROM PAOLO RINALDI, ED., *WALTER ALBINI: LO STILE NELLA MODA*, MODENA: ZANFI, 1988

by steven meisel

Château de la Mode

Château de Vaux-le-Vicomte and Château de Grousay, two extraordinary French residences belong to different centuries—but each is a testament to the singular aesthetic of a visionary connoisseur. Vicomte, a Baroque gem that served as the architectural inspiration for Versailles, was so magnificent that its owner, Nicolas Fouquet, was jailed by a jealous Louis XIV. Count Carlos (Charles) de Beistegui, who bought the 19th-century Château de Grousay in 1939, fared somewhat better. The heir to a Mexican silver fortune, Beistegui had a flair for the theatrical, and Grousay—where he designed elaborately themed rooms in grand neo-classical style—was his stage. But Beistegui's greatest production was his 1951 costume ball at the Palais Labia on the Grand Canal in Venice, one of the most memorable social events of the last century. Cecil Beaton's photographs of the fete capture a divinely decadent world—one that's also celebrated in the spring couture. Tasteful extravagance is alive and well in these beaded capes, minidresses and frothy organza frocks—all photographed against the sumptuous backdrops of Grousay and Vicomte.

PHOTOGRAPHED BY MICHAEL THOMPSON

Carlos (Charles) de Beistegui at
the Venice Ball at his Palais Labia,
wearing an 18th-century sausage-curl
wig. Photographed by Cecil Beaton.

Yves Saint Laurent's cotton
shirt with a silk tie and wool
pants. Photographed in Château
de Groussay's theater.

Photograph by
Cecil Beaton

Daisy Fellowes at the Venice ball, representing America in the 18th century. Photographed by Cecil Beaton.

____THE ROOF TERRACE AND THE LARGE SALON IN CHARLES DE BEISTEGUI'S APARTMENT, 136 AVENUE DES CHAMPS-ELYSÉES, PARIS, 1929-1932, RENOVATION DESIGN LE CORBUSIER AND PIERRE JEANNERET. FROM STEPHEN CALLOWAY, *BAROQUE: THE CULTURE OF EXCESS*, LONDON: PHAIDON, 1994

TALL

AND

WELL

STACKED

TEXT
MITCHELL
OWENS
PHOTOGRAPHS
DERRY
MOORE

It was a domestic scenario straight out of Puccini, with bits of Stendhal and Maupassant grafted on for atmospheric good measure. "A life of decadent hardships," its hero mused, "with the thick smell of soup and a desperate love for a woman with a beautiful face and an abominable body, or vice versa, an abominable face and a beautiful body."

But what about the setting? What would be most appropriate for conducting this *via bohemia*? A garret, certainly, an urban space of minimal square footage, tucked into bat-ridden eaves, chilly at night, and quiet but for the torturous drip-drip-drip of a leaky tap. And of course, the garret would be reached by a staircase – narrow, even rickety, perhaps slightly unsafe – a shadowy ascent of soot-settled corners, one steep, creaking flight after the next, and balusters loose in their sockets.

Flights of Fancy: Mongiardino's rendering, in cross section, of the Bussei house, his favorite, which he had made in marzipan cake for his eightieth birthday party.

MONGIARDINO INSTRUCTIONS FOR USE

CHAPTER I _ BY WAY OF THE STAIRS _ Yes, it could all start like this, here, in a neutral place belonging to everyone and no one, twenty-three landings, sixteen doors (one false) different only in their handles, like climbing up a lighthouse. Yes, it will start here: between the third and fourth floors, with the plan and section in front of us as we try to understand.

CHAPTER II _ THIRD FLOOR _ Double-height bedroom, fit for a queen, marble bust in one corner, four-poster bed, bathroom in the gallery, claw-foot bathtub.

CHAPTER III _ GROUND FLOOR _ Twentieth-century café and dining room, built-in velvet-covered benches, polished dark boiserie with arches, cornices and slender columns in front of mirrors flashing back crazy perspectives, with an oblique drape fluttering in front of stained glass, floral railroad lamps, with internal steps leading to the sitting room.

CHAPTER IV _ SITTING ROOM _ Secret, damasked reading room on the first floor, with mock mahogany upholstery, ceramic stove, nineteenth-century furniture.

CHAPTER V _ ATTIC _ Private suite, ghostly drapes over red damask on the walls and floor, and even the fireplace. Clothes in the ancient trunk. The white drapes follow us up the last, truly the last flight of stairs, the twenty-second, and disclose truly the last corner at the top of the house, crammed full with a bathtub paved in gold mosaic, surrounded by blue walls, a bath without a room.

CHAPTER VI _ FOURTH FLOOR _ Bedroom, perhaps for guests, plain but with ochre pilasters setting off the red tapestry, the bed sturdy and high.

CHAPTER VII _ SERVICE ROOM _ On the second floor, mysterious, crowded with incongruous furniture, stage sets awaiting a performance.

CHAPTER VIII _ CELLARS, 1 _ First basement level, the kitchen with lowered vault, catacomb-like, with white faceted tiles on the walls.

CHAPTER IX _ ANTONELLI _ In 1880 Alessandro Antonelli, professor of fine arts, architect and speculator, built on an impossible triangular site, this *slice of polenta*, just over 3.5 m wide, 16 m long, six floors above ground and two below, circa 30 m^2 per floor, in the city of Turin.

CHAPTER X _ CELLARS, 2 _ Antechamber with brick-lined vault and gold mosaic on the walls, then the private baths, oval eye of the day, quartz floor, lowered marble ceiling with grooves to carry condensation into an elegant cornice, perfumes from mysterious conduits.

CHAPTER XI _ BUSSEI _ In the living room studio on the fifth floor, where he collects his albums of poetry, epigrams and photographs: the master of the house, silver-haired, the elegance of a prince Edward, walking stick. Dandy?

CHAPTER XII _ MONGIARDINO _ Master architect and stage-designer, a Renaissance man, with his white beard and the eyes of a man born in Genoa, looks like the keeper of a lighthouse rendered as luxurious as a transatlantic liner. **RM**

___ __ PLAN AND SECTION OF THE **BUSSEI HOUSE IN TURIN**, FURNISHED BY RENZO MONGIARDINO. DRAWINGS FOR THE MARZIPAN MAQUETTE FOR THE ARCHITECT-INTERIOR DESIGNER'S EIGHTIETH BIRTHDAY PARTY. PAGES FROM "TALL AND WELL STACKED," *NEST*, NO. 2, FALL 1998

_ _ _ ROOM FOR THE ANTIQUE CERAMICS COLLECTION AT HÔTEL LAMBERT, PARISIAN RESIDENCE OF THE ROTHSCHILD BARONS, FURNISHED BY RENZO MONGIARDINO.
PHOTO DERRY MOORE

___ **DOLCE & GABBANA STORE, OLD BOND STREET, LONDON**, DESIGN DOLCE & GABBANA IN COLLABORATION WITH DAVID CHIPPERFIELD. PHOTO DENNIS GILBERT/VIEW

__ __ **EASY CHAIRS HANGING TOGETHER**, DESIGN JÖRG SIELAFF, NEU ISENBURG. FROM *MOBILIA*, NO. 169, AUGUST 1969

___ GIANFRANCO FERRÉ'S OFFICE WAITING ROOM, **SPAZIO GIANFRANCO FERRÉ, VIA PONTACCIO 21, MILAN**, 2001, DESIGN GIANFRANCO FERRÉ IN COLLABORATION WITH FRANCO RAGGI. PHOTO PAOLA DE PIETRI

___ ___ *CITTÀ CHE SI RISPECCHIA*, 1955, DECORATIVE DESIGN FOR SCREEN BY PIERO FORNASETTI ___ ___ **SERIES OF PLATES WITH ARCHITECTURAL DESIGNS**, CREATED BY PIERO FORNASETTI AS A PROMOTIONAL GIFT FOR THE BRENTA CONSTRUCTION COMPANY. FROM PATRICK MAURIÈS, *FORNASETTI: LA FOLLIA PRATICA*, TURIN: UMBERTO ALLEMANDI & C., 1992

____ **WINDOW DISPLAYS FOR LA RINASCENTE DEPARTMENT STORE, MILAN, 1959-1961**, ON THE THEMES: *MOSTRA DELL'INDIA*, DESIGN G. ORTELLI, R. SAMBONET, A. FAGGIAN; *NATALE*, DESIGN G. ORTELLI; *TESSUTI MINICARE*, DESIGN G. ORTELLI. FROM BRUNO MUNARI, ED., *VETRINE NEGOZI ITALIANI*, MILAN: L'UFFICIO MODERNO, 1961

DISPLAY AT LA RINASCENTE, MILAN ___ I started work at La Rinascente, thinking it was going to be a temporary job and that I would go back to studying medicine again. But when I got in there I became fascinated by the abyss that stretched between what people were beginning to want and what industry had to offer them. . . . In the beginning I was assistant to various architects who were responsible for the arrangement of exhibitions, window displays, et cetera. At that time people like Max Huber, Roberto Sambonet, Giancarlo Iliprandi, Bruno Munari and Giancarlo Ortelli were working for La Rinascente. They used to travel around the world and come back with material to be used for the big market-exhibitions that cost the corporation a fortune. But they introduced the concept of culture to the department store public. **Giorgio Armani**, in Silvia Giacomoni, *L'Italia della moda*, Milan 1984

_____ **TADINI LAMBERTENGHI STORE, VIGEVANO**, 1960, DESIGN VITTORIO GREGOTTI, LODOVICO MENEGHETTI, GIOTTO STOPPINO, AND **MARTINISI STORE, MILAN**, 1960, DESIGN MICHELE ACHILLI, DANIELE BRIGIDINI, GUIDO CANELLA. FROM BRUNO MUNARI, ED., *VETRINE NEGOZI ITALIANI*, MILAN: L'UFFICIO MODERNO, 1961

3 1 7

__ __ **RED EAR JEANS SHOP/PAUL SMITH, TOKYO**, 2001, ARTISTIC DIRECTOR PAUL SMITH, WALL AND FLOOR DECORATIONS BY RICHARD WOOD, DESIGN SOPHIE HICKS

___ ___ **PAUL SMITH STORE, MILAN,** 2001, ARTISTIC DIRECTOR PAUL SMITH, DESIGN SOPHIE HICKS

__ __ FROM THE FILM *THE COOK, THE THIEF, HIS WIFE AND HER LOVER*, 1989, DIRECTOR PETER GREENAWAY. PHOTO © M. CLOSE/CORBIS SYGMA/GRAZIA NERI

_____ **THE ALCOVE IN CESARE RIVETTI'S HOUSE, TURIN**, 1949, DESIGN CARLO MOLLINO. AT THE FOOT OF THE BED, A SOFA WITH BACK IN THE FORM OF A SUSPENDED BUTTERFLY WING; ON THE FAR WALL, A PANEL WITH PHOTOGRAPHIC ENLARGEMENT (CLOUDS FROM AN ENGRAVING) AND PSYCHE, PHOTO MONCALVO. FROM _DOMUS_, NO. 245, APRIL 1950

BACHELOR APARTMENT __1-2. The *garçonnière* occupies the first floor of a small mansion located between the street and the river embankment. It has an elongated wedge-shaped plan. Its service rooms are situated on the street side so as to insulate the living and bedroom zone, which faces the river, against noise. At the end of the corridor is the room for erotic rites. _3. A Japanese-style sliding wall divides the entrance hall from the living room. On the slender column is a female bust in the art nouveau style. _4. In the living room, pink velvet drapes conceal the walls, while mirrors distort perception. On the floor, light brown carpeting and two zebra skins. Murano glass chandeliers and Chinese paper lanterns. At the other end, the dining area. _5. One wall of the living room is decorated with the blowup of a sylvan landscape. A rococo door serves as the frame for a mirror, in which a faux marble fireplace floats. _6. In the alcove, a four-poster bed with velvet drapes and a fur bedspread. _7. In the bedroom, leopard-spotted wallpaper provides a backdrop for the plaster cast of a female bust. _8. Butterflies under glass on the doors of the built-in armoire.

__ __ **MOLLINO HOUSE ON VIA NAPIONE 2, TURIN**, CIRCA 1961-1970, DESIGN CARLO MOLLINO. PHOTO 1987 M.L.

3 2 3

CARLO MOLLINO __ Carlo Mollino's personality is a rich mixture of aptitudes and parallel pursuits. Architect, photographer and automobile buff, inventor of patents, acrobatic aviator, skier, university lecturer, furniture and interior designer, writer and experimenter with a taste for precision, he was a remarkable eccentric and individualist. In the second half of the thirties Mollino was already actively engaged in reversing the process launched by modernism, which had dropped decoration and the caressing of the senses to exalt nudity and visual harmony of proportions, discarding the sensual in favor of the highbrow, the tactile for the visual. Mollino set out to reverse that process. When he designed interiors with padded walls, sinuous lines, alcoves and red lip-shaped sofas that glorify semi-darkness and tactile atmospheres, he seemed to share the disappointment felt by the surrealists and Tristan Tzara with the "aesthetic of castration" practiced by the new orthodox modernists.

Mollino viewed the home as a background to life, a support and mirror of its inhabitant's psyche. He saw it as a danger zone, where the architect's action is liable to be confused and to clash with that of the person living there. Mollino ventured in where architectural culture usually fears to tread, weighing up the connections between the inhabitant's inwardness and the array of objects and decorations that make up an interior landscape. He was that rare instance of an architect who treats the home as a self-portrait (not exactly a building, but an experience). Mollino's interior designs thus present themselves as the narration and description of characters ruling over a closed world, where every possible space must coexist: childhood, old age, current events and memory, evidence and modesty. All this cannot be expressed by a hierarchic order, because "all things are equally close and each implies an infinite number of others; all of them vie with one another and do not want to be forgotten." Mollino's favorite figure is the bachelor, and the bachelor apartment becomes a space in which to experiment with a special reduced living space and the cultural dimensions associated with desire. **ML**

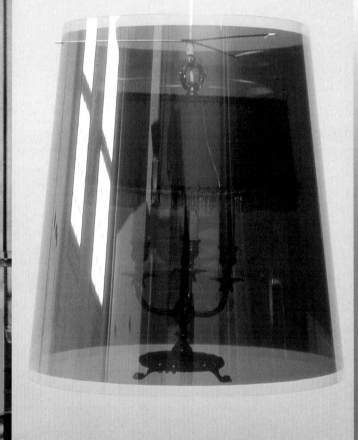 

__ __ *CINDERELLA'S SLIPPER*, 2000, CHANDELIER COMPOSED OF 88 BLOWN-GLASS SHOES, FOR **BOUTIQUE MOSCHINO**, VIA SANT'ANDREA 12, MILAN, DESIGN JO ANN TAN/STUDIO MOSCHINO

___ __ **LUCIEN LELONG'S MAISON DE COUTURE**, PARIS, LATE THIRTIES, DESIGN JEAN-MICHEL FRANK. FROM LÉOPOLD DIEGO SANCHEZ, *JEAN-MICHEL FRANK*, PARIS: ÉDITION DU REGARD, 1997 ___ __ **INTERIORS OF HOTEL SANDERSON, LONDON**, 2000, REMODELED BY PHILIPPE STARCK AND ANDA ANDREI. PAGES FROM BROCHURE AND FROM "THE WHITE HOTEL," *VANITY FAIR*, MAY 2000 (PHOTO TODD EBERLE)

THE WHITE HOTEL

The Sanderson, Ian Schrager's second London hotel,
is his highest concept yet: an ethereal, transparent "urban spa" in which walls
are replaced by glass and sheer, sexy layers of curtain.
As it opens, PETER YORK talks with Schrager about how he and his
phenomenally gifted partners, designers Philippe Starck and Anda Andrei,
have created yet another magical stage set for
the world's high-profile travelers

SILVER LINING
The bathhouse relaxation area
at the Sanderson in London, which
Philippe Starck has lined
with sheer white curtains and filled
with a mix of 18th-century
furniture and chrome and mirrored
pieces of his own design.
The hotel, which is housed in a
landmark 1958 building near Soho,
is Ian Schrager's second
venture in London.

PHOTOGRAPHS BY TODD EBERLE

___ **MOVIE THEATER AND BALLROOM IN BARON ROLAND DE L'ESPÉE'S HOUSE**, PARIS, LATE THIRTIES, DESIGN JEAN-MICHEL FRANK, WITH SOFA DESIGNED BY SALVADOR DALÌ.
FROM LÉOPOLD DIEGO SANCHEZ, *JEAN-MICHEL FRANK*, PARIS: ÉDITION DU REGARD, 1997

__ __ **ALGIERS HOTEL RECEPTION, MIAMI BEACH**, 1951, DESIGN MORRIS LAPIDUS, PHOTO GOTTSCHO-SCHLEISHNER, INC. FROM MORRIS LAPIDUS, *TOO MUCH IS NEVER ENOUGH: AN AUTOBIOGRAPHY*, NEW YORK: RIZZOLI INTERNATIONAL, 1996 __ __ **INTERIOR OF THE RAINBOW SHOP, BROOKLYN, NEW YORK**, 1939, DESIGN MORRIS LAPIDUS. COURTESY ESTATE OF MORRIS LAPIDUS

DUEPEZZI FANTASIA, ROSA CHA. SANDALI PLATFORM, ELSE ANITA.

BEST EXIT: MORRIS LAPIDUS (1902-2001) __ God bless Morris Lapidus for showing us how to go out in style. Five decades ago the architect was excommunicated from modernism for having too much fun with a series of Miami Beach hotels. He carried on so quietly that many assumed he had died, until he was swept up in the sudden love for all things mid-century. Lapidus began his belated victory lap by claiming Frank Gehry had stolen his licks. And when he was honored at the White House last year, he didn't wallow in his glory. A few minutes before the ceremony Lapidus was railing to the press about being slandered in the *New York Times*. (The article in question was published in 1964.) At an awards dinner in New York in November 2000, he stood up from his wheelchair, walked very slowly to the podium, and waged a crooked finger at the entire design world. "What's the most important thing in architecture?" he asked gravely. "It's people. People! Don't forget that." By January he was dead. **Philip Nobel**, from "Best from 2001," *Artforum*, no. 4, December 2001

SURFACE QUALITIES __ Architecture has simplified its surfaces, but is facing them with incorruptible materials, because with the lack of overhangs, stones and gutters, plaster ages badly, especially in the atmospheres of towns heavy with fuel oil residues. It is necessary to have facings that the rain itself will wash, and that match both the modern materials of the window frames, such as aluminum, and traditional materials like wood . . . these facings, old and new, are now beginning "to move"; that is to say, by their relief they move the surface that they represent . . . so the facing acquires (and causes the architecture to acquire) new qualities – plastic qualities under the sky and the sun, and in nocturnal lights, shining and changing their appearance as the shadows move (and to all this may be added color, which in ceramic has every possibility). **Gio Ponti**, *Domus*, no. 328, 1957

__ __ INTERIORS AND SOUTH FACADE OF **ALBERGO PARCO DEI PRINCIPI, ROME**, 1964, DESIGN GIO PONTI. FROM *DOMUS*, NO. 425, APRIL 1965

3 3 3

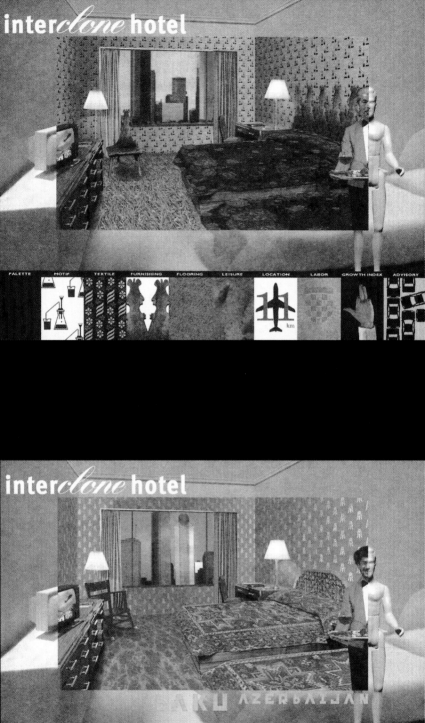

DILLER + SCOFIDIO, *INTERCLONE HOTEL*, 1997, VIDEO INSTALLATION AT ATATÜRK AIRPORT, 5TH ISTANBUL BIENNIAL, ISTANBUL

inter*clone* hotel

HO CHI MINH CITY VIETNAM

PALETTE MOTIF TEXTILE FURNISHING FLOORING LEISURE LOCATION LABOR GROWTH INDEX ADVISORY

inter*clone* hotel

TIJUANA MEXICO

PALETTE MOTIF TEXTILE FURNISHING FLOORING LEISURE LOCATION LABOR GROWTH INDEX ADVISORY

___→ SAM TAYLOR-WOOD, *XV SECONDS*, 2000, INSTALLATION FOR THE FACADE OF SELFRIDGES, LONDON. COURTESY JAY JOPLING/WHITE CUBE, LONDON

3 3 7

__ __LVMH TOWER, NEW YORK, 2000, DESIGN CHRISTIAN DE PORTZAMPARC. PHOTO © PETER MAUSS/ESTO

__ __ **MAISON HERMÈS, TOKYO,** 1998-2001, DESIGN RENZO PIANO. PHOTO © MICHEL DENANCE

isolated heroes nr.1 : robbie june 1988

__ __ INSTALLATION FOR THE EXHIBITION *RADICAL*, 60 PHOTOS ON REVOLVING BILLBOARDS BY 20 "RADICAL" DESIGNERS, ANTWERP, 2001

__ __ **GALERIE LAFAYETTE, BERLIN,** 1991-1996, DESIGN JEAN NOUVEL, EMMANUEL CATTANI. PHOTO M.L.

___ MARTIN PARR, **BLOOMINGTON MALL, MINNEAPOLIS**, 1994. PHOTO © MARTIN PARR/MAGNUM/CONTRASTO

___ __ **NIKETOWN, NEW YORK**, 1996, DESIGN GORDON THOMPSON, JOHN HOKE, JOHN FARNUM AND BRITT BREWER. COURTESY NIKE, INC.

__ __ DINOS & JAKE CHAPMAN, *CHOCOLATE CHA-CHA*, 1996. PHOTO EDWARD WOODMAN, COURTESY GIO' MARCONI, MILAN

__ __ DILLER + SCOFIDIO, *LOGOTYPES*, VIDEO STILLS. FROM *LESS AESTHETICS MORE ETHICS*, EXHIBITION CATALOGUE, 7. MOSTRA INTERNAZIONALE DI ARCHITETTURA, LA BIENNALE DI VENEZIA, VENICE: MARSILIO, 2000

3 5 3

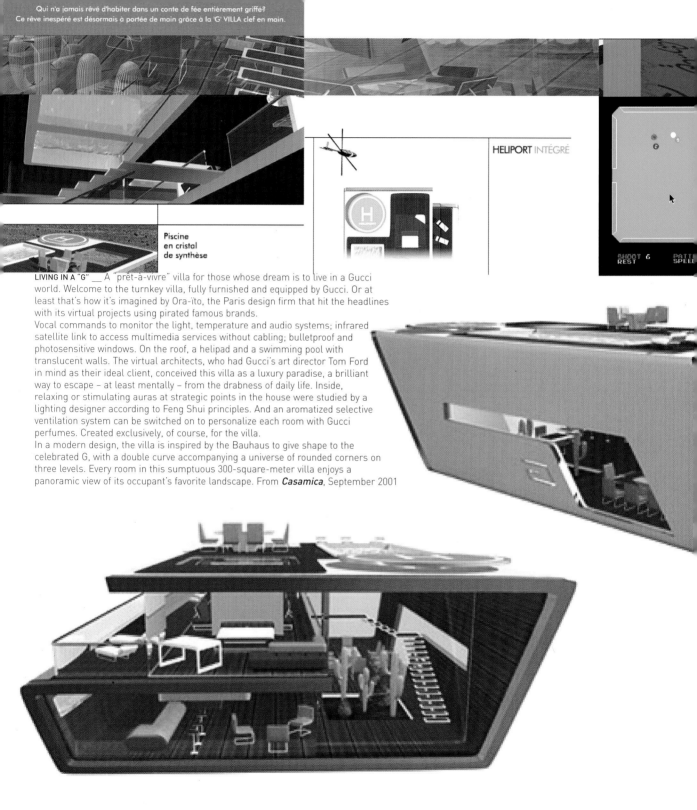

HELIPORT INTÉGRÉ

Piscine
en cristal
de synthèse

SHOOT 6
REST

PATTE
SPEE

LIVING IN A "G" __ A "prêt-à-vivre" villa for those whose dream is to live in a Gucci world. Welcome to the turnkey villa, fully furnished and equipped by Gucci. Or at least that's how it's imagined by Ora-ïto, the Paris design firm that hit the headlines with its virtual projects using pirated famous brands.

Vocal commands to monitor the light, temperature and audio systems; infrared satellite link to access multimedia services without cabling; bulletproof and photosensitive windows. On the roof, a helipad and a swimming pool with translucent walls. The virtual architects, who had Gucci's art director Tom Ford in mind as their ideal client, conceived this villa as a luxury paradise, a brilliant way to escape – at least mentally – from the drabness of daily life. Inside, relaxing or stimulating auras at strategic points in the house were studied by a lighting designer according to Feng Shui principles. And an aromatized selective ventilation system can be switched on to personalize each room with Gucci perfumes. Created exclusively, of course, for the villa.

In a modern design, the villa is inspired by the Bauhaus to give shape to the celebrated G, with a double curve accompanying a universe of rounded corners on three levels. Every room in this sumptuous 300-square-meter villa enjoys a panoramic view of its occupant's favorite landscape. From *Casamica*, September 2001

BILLARD MONOGRAMMÉ G

__ __ MASATO NAKAMURA, *QSC+MV/V.V*, 2001, VARIOUS MATERIALS, INSTALLATION FOR *FAST AND SLOW*, JAPANESE PAVILION, 49. ESPOSIZIONE INTERNAZIONALE D'ARTE, LA BIENNALE DI VENEZIA, VENICE

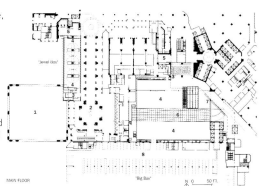

GUGGENHEIM __ For better or for worse, all through the nineties the Guggenheim came to symbolize the expansion of museums into omni-comprehensive cultural industries. With its branches in New York, Venice and Berlin, and its cathedrals of contemporary art in Bilbao and Las Vegas, the Guggenheim has turned museums into grandiose financial and architectural operations, orchestrated by masters of the corporate avant-garde such as Frank O. Gehry and Rem Koolhaas. Detractors even coined the term McGuggenheim to describe this intricate mixture of entertainment, spectacle and global ambition, which seems to owe more to McDonalds' strategies than to traditional museology.

Most recently – as a result of the recession that has followed the September 11 events – the Guggenheim announced drastic cuts to its personnel and programs, involuntarily generating yet another neologism: GuggENRON – from the ENRON scandal that has undermined the Bush administration – might become the new keyword to understand an unexpected shift of paradigms in our contemporary culture. **MG**

1. *Hotel porte-cochère*
2. *Hotel lobby*
3. *Museum reception*
4. *Gallery*
5. *Museum shop*
6. *Trench*
7. *"Mega-door"*
8. *Garage*

___ COR-TEN STEEL SIGN OF **THE HERMITAGE GUGGENHEIM GALLERY**, ON THE GROUND FLOOR OF THE **VENETIAN HOTEL, LAS VEGAS** __ __ GENERAL PLAN OF THE **GUGGENHEIM LAS VEGAS**, 2001, DESIGN REM KOOLHAAS/OMA, CLIENTS: VENETIAN CASINO RESORT, GUGGENHEIM MUSEUM. THE TWO EXHIBITION AREAS ("JEWEL BOX" FOR THE HERMITAGE GUGGENHEIM GALLERY AND "BIG BOX" FOR TEMPORARY EXHIBITIONS) ARE DIVIDED BY THE GRAND LOBBY OF THE VENETIAN HOTEL.__ __ **GUGGENHEIM LAS VEGAS**, 2001, VIEW OF THE LARGE EXHIBITION HALL ("BIG BOX") DURING THE EXHIBITION *THE ART OF THE MOTORCYCLE*, EXHIBITION DESIGN FRANK O. GEHRY. PHOTO © 2001 TODD EBERLE

FREMONT STREET, LAS VEGAS. PHOTO © TIMOTHY HURSLEY

___USA AT NIGHT, COLOR-CODED IMAGE FROM SATELLITES OF THE AMERICAN DEFENSE METEOROLOGICAL SATELLITE PROGRAM. PHOTO © US GEOLOGICAL SURVEY/SCIENCE PHOTO LIBRARY/GRAZIA NERI

TRUMAN __ Truman in the mirror, and ourselves reflected in him. We love him. We pull for him because he is true, genuine. "There's no more truth out there than there is in the show," says Christof, the director-creator. Only in the world he created specially for the True Man, Truman Burbank, is there nothing to fear. The film ends but we stay on in the show. Today we can't help wondering where he is now, what became of him. Outside. Will he have become a Sunday TV guest or did he manage to escape? But did he really want to disappear? According to the many Christofian interpretations of the movie, by leaving the program Truman liberates us, too. But that is not the case. Perhaps we are more aware that the media system is not a monolith, knowing how often it has been mocked by hackers or terrorists, or by artists real or alleged, but we also know there is nothing that can protect us any more, and that the message is our life. **AT**

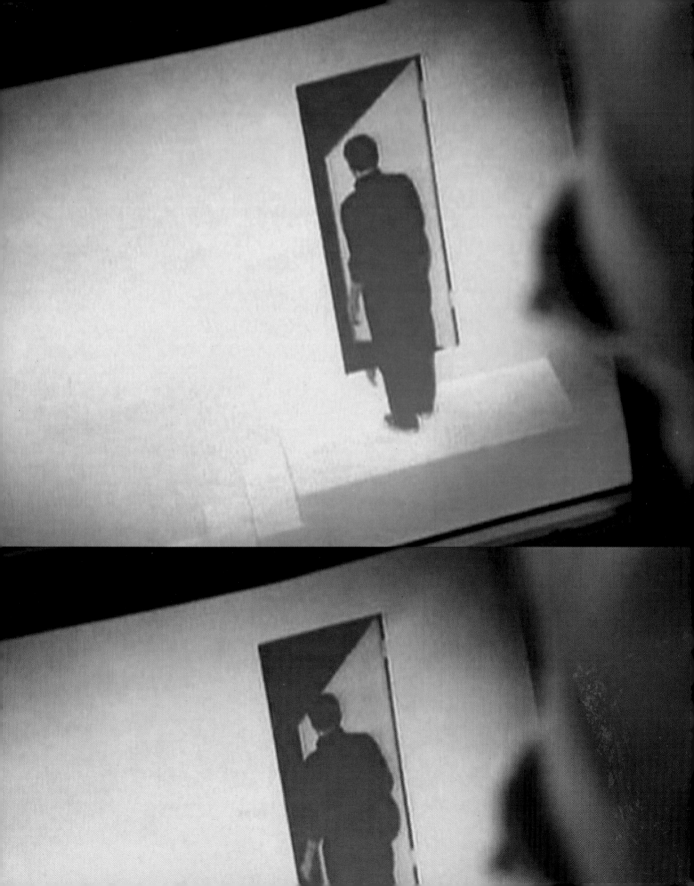

TOTAL LIVING IS A PITTI IMMAGINE PRODUCTION
EDITED BY **MARIA LUISA FRISA, MARIO LUPANO, STEFANO TONCHI**

RESEARCH COLLABORATORS: BRUNELLA CACCAVIELLO, IRENE CANOVARI, LIVIA CORBÒ, EMANUELA DE CECCO, LORENZA PIGNATTI, BRADLEY RIFE, ANGELO TEARDO

FOR COMMENTARY ON THE VISUAL SEQUENCES:
__TEXTS BY IRENE CANOVARI, EMANUELA DE CECCO, RICCARDO DIRINDIN, MASSIMILIANO GIONI, MARIO LUPANO, ROBERTO MONELLI, LORENZA PIGNATTI, VITTORIO SAVI, MICHELE SERNINI, ANGELO TEARDO, STEFANO TONCHI
__CITATIONS FROM TEXTS BY MARIUCCIA CASADIO, PIPPO CIORRA, GIACINTO DI PIETRANTONIO, SILVIA GIACOMONI, PHILIP NOBEL, GIO PONTI, PIERRE RESTANY, THOMAS RUFF, VALERY STEEL

ICONOGRAPHIC MONTAGE BY MARIO LUPANO WITH ALESSANDRO GORI

___ ___ ARCHITECTURE AND DESIGN

EERO AARNIO, MICHELE ACHILLI/DANIELE BRIGIDINI/GUIDO CANELLA, ALCHIMIA (CON CARLA CECCARIGLIA, GIORGIO GREGORI, ALESSANDRO GUERRIERO, ALESSANDRO MENDINI), TADAO ANDO, ANDA ANDREI, COSIMO ANTONACI, ARCHITECTURE & ASSOCIÉS, ARCHIZOOM, BAAS ARQUITECTOS (JORDI BADIA E MERCÈ SANGENIS), JONATHAN BARNBROOK, EDWARD BARNES E HENRY DREYFUSS, FABIEN BARON, LUIS BARRAGÁN, CRAIG BASSAM, JURGEN BEY, ERWAN E RONAN BOUROULLEC, EMMANUEL CATTANI, DAVID CHIPPERFIELD, JOE COLOMBO, DILLER + SCOFIDIO, DROOG DESIGN, ANDRES DUANY E ELIZABETH PLATER-ZYBERK, CHARLES EAMES, THOMAS ERIKSSON, PIERO FORNASETTI, JEAN-MICHEL FRANK, ALBERT FREY, FUTURE SYSTEMS, MICHAEL GABELLINI, CHAFIK GASMI, RICHARD GLUCKMAN, FRANK O. GEHRY, MATHIAS GÖRITZ, EILEEN GRAY, VITTORIO GREGOTTI/LODOVICO MENEGHETTI/GIOTTO STOPPINO, HERZOG & DE MEURON, SOPHIE HICKS, TOYO ITO, PHILIP JOHNSON, TAKAO KAWASAKI, GORDON KIPPING, PIERRE KOENIG, REM KOOLHAAS/OMA, SHIRO KURAMATA, ANNE LACATON E JEAN-PHILIPPE VASSEL, MORRIS LAPIDUS, JOHN LAUTNER, LE CORBUSIER, ADOLF LOOS, ANTTI LOVAG, ROBERT MALLET-STEVENS, MARMOL & RADZINER, RICHARD MEIER, LUDWIG MIES VAN DER ROHE, CARLO MOLLINO, RENZO MONGIARDINO, TOSHIKO MORI CON GWENAËL NICOLAS, JASPER MORRISON, RICHARD NEUTRA, OSCAR NIEMEYER, NL ARCHITECTS, PATRICK NORGUET, JEAN NOUVEL, ORA-ÏTO, G. ORTELLI/R. SAMBONET/A. FAGGIAN, MATHIEU PAILLARD, VERNER PANTON, JOHN PAWSON, LENA PESSOA, RENZO PIANO, GIO PONTI, CHRISTIAN DE PORTZAMPARC, FRANCO RAGGI, KARIM RASHID, ITALO ROTA, PAUL RUDOLPH, KAZUYO SEJIMA E RYUE NISHIZAWA, CLAUDIO SILVESTRIN, J.W. FRED SMITH, BILL SOFIELD, PHILIPPE STARCK, STUDIO BACIOCCHI, STUDIO GIANFORMA, STUDIO MORSA, SHIN TAKAMATSU E MAMORU KAWAGUCHI, JO ANN TAN, PATRICIA URQUIOLA, VUDAFIERI PARTNERS, PETER WHEELRIGHT, PETER ZUMTHOR

___ ___ FASHION

ARMANI CASA, GIORGIO ARMANI, BALLY, ENNIO CAPASA, PIERRE CARDIN, CALVIN KLEIN HOME, ROBERTO CAVALLI, HUSSEIN CHALAYAN, COMME DES GARÇONS, COSTUME NATIONAL, DIESEL, DIOR HOMME, DOLCE & GABBANA, LINDA DRESNER, GIANFRANCO FERRÉ, TOM FORD, GUCCI, HERMÈS, CALVIN KLEIN, DAVID HICKS, KARL LAGERFELD, HELMUT LANG, RALPH LAUREN, LUCIEN LELONG, MANI, MARNI, ISSEY MIYAKE, MOSCHINO, NIKE, PRADA, EMILIO PUCCI, YVES SAINT LAURENT, JIL SANDER, SEPHORA, HEDI SLIMANE, PAUL SMITH, KATE SPADE, VALENTINO, VERSACE, VERSUS

___ART

DOUG AITKEN, RICHARD ARTSCHWAGER, ATELIER VAN LIESHOUT, VANESSA BEECROFT, ANUSCHKA BLOMMERS & NIELS SCHUMM, LOUISE BOURGEOIS, ANGELA BULLOCH, DINOS & JAKE CHAPMAN, LORIS CECCHINI, GREGORY CREWDSON, PHILIPPE-LORCA DICORCIA, SYLVIE FLEURY, ANDREAS GURSKY, DAMIEN HIRST, JENNY HOLZER, PIERRE HUYGHE, DONALD JUDD, ILYA KABAKOV, YAYOI KUSAMA, ARMIN LINKE, OTTONELLA MOCELLIN, MASATO NAKAMURA, JORGE PARDO, NICOLA PELLEGRINI, MARC QUINN, TOBIAS REHBERGER, THOMAS RUFF, NINA SAUNDERS, CINDY SHERMAN, LAURIE SIMMONS, SAM TAYLOR-WOOD, RIRKRIT TIRAVANIJA, PETER WHEELWRIGHT, KRZYSZTOF WODICZKO, ANDREA ZITTEL

__ __PHOTOGRAPHY

PETER AARON, SLIM AARONS, NOEL ALLUM/DAN CORNISH, ALDO BALLO, FABIEN BARON, GABRIELE BASILICO, CECIL BEATON, ANUSCHKA BLOMMERS & NIELS SCHUMM, HARRY BENSON, KOTO BOLOFO, ANTOINE BOOTZ, GUY BOUCHET, PIERRE BOULAT, MICHAEL BÜHLER, SANTI CALECA, LORENZO CAMOCARDI, DANILO CERRETI, PASCAL CHEVALLIER, M. CLOSE, STEPHANE COMPOINT, THIBAUT CUISSET, RICHARD DAVIES, D. JAMES DEE, RAUL DE MOLINA, MICHEL DENANCE, PAOLA DE PIETRI, ARALDO DI CROLLALANZA, PHILIP-LORCA DICORCIA, PHILLIP DIXON, M. DOMAGE, CHARLES DUPRAT, TODD EBERLE, ANNABEL ELSTON, ENRICO FERORELLI, FARABOLAFOTO, DENNIS GILBERT, BOB GOEDEWAGEN, GOTTSCHO-SCHLEISHNER, RETO GUNTLI, MASAYUKI HAYASHI, ALEXEI HEY, STEVE HIETT, HORST P. HORST, EDWARD HUEBER, TIMOTHY HURSLEY, INTERFOTO, DAVID JOSEPH, YORAM KAHANA, KURITA KAKU, JEAN-PIERRE KHAZEM, CHRISTOPH KIRCHERER, WILLIAM KLEIN, MORGANE LE GALLE, DAVID LEVINTHAL, PETER LINDBERGH, MARIO LUPANO, ALEX S. MACLEAN, MARCUS MÅM, ATTILIO MARANZANO, PETER MAUSS, RAYMOND MEIER, STEVEN MEISEL, JOHN MIDGLEY, DERRY MOORE, MONCALVO, JEAN-MARIE DEL MORAL, MICHAEL MORAN, GRANT MUDFORD, NAKASA AND PARTNERS, JEAN-CLAUDE N'DIAYE, NEW E.R.A., OCCHIOMAGICO, MICHAEL O' NIELL, ALESSANDRO PADERNI, MARTIN PARR, SEBASTIANO PAVIA, JONATHAN PLAYER, ST. JOHN POPE, DUSAN RELJIN, JEFF RIEDEL, FRANCO ROSSI, SYLVIE RUAU, PHILIPPE RUAULT, M. RÜCKER, ARMANDO SALAS, ERIK SAMPERS, SAMUELSON, SANAA, JASON SCHMIDT, INGE SCHOENTHAL FELTRINELLI, MIKIO SEKITA, ELFIE SEMOTAN, ASGER SESSINGØ, JULIUS SHULMAN, SIDALI-DJENIDI, LORD SNOWDON, SANDRO SODANO, JOSEPH SOHM, EZRA STOLLER, GINO SULLIVAN, HISAO SUZUKI, MARTIN THOMPSON, MICHAEL THOMPSON, TONI THORIMBERT, MARCUS TOMLINSON, ELLEN VON UNWERTH, FABIAN W. WAINTAL, PAUL WARCHOL, BRUCE WEBER, EDWARD WOODMAN, GIONATA XERRA, YUTAKA YAMAMOTO, MAX ZAMBELLI

__ __MAGAZINES

ABITARE, AMICA, ARCHITECTURE INTÉRIEURE CRÉÉ, BIG, CAP, CASABELLA, CASE DA ABITARE, DOMUS, ELLE DÉCOR, DUTCH, ESQUIRE, FASHIONS OF THE TIMES-THE NEW YORK TIMES MAGAZINE, FLAIR, FLAUNT, GA DOCUMENT, I.D. MAGAZINE, INTERNI, INVIEW, L'OFFICIEL, LO STILE, MEN'S FASHIONS OF THE TIME-THE NEW YORK TIMES MAGAZINE, MARTHA STEWART LIVING, MOBILIA, NEST, THE FACE, TRANSCRIPT, VANITY FAIR, VOGUE, VOGUE ITALIA, W, WALLPAPER*

TOTALIVING

A young woman lying on a rudimentary bed, poised between modern functionality and hospital simplicity. A texture of black and white stripes that not only decorates and punctuates the room, but envelops and constrains the female body on its pallet. *Sister Ponti* is the title of this work by Vanessa Beecroft, inspired by the studio, an obsession in black and white, which Giò Ponti designed in 1936 for the president of Ferrania in Rome. The image is perfect: beautiful and awesome, glossy and obscure, quiet and loud. Its overbearing graphic glamour attracts and repels.

Sister Ponti is the metaphor, the manifesto and the cover – spectacular and revealing – of this book. Immediately afterwards, without any mediation of words or concepts, comes a dense montage of images of miscellaneous origins and intensity. These are followed by a collection of writings by scholars, critics and journalists who, as in a Robert Altman film, depict the many-colored stage of life. Urban utopias, modern houses turned icons of the luxury life, architectures of fashion, series-made museums and advertising sets, models of life, televised lives . . . real life within the show, like the one directed by Christof, creator of the True Man, Truman Burbank. Infant, child, adolescent, young man and adult conserved-observed, Truman lives his existence unknowing and happy, in the small town made to measure.

Fascinated and critical, we watch the continuous flow of images, the lapping and overlapping of places, ideas, people. We think we are different, immune, whereas we unconsciously watch ourselves leading our lives. Total existence is not only the gilded haven of a residential area, it is the eye of an expanded Big Brother, the closed circuit camera filming us at the bank or in the supermarket. Perhaps it is the pattern imposed on us by a total entertainment society.

Reality as we experience it today is crisscrossed by the standardizing and pervasive behavior patterns set by labels and definitions of fashion as industry and cultural form. An ever more sophisticated reality seeks to assert its own particular lifestyles and to dictate our clothes, behavior, spaces, even atmospheres. Anyone can choose from its variegated catalogue to create his or her character and to inhabit global fashion entertainment.

Advertising, fashion, press and television have grown overwhelmingly and tend to shape our every desire and need. The creation of an imaginary world that can be bought has become as necessary as the creation of ever-changing products. Paradoxically though, if the supply of fashion is accelerated, nobody can impose a homogeneous fashion on anyone any more. We imitate whomever we like, when and how we like. The aspiration to luxury gets commoner and everybody wants for himself or herself what is best and loveliest.

The new forms in which lifestyles are offered also reflect the complex overlappings and interconnections between the systems of fashion, design, architecture, art and communication. The roots of this phenomenon may lie in the past and coincide with total design, but the media paroxysm is new, and so is the ever-wider uniformity of individual behavior.

The subjects and the points of departure for reflection are many and contradictory. *Total Living* is an attempt to photograph, without bogus moralisms, prejudice or ideologies, a present already on the move. MLF/ML/ST

DETAIL FROM THE
DKNY ADVERTISING CAMPAIGN, SPRING 2002

Nothing has made a greater contribution to the development of contemporary architecture than its discovery of fashion, of lifestyle. For about twenty years now, ever since it finally joined the culture industry, architecture has been moving into a new dimension within the modernism debate. Architecture is no longer a moral institution, the "mother of the arts." It has gone back to life, and taken on the task of "equipping" it. It has done this in all periods of world history, but at least these were periods that included several decades, and they were then defined as styles in retrospect, by historians.

Yet it is still a moral problem in the current debate about architecture to mention fashion and architecture in the same breath. Architecture has a claim to eternity and to the ultimate truth, while fashion is short-lived and superficial. But this distinction has now been removed in the new discourse called "cultural studies," where the old definition of historical periods in terms of style has been replaced by a new everyday cultural observation of consumerist phenomena and developments.

It therefore no longer makes sense to refer to the phenomena of dressing in architectural history. Gottfried Semper, who first aired this subject of the diverse surfaces of historical architecture, is no longer at the center of the debate. Today architecture is concerned with the pre-formulated formal worlds of clients. Here the commissioning body's branding and program are the guidelines that architecture has to address.

Today both fashion and architecture are part of the culture industry. The boundaries between art and consumerism have shifted, and can no longer be clearly defined. The art of architecture has been realized in cultural buildings in the past twenty years, and has made a considerable impact on the public. For this reason the art of architecture was principally responsible for the change in function that museums have undergone: they have been transformed from temples of history into adventure worlds, intended to attract huge visitor numbers. The next step, from culture museums to temples of consumerism, was then simply the logical consequence.

Scene One: New York 1998, Guggenheim Museum SoHo. A major exhibition of post-war French art is being shown. The only way to get to the museum ticket desk is by making your way through the Guggenheim's large and famous museum shop. This is a shop on such a scale that it is distinguishable from the Dean & Deluca delicatessen, which is diagonally opposite, only by its stock. The exhibition starts with some small sculpture before you get past the entrance checkpoint. Small objects are presented on hip-high plinths. There is some excitement at the shop till. A customer at the shop, or was he a visitor to the museum, has suddenly taken one of these small sculptures, an exhibit, off its plinth and is trying to buy it. His mistake is explained to him: he has mistaken a work of art for an item on sale in the shop.

Scene Two: Not far from Guggenheim SoHo is fashion designer Helmut Lang's New York shop. Inside is an installation made up of serial hermetic cubes. They could be the work of the artist Donald Judd. The backs are open, and selected items of clothing are laid out. By the till is an installation using moving illuminated letters. It looks like an installation by Jenny Holzer, but given that it is by the till (!) it must be an advertisement for and by Helmut Lang. Disappointment or a deliberate attempt to disturb? It seems to be an advertisement for Helmut Lang, but in fact it really is an installation by Jenny Holzer.

Scene Three: New York 2000. Guggenheim Museum SoHo. The Guggenheim museum shop still exists. But the exhibition galleries have already been leased to Prada, the fashion company. These are scenes that have been observed in the world of architecture, art and fashion. Scenes showing fluid boundaries, changing value-allocations. The only thing that is important here is that over the past decade a cultural shift has taken place that is as remarkable as it is interesting. We can't forget that the "museum" has been the ultimate building contract for postmodern development in the last few decades. Museums became known as the new cathedrals of society. They drew on the theatrical power of architecture. The Guggenheim Museum in Bilbao, says Frank O. Gehry, could never have been built as it was if Hans Hollein's Museum Abteiberg in Mönchengladbach had not unleashed the power of theatrical presentation in the eighties. From then onwards it became possible for art to be presented, to be staged, by architecture.

But in these last few decades haven't museums themselves, by dint of their architectural importance, become places where lifestyles are staged? In looking back, we discover that today judgments have become very different. Architecture's performance potential has expanded from the world of art and the museum toward fashion and advertising.

We have become aware in the meantime that it is difficult to distinguish between visiting a museum and visiting a department store. In the underground foyer of the Louvre, all there is in the otherwise indistinguishable area between the museum and the shopping mall is a security check. The whole design of the entrance floor, in its material quality and appearance, does not make any distinction between the areas used for cultural and commercial purposes.

In complete contrast with this, when visiting a temple of fashion you have to maintain the silent humility of cultural worship. For example, the British architectural minimalist John Pawson has developed an almost holy ambience for the Calvin Klein flagship stores (Tokyo, Seoul, New York, Paris), which makes every purchase into a confession with subsequent absolution. The saleswomen are untouchable ascetic priestesses and the gracious way the credit card is returned after a purchase has been made is like the relief afforded by acceptance of the host after transubstantiation has taken place, confirming one's membership in the religious sect.

The boutique as the chapel of consumerism. Fashion as an object of worship. The museum as a department store. The concepts are starting to shift, the functions are changing. And do we hear the insistent question about the role of architecture here?

First of all we have to question one of the myths of modernism. Modernism – but every "style" before it as well – also expressed lifestyles and fashions in its day. In fact it had to, as otherwise no social agreements and codes could have been associated with the movement. Le Corbusier took great care in choosing the car models that were to be photographed to make up the foreground of his buildings. And of course architecture and fine art, design and fashion were linked culturally and aesthetically at the Bauhaus and at Vchutemas in the Soviet Union. It was not until modern architectural history was infiltrated by art historical categories that the concept of "fashion" became reprehensible; from then onwards, architecture had to record a striving for truth and honesty, for progress and enlightenment as style. And for this reason, architectural achievements were increasingly rarely placed in an overall cultural context, which of course had to include fashion and everyday life as well.

Allegedly it was postmodernism that brought about a break with this taboo. Not in its references to architectural history, but in its openness to everyday phenomena. Venturi, Scott Brown and Izenour's publication *Learning from Las Vegas* opened up the view of architecture, just as did Morris Lapidus's rediscovery of the effective aesthetics of American shops and hotels. But even before this, the American sixties avant-garde had left the interior decoration discourse in favor of pop culture. Archigram, Archizoom, Coop Himmelblau, Hausrucker & Co and others deliberately used the marketing instruments of mass media for the first time to convey their architectural ideas. But it was also always about the architectural creation of atmospheres, moods, suitable ambiences, and products and signs that could compete with a general "world of goods."

The eighties and nineties then showed an abundance of signs of the new "dialogue" between architecture and the market, or better, architecture and lifestyle. As early as 1983, the décor for the film *9 1/2 Weeks* brought together a variety of images that were later to influence architecture as well: the cool loft atmosphere, the blinds and the sophisticated lighting. Finally Mickey Rourke and Kim Basinger wander around Rei Kawakubo's Commes des Garçons boutique in Manhattan, thus shocking Manhattan's bourgeois who shopped at established places like Bergdorf Goodman department store.

The opening sequence of the film *The Big Easy* a few years later was also legendary: here a corpse was found in the pool of Charles Moore's "Piazza d'Italia" in New Orleans. Dennis Quaid as the detective jumped incisively to the – incidentally wrong – conclusion that in a place with a name like this it could only be a Mafia murder. A classic product placement for architecture, just as in the last scene of the same film a little Apple Macintosh SE decorated the desk, completely unnecessarily and superfluously.

When the film industry starts to name the locations graced by the new architecture in its pictorial language, then the step to the architects themselves is a short one. The increasing spread of the phenomenon of the "star architect" made the individuals themselves well enough known, and ripe to be used in other ways. Sir Norman Foster advertises Rolex watches and Michael Graves promotes good shoes, "almost as though they're handmade." This was the time when Disney recognized the power of the star architects – Aldo Rossi, Michael Graves, Arata Isozaki, Robert A. M. Stern, Frank O. Gehry, etc – and used it as a marketing instrument. But this was only in the adult sphere, for hotels, offices, etc. All the other areas are still, as they always have been, developed and planned by Disney's "Imagineering" department.

This meant an end to the days that Jacques Herzog once called the epoch of gray and brown managers. He meant the sixties, when gray-suited managers also commissioned gray business architecture. And the seventies, when managers started to wear brown corduroy suits and floral ties with colored shirts. Business architecture became more colorful and louder then as well.

Today, business architecture has splintered into a variety of identities, which then turn up as signs of the company's presence in the same form all over the world. It is not only the MacDonald's corporate identity that is the same all over the world, thus meaning "home" everywhere for Laurie Anderson, as the pop artist once said. Large chains of shops like Benetton, Body Shop, Esprit, etc., have long since set a new orientation pattern with their elaborate corporate design in all the world centers. At the same time, the design and furnishing of auto shows follow painstaking stage directions, stored away in company manuals that are as secret as they are thick.

The fashion industry has also expanded into corporate culture. They have become lifestyle producers, and are thus in a position to go beyond mere clothing to equip people for anything. But it is interesting that consumers scarcely ever stick to one provider, one brand, but are happy to mix and match. To compensate for this, the fashion firms, particularly in Milan, have also started to be active in the urban field. They have followed the example of Donna Karan, who has created one of Manhattan's major and most photographed landmarks with her enormous DKNY firewall in New York's SoHo. In Milan, Missoni and then Armani led the way with radiant artificial models on similar billboards the size of buildings, which have surprisingly become even more important as city landmarks than any new architecture, however radiant it may be.

And so what is left for architecture in this permanently expanding world of Corporate Culture and Corporate Design? Well, there is still housing – in Europe anyway – and occasional educational or cultural buildings as well. But beware: for so-called "public" or "social" housing we'll have to wait for progressive liberalization and opening up of the market in Europe as well. This will increasingly give rise to a popular component that will soon regress to the US model of new urbanism. And educational and cultural buildings now only seem to be autonomous. All they do is follow the media market rules of public attention at an ostensibly higher level. Bilbao is proudly proclaiming that investment in Frank O. Gehry's Guggenheim Museum has paid off for the Basque government after a mere three years, thanks to increased income from tourism and the resultant higher tax take. This means that the building, which was not really built to last, could follow the rules of tourism and be left to decay slowly in its own right now that it has provided an economic return. The administrators of Mies van der Rohe's Tugendhat House in Brno are trying to achieve the opposite effect. The use of the location for TV commercials – there are two running at the moment, for an insurance company and a brewery – is intended to finance necessary refurbishment. And at the same time as the Tugendhat House is being aggressively marketed, it has been declared a UNESCO World Heritage Site.

Of course the Bilbao Guggenheim has been and is being used as a location – in its role as a "spectacle" – for various advertising campaigns for cars and consumer articles. But who would have thought that a similar effect would be created by a remote, reticent building like Peter Zumthor's Thermal Baths in Vals? Fashion shoots, music clips, advertising – it is used as a background for all these purposes to convey a special, "spiritual" atmosphere, and at the same time, rather like Disney's commitment to star architects, to convey some knowledge of architecture to the lifestyle client. Why else would all these advertising teams have put themselves through the arduous journey into the Swiss mountains, where the inhabitants insist on keeping their narrow and dangerous road so that not too many tourists discover their idyllic location. The advertising people count on the fact that the potential buyer of the jeans in front of Zumthor's stone wall also knows who designed the walls. Despite this social and cultural use of his object, or perhaps because of it, Zumthor can continue to style himself the lonely monk of the mountains. In this way he underlines a kind of self-marketing that is not dissimilar to the approach used by the shy and retiring Helmut Lang. Perhaps Peter Zumthor, like Helmut Lang in fashion, is on the lookout in architecture for the unique and eternally valid T-shirt.

But there are already signs that this new use and evaluation of architecture has been penetrated intellectually. Rem Koolhaas and Jacques Herzog, two star architects of the "second generation," are definitely no longer interested in the signature building strategy of the first generation of star architects. They do not see the image, they see the structure. From now on they want to consolidate their star status to the extent that the "firm" and not the design is in the foreground. This is also illustrated in the present company names OMA and HdM. As a well-calculated marketing strategy, they have announced the foundation of a joint office for the building of a new hotel in Manhattan. This announcement alone has already made enough impact and attracted considerable attention, and even the fact that this project has now come to nothing is of only secondary importance. Could it be that the hotel owner, who has become famous and successful with his designer hotels by Philippe Starck, was suddenly afraid that the OMA and HdM would have a rather higher fashion quotient than his own? Both OMA and HdM are drawing here on the strategies of the fashion industry, where branding and marketing power are the crucial factors, but the creative input grows out of the "firm" itself, almost anonymously, although the fashion industry considers it important that the "creative talent" they have brought in for the season is known at least to insiders. OMA and HdM certainly also see the linking of the two "brands" as a possible means of access to bigger contracts and markets.

In my analytical essay "Superfluous Architecture" (1994), I assigned architecture, in this new total marketing environment, the role of conducting research, doing laboratory work, and professing faith in a new realism. In the meantime, everything that is marketed as architecture has become event or entertainment architecture. The question of whether architecture – uniquely among the culture industries – could refuse to accept the world crown of media consumerism has been settled. Every cathedral, every museum, is a shop. And at the moment it seems that the OMA and HdM strategy is the only one that can simultaneously gain control of, question, and accelerate this development, reflectively and with their eyes open. For there is one thing that recent years have shown quite unambiguously in architecture: even refusal leads to being assimilated. All architecture is "promotional architecture," or it is not architecture at all. It doesn't matter what the architecture's own aspirations are, its values and its attentiveness to the media correspond with the seasonal excitement that marks the fashion industry.

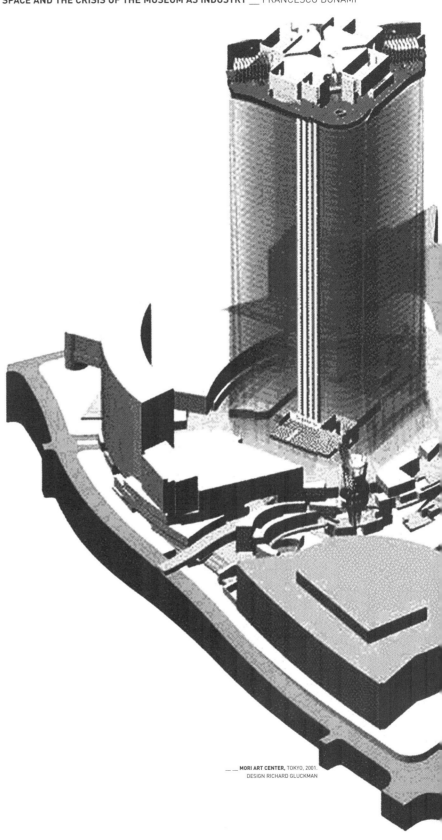

__ __ **MORI ART CENTER,** TOKYO, 2001.
DESIGN RICHARD GLUCKMAN

Once upon a time . . . Once upon a time there was a world of museums where the so-called curators curated exhibitions. The museums, or at least those of modern and contemporary art, were buildings whose function was to host the most stimulating avant-gardes of the world of art and creativity. The curators met challenges and set forth challenges of their own.

People like Pontus Hulten, Harald Szeemann, Kaspar König, Suzanne Pagét, Rudi Fuchs, Germano Celant or Jan Hoet, while laying the groundwork for future strategies and career paths, didn't hesitate to question and challenge the art system, creating new places and situations from which to head for the future. Art itself, though at the center of the transformation process, didn't demand sterile spaces and safe distances from the people and things around it. Images of exhibitions in the sixties and seventies show a crowded, vital, at times chaotic context where the spectators, artists and curators, nevertheless, intermingled with the objects and situations presented, in a kind of equilibrium that was less reverential than today's customary isolation of every object, whether it is delicate or not, precious or not: today isolation is seen almost as a guarantee of importance and value. In the seventies, on the other hand, the present of the object was more important than its future, and the present of the space was stronger than its history. Then something happened at the beginning of the eighties. Museums and curators began to go their separate ways, the former becoming less a home than an industry, the latter increasingly nomadic, homeless. Strategy took over, neglecting projects and challenges, avoiding intellectual adventures. Fewer and fewer spaces stayed on the front line, such as P.S.1 in New York, Portikus in Frankfurt and a few other small institutions scattered in the middle of Europe or the United States. The others became increasingly senile, predictable, slow, in a multiplication of the elephants and accelerating extinction of the fleas. By fleas I mean those small, quick, living structures that latch onto research and never let go, while the elephants are the increasingly cumbersome institutions that cause disaster when they fall and cost a fortune if they don't. The new fleas are a new generation of independent curators who use extemporaneous, daunting and at times obscure exhibitions to create a parallel world, far from the official one. The dialogue stops, different languages emerge and a new intellectual Babel seems to rise up in the ever-less-central center of the art system. At the end of the last century and millennium the Guggenheim Museum in Bilbao was born, a new Mecca, a deceptive wonder; you walk around it, you go inside but you can never penetrate it with soul and thought; nevertheless that gigantic piece of shiny foil dumped there between the city and the river changes the rules of the game.

The museum, as Alfred Barr or Pontus Hulten thought of it – a mental place equipped with space – is perhaps forever finished, only to become a cathedral symbolizing a world that has sold its soul to mere appearances. The museum's reason for being is no longer art and artists, curators and directors as catalysts for ideas and artworks become irrelevant, and in fact in Bilbao there is no director in the old sense of the term, but instead a manager-administrator. For a certain period this transformation of the museum seemed like a revolution, but as time goes by it looks more and more like a crisis posing as a breakthrough. The Guggenheim system seems like a faulty mechanism, like many other museums whose physical growth doesn't go hand in hand with intellectual growth or psychological maturity. But the virus is loose and new cathedrals rise up, increasingly grand and ambitious; new materials, technologies and perspectives capture the imagination of mayors, directors and wealthy patrons. As the new fibers and metals clad the facades, the jackets and shirts of the curators seem to age, their computers break down every half hour, their desks are covered with canceled and forgotten projects, their shoes wear out, their health deteriorates due to air travel in overcrowded cattle class, their backs ache from sleeping in cheaper and cheaper hotels. The stars of the show are the architects who design museums and spaces, one after another, that most artists would reject or want to modify, spaces where visitors run the risk of getting lost or remaining imprisoned in that new shopping mall known as the Museum Store. Everyone focuses on tomorrow, the day after tomorrow is too far away, too abstract.

In Tokyo the Mori Art Center begins to rise up into the skyline. It will be the tallest building in Tokyo and up on the top levels the visitor, after paying twenty-five dollars, will find a restaurant, as well as a fantastic museum designed by Richard Gluckman, the one who did DIA in New York. But Richard Serra will never make it up there, because the elevators specified by the Japanese engineers are too small. Many artworks will thus be denied a view of the skies of Tokyo. Once again art becomes just an appendage to something else, in this case a view, in Bilbao of the museum itself, in Los Angeles, at the Getty Center, of the central plaza where people stand in line waiting to buy a Coke or a mocaccino at Starbucks. In other museums other design fantasies will get the better of the art.

In Milwaukee, in the new wing of the museum designed by Calatrava, a complex device similar to the sails of a tall ship distracts observers even from the internal space of the museum itself. Everyone's outside, busy watching the wings rise and fall, though no one knows for what purpose. In Stockholm at the Moderna Museet the floors and skylights deliver the coup de grâce to the art; in the Kunsthal of Rotterdam the grates of the staircases command more attention than the paintings on the walls; at the Museum of Contemporary Art of Chicago the monumental flight of steps prevents you, in its horror, from ever reaching the door of the museum; while at the new Tate Modern in London the grills of the flooring get the upper hand over anything that is happening nearby, while a lovely bookshop breaks up the narrative itinerary of any exhibition, on which some distracted curator may very well have worked for five years. Many visitors only see half the show, assuming the bookstore is the arrival point of the experience.

As the museums grow, anti-institutional curators wander the planet, like those in search of an institution that wants to welcome them with their fantasies, their flexibility, their folly, a folly that continues to put the creative process, artists and their work, at the center of the space and of life. This form of nomadism, of curatorial enterprise, has generated exhibitions whose theme centers on the spaces themselves, positing movement as a form of research essential to the discourse of contemporary art. One speaks of the city as an urban test tube for future experiments in *Cities on the Move*, curated by Hans Ulrich Obrist and Hou Hanru, or in *Mutations* and *Laboratorium*, exhibitions where Obrist has continued with his essential role as an institutional provocateur. *My Home Is Yours, Your Home Is Mine*, curated by Jérôme Sans and, once again, Hou Hanru, bases its research on the meaning of home in a world that is increasingly in movement, increasingly unstable, where concepts like family and place of residence become weaker and weaker.

But before these events, a few years ago another exhibition opened the way for reflection on what home means today. *No Place Like Home*, curated by Richard Flood at the Walker Art Center in Minneapolis, was a reflection on exile – both physical and mental – on the alienation which the contemporary world with its contradictions, violence and tragedies creates in the identity of the individual and the contemporary artist. Just what home are we talking about when we say "return home" today? The physical space, our original language, our work, our friends, solitude, the street, the hovel, the shantytown? It is hard to understand, the pacific migrations prompted by work or pleasure, for short periods, are much greater in number than those movements caused by war or poverty. Minneapolis, home of the Walker Art Center, is a city lost in the Midwest of the United States, where the temperatures plunge below zero in the winter; by the lake an incredible number of different ethnic groups have found home, from Cambodia, Ethiopia, China, and on the frozen lake every winter a little city appears, of huts where people spend their weekends ice fishing, and drinking beer in the evening in a small bar that has also been erected on the frozen surface of the lake.

Walker Art Center is perhaps one of the few museums that attempts to insert art and the creative process into the whole of contemporary society. The monumental addition designed by Herzog & de Meuron will try to transform the Walker into something else; even the name – a Center, not a Museum – means this is an institution that makes an effort, even within its own contradictions, to be something else.

But physical space can also be a deadly trap, its expansion can make efforts to focus on fundamental contents in the dialogue with our society into a futile exercise. Moreover, physical space clashes with the obsession with the virtual dimension that seems to have run out of control among museums. While the number of "bodies" that crosses the threshold of the museum is still an obsession of any director worth his salt, the investment being made in the virtual dimension is enormous, raising the suspicion that those behind it think going to the museum is boring, that things might seem more interesting when seen at home. This is obviously not true; the number of visitors to museums in the United States is larger than the number of people who attend sporting events, while the famous "virtual Guggenheim" is about to crash, in spite of the millions of dollars invested in the project. So to imagine that everyone does everything and goes everywhere is a childish illusion. The Guggenheim has also had to come to terms with the hard reality of a lukewarm public reaction in Las Vegas to its latest museum project (Gehry, Koolhaas and the motorcycles). Five thousand visitors per day were expected, but only one thousand have materialized, and the tragedy of September 11 certainly hasn't improved the mood of folks who go to Vegas primarily to gamble and dine in the shadow of the Pyramids or by a Venetian canal. The contemporary ocean is populated by these ghostly galleons called museums, and by the lifeboats in which the curators, more emaciated than ever, try to save their skins. What will become of both categories? One possible answer is being hypothesized in Paris with the Palais de Tokyo, a public space planned for multiple events, based on the fluidity of languages. Will this space become a truly innovative structure that will open new perspectives for the presentation of the creativity of the future, or will it simply remain an endless opening? It's probably a wager worth making. But one place alone will not be able to generate the oxygen required for the idea of the museum or the contemporary center to be finally transformed into something that is really in step with the society of our time, with its constant transformations, where realities multiply day after day, borderlines dissolve creating new, hybrid, more complex cultural realms composed of a density not only of ideas but also of objects, art, sounds.

If Calvino listed six reminders for a new millennium, it might be interesting to define six museums, six places where an idea from the eighteenth century – the museum – in a nineteenth-century body can discover both a new body and a new idea. The Guggenheim Museum has tried and is failing, the Walker is trying, the Palais de Tokyo, the Mori Art Center, the new – when it's finished – Center for the Contemporary Arts designed by Zaha Hadid in Rome are trying, along with the Tate Modern. But maybe, like Calvino, we ought to think less about spaces and more about adjectives that can give the space its own identity, its own history to construct and model to define. So I'd like to conclude by outlining six possible adjectives with which we can imagine a museum, a center and, in general, an institution of contemporary art that could, in the future, be important for our growth as contemporary citizens.

Rapid. A contemporary art institution should be rapid in grasping what is happening in the research on contemporary language. There are artists who characterize very brief but essential periods, and showing them at the right moment is fundamental for the identity of the institution.

Self-reflecting. The future and the present of a contemporary institution should reflect one another. To construct a collection through the production and presentation of artworks so that by observing the collection it is possible to understand the history of the institution and, by observing the projects, to imagine the future of its collection, the future of its history.

Agile. A contemporary institution should be agile, slim, both in terms of economics and of organization and programming. Today large quantities of money are squandered in the definition of image and in the paradoxical organization of growth, leading to growing weakness in the efficacy and cultural visibility of the programming.

Transmitting. The capacity to transmit the quality of projects depends more on the projects themselves than on marketing and development efforts. The intrinsic communicative power of art is being underestimated. A work capable of pushing society's buttons doesn't need advertising, it is advertising. A contemporary institution must be able to transmit the energy of its content in a simple, oral way, like gossip.

Receiving. The capacity to receive and to process information from the outside is essential for a contemporary institution. A program cannot be based on in-house, personal tastes, it requires analysis of external creative reality. The identity of the institution depends on its capacity to create its own specific role and, at the same time, to bear witness to its own time and its own context. Welcoming. Not only as a space, but also as a philosophy and a process. To welcome not only visitors but also other ideas, other realities that would otherwise be excluded from the construction of an effective social and intellectual fabric. A contemporary institution should be a temporary point of transit for visions that may also contradict its identity, and which can, in their contradictions, take part in the inevitable and necessary process of transformation.

___ **VILLA STEIN**, GARCHES, 1926-1928.
DESIGN LE CORBUSIER

Despite apparently univocal and determinant relations, total living is not a product of our time and its culture. Media paroxysms, dynamic consumer convulsions and increasingly uniform individual behavior only add new assumptions to a phenomenon whose origins lie elsewhere and correspond to that of integral design. The recent issues of total living, of the dynamics of lifestyles, have led to its explosion and fragmentation into a multitude of events. This has made it all the more visible, but also extremely difficult to conceptualize clearly. In a context of this kind, its root, the dialectic between a sphere of taste and the action of design, is totally unrecognizable, submerged and hybridized as it is, by an infinite number of other factors. The chaotic obscurity of today's declension of total living can nevertheless be contrasted by a sufficiently distinct reconstruction of the stages on which it is founded: a succession of alterations and germinations of its architectural origin, belonging at this point to the ancient times of media, consumption and industrial production.[1]

Those events began with the early age of media, when the accent was on architectural design disciplines. At the end of the nineteenth century and in the early years of the twentieth, in a climate of international art nouveau, a number of new decorative arts magazines came to the fore. They became not only central to the discipline, but also began to circulate widely and to foster cultural exchanges among artists. Furthermore, they served to widen, especially in geographic terms, the numbers of readers interested in the movements of taste. However, the wide circulation of those magazines also made them liable to be reduced to mere instruments of fascination, if the gap between where they were published and where they were read grew too wide.

Once a month, on the fifteenth, there arrived from England for Jolanthe the magazine *The Studio, an Illustrated Magazine of Fine and Applied Art.*

On those evenings after dinner, Jolanthe would always sit in a low armchair in the corner, close to the soft light of the English standard lamp which she had named "Edith" and which she treated with tenderness and gratitude on account of its pleasant light.

She would spread *The Studio* upon her delicate knees and slowly turn its pages, often flicking back again and stopping for a further pause.

Sometimes the pauses were very long.

Then her husband would say, Jolanthe . . .

And she would continue to turn the pages.

She never called him, never said, Look . . .

He remained seated at the big table, calmly smoking and resting after the day.

She sat in the low armchair and turned through the pages.

She looked at the dreamy women painted by Burne-Jones who seemed to touch the ground only with their toes. She gazed, too, at marvelously wiry, naked, marmoreal bodies, at a variety of objects in ivory and worked copper, models in iron and gold, infinite luxuriant meadows and sporadic giant trees . . .

. . . Sometimes her husband would move over to the standard lamp, adjust its light, remove the enormous green silk lampshade and retire to bed.

This fifteenth of the month had become a holiday, and at all events a different kind of day.

"I am in England," she felt, "in England!"

. . . Once she even dressed up as a Burne-Jones figure. She put on a light cloak of white silk with a thousand pleats over her naked body and a long parting in her hair. Holding the long stem of a flower in her hand.

. . . And so the three of them lived in mutual peace: Jolanthe, Jolanthe's husband, and *The Studio*, the beautiful English magazine.

In the same fin de siècle Vienna in which Peter Altenberg tells the story of this ménage, entitling it *The Friend*,[2] and in which Jolanthe was, in all probability, dreaming of the England of William Morris and yearning to be transfigured into a Burne-Jones figure, another story was unfolding. This time, however, with a different main character. The reasons for his attraction toward art are different, and so is the outcome of the relationship with the person who offers it to him. It is the story of a rich and satisfied bourgeois, who one day feels, however, that his happiness may have been marred by his estrangement from "a great enchantress: art." To rectify this, he approaches a "famous architect," who carries out his client's wishes by getting rid of all his old furniture and sending in "an army of parquet craftsmen, decorators, lacquer-workers, bricklayers, housepainters, carpenters, plumbers, boilermen, upholsterers, painters and sculptors." Thus art was suddenly "captured, packaged and neatly arranged between the rich man's domestic walls," and he finally attained happiness. The first act of *About a Poor Rich Man*, the famous and brilliant satire by Adolf Loos,[3] closes here. The rich man's *friend* – this time certainly more a problem-solver than the partner in a loving relationship – has in any case already made his appearance. He is an exponent of the Viennese Secession, a movement that was in some measure a continental equivalent to the arts-and-crafts in England, which, by the reflected light of *The Studio*, had so enthralled Jolanthe.

In the connection between these two Viennese tales, a hitherto unconsidered phenomenon seems to take shape fairly clearly. We have seen how *The Studio* afforded a knowledge of and kindled the desire for a universe of forms, the heart of whose existence is situated elsewhere; a desire which in Jolanthe seems moreover to consist of a purely nostalgic pleasure, augmented precisely by the remoteness of the objects of her admiration. In any case the only thing perceptible in the young Viennese woman's home is the isolated, virtually alien presence of the venerated English lamp. And Jolanthe herself, in order for once to make her fantasies more tangible, can only translate them into a timid disguise, a projection of the silent and exclusive rapport with her own dream. A desire of this kind may, however, also be turned without delay into a pleasure, produced by the greatest possible proximity, as in the case of the rich man. The latter, in fact, decides to disguise his house. Accordingly he summons the services of an architect. The result is what he had wanted, for the rich man, "whenever he grasped a handle was in fact resting his hand on art, and whenever he slumped into an armchair he was in effect sitting on art; he sank into art whenever he laid his weary head on his pillows and his feet trod on art every time he walked across one of his new carpets."[4]

The impression, in short, is that with Altenberg and Loos the media transmission of taste had got off to a start, but with very little wind in its sails, considering that from then on the story runs parallel to that of the consumer system and that their two destinies are interwoven. Under those conditions the fulfillment of a desire to be enveloped by a system of forms was still subject to traditional procedures. It is true that certain media do allow the production of total living models as such. But their reproduction by the public can only occur through the direct action of their creator. So the latter, as long as the commercial relationship is grafted onto that sort of model, must duplicate; they must directly overlap a media enterprise that may perhaps be effectively in place, but has only a relative reach. This means, in more precise media terms, that the producer is still the sole cultural body actually able to guarantee the client the homogeneity of the totalizing formal apparatus created – a homogeneity that must always imply originality or naturalness if a model of total living is to be perceived as such. Despite all this, however, the germ of a different dynamics is already active.

We had left the rich man at a time when nothing of his condition had yet turned wretched, despite the title of the story. His fate, however, was already sealed. The universe created by the architect is, as we have seen, one of art everywhere. Soon, however, its paroxysmally fixed effusion, unchangeable and hostile to intrusion, is revealed. The freedom granted by the rich man to the architect turns out to be equal to that personally lost through his own naivety or frantic desire to appropriate art. "The happy man felt all of a sudden deeply, infinitely unhappy. . . . For it had occurred to him that now he would have to learn to go around carrying his own corpse. Yes! It was all over! It was *complete*."[5]

Within that context the most celebrated and striking aspect of Loos's satire is also the least interesting, namely his mockery of the all-embracing design advocated by such figures as Josef Hoffmann and Joseph Maria Olbrich, *famous* architects of the Secession. It is, however, worth recalling just what that aspect implied: on the one hand, the conceptualization – recognized as having a general quality – of a canonical total living, from a purely architectural source;[6] and on the other, the obviously opposing theory of a stripping of design, which in other parts of Loos's writings is explicitly formulated.

That same opposition to the Secessionist practice of architectural design also occurs though at another level. The theme of modernity and of the style by which it is expressed can be glimpsed through a passage from the parody of the poor rich man. This is crucial to the Viennese architect's theoretical work. According to Loos, in the manufacture of ordinary objects, modern style lies in the desire for a form true to the spirit of the time, under which craftsmen can work freely, in other words only without the unfortunate and ill-tolerated creative protection offered by architects. In consequence, Loos, in a typical essay, declares it compulsory for the *modern* architect to leave furniture production "to the upholsterer and to the cabinet-maker." For what they make is just as "modern as our shoes and our clothes, our leather luggage and our automobiles." He goes on to prescribe the following to the modern enlightened rich: "As for brass beds and iron beds, tables and chairs, armchairs and seating in general, desks and coffee-tables – all things made in a modern way by our craftsmen (never by architects!) – let everyone procure these for themselves according to their own wishes and inclinations. Every item will match the rest because it is modern."[7]

This invitation to build a *modern* material universe thus pays homage to a hasty Zeitgeist. It signifies both a rejection of the designed object[8] and approval of the substance of what remains. As far as Loos the anarchist, the anti-Secessionist controversy and the theorizing of a zero degree of design are concerned, this principle clearly constitutes a paradox; the paradox of a total living no less substantial for having been conceived in the negative. From the point of view of the production of total living, which had been left in a germinal state, this position is, on the other hand, fundamental. What Loos had in fact developed as pure theory was carried by Le Corbusier into the media translation of architecture, along one of the many lines of continuity and mutual indebtedness to be observed between the two architects.

Loos therefore caused (*modern*) architecture to be numbered among contemporary practices of material production that had absolutely nothing to do with interior hierarchies; and he did so by referring explicitly to the construction of private universes. Le Corbusier's work was instead carried out within a self-representation of architecture and its most modern expressions. The original place and its elements are clearly identified: a purist villa designed by him (the Villa Stein at Garches, 1927), and a Voisin automobile (his 14 CV sedan) in a series of photographs arranged by Le Corbusier himself. It is not necessary to make a journey into the representation of architecture dating back to Otto Wagner's perspectives, animated by figures dressed in the fashion, to realize that in these images the communicative impact of photography is geared to an unusual complementarity between the objects depicted.[9] The gap is obvious even compared to the earlier or contemporary drawings of Le Corbusier himself, in which the car or other products of modern life appear very frequently. By the second half of the twenties, however, it had become possible to achieve media effectiveness with the aid of a further tool; and the movie *L'architecture d'aujourd'hui*, directed by Pierre Chenal in collaboration with Le Corbusier between 1927 and 1930, documents architecture while generating from the model of those photographs a range of possible subjects: such as the arrival of the Voisin 14 CV at the Villa Stein, shown and now re-included in a series of activities from modern life staged in the architect's houses.[10] The model for the presentation of the Villa Stein through photographic images is, however, repeated by Le Corbusier in almost all the works he did over the next few years, and it was imitated time and time again by modern architects everywhere. It goes without saying that those many straight imitations do not include the picture of the Villa Müller in Prague by Loos (1928-1930), in which a sedan occupies the foreground.

The photographs and sequences of *Architecture d'aujourd'hui* are naturally only a paradigm.

Generally speaking, in fact, a phenomenon at last and effectively occurs whereby, a certain degree of maturity having been reached by the media and by the consumer system, architecture is abstracted from the mere action of design and produces lifestyle models for a public that can acquire them by independently, at least in the first instance, reproducing them.

The control by architecture over that new form of production of total living, brought about by architecture itself, was short-lived and probably of little more than virtual substance. After Le Corbusier, in fact, the crossing by architects from disciplinary self-representation to the media control of their work – even for the purpose of defining it as a lifestyle factor – was no longer repeated. And the fate of Le Corbusier's project was announced during the very years in which he had devised the models mentioned, when these were adopted by Mercedes-Benz in the advertising campaign for a new range of cars. Accompanied by female models dressed in the latest fashion, they were photographed against the backdrop of the Weissenhofsiedlung in Stuttgart.

Some twenty years later, destiny made itself unequivocally clear. In the postwar United States, again in the sphere of modern architecture, albeit notoriously impoverished by moral, social or other motives and injected instead with a carefree air, the production of models for material existence became very widespread. The architects, generally in agreement with a given movement of taste, remained, however, aloof from efforts made to involve their work in the media-related unfolding of that movement. Conversely, the corpus of a celebrated architectural photographer of the fifties and sixties, Julius Shulman, also forms that of a photographer of the American way of life. And although a man like Shulman took up the heritage of Loos-Corbusian harbingers, he ended up having to follow a path leading almost backwards into architecture, when it showed a desire for the automobile not to be included, but excluded, from images reproducing its works. This happens in the case of an architect of European origins who had also, surprisingly, been a pupil of Loos:

> Photographing architect Richard Neutra's Maslon residence in Cathedral City, California, was a unique event in my life. . . . I had first photographed the house for Neutra. As was his practice, he, with two associates, removed most of what he considered undesirable furniture. Neutra was concerned with the design statements of his architectural elements. He preferred to have the photographs published in European books which favored the stark drama of his work. However, the furnishings of the Maslons were attractive and of considerable comfort. I was disturbed by Neutra's blatant disregard for the personal aspect of the interiors and arranged with Mrs. Maslon to return at a favorable time to take new photographs illustrating her lifestyle. This was achieved. The resultant scenes, coupled with the renowned Maslon collection of contemporary art masterpieces (paintings and sculptures), illustrated how the Maslon lifestyle was enhanced further by the park-like environment of the richly landscaped golf course viewed through the glass walls of the house.[11]

What is revealed by Neutra's desire for architectural purity is that the production of models for total living had by then fully assimilated the architecture by which it had been generated, and that it could handle it with the greatest of ease. What on the other hand is latent in it is the hope that architectural design may remain immune to such models; that architects may once again measure their strength with clients extraneous to the media and their action. In other words, that the original creation of material universes may not itself be disconnected from them. The advance of the media civilization and its reflections on architecture in the decades leading up to the present, show how vain that hope was.

1 __ Naturally the original form of expression of total living is defined as architectural only for the sake of convenience. This formula is in fact intended generically to sum up the different possible ways of carrying out a design that, aside from its own source, gives total form to a private dominion (and in the first place to its public projections). It should also be borne in mind, with reference to any period, that totalization must be understood as saturation in terms of quality rather than quantity, that is to say, of an absolutely dominant characterization that leaves aside the quantity of means with which it is achieved: it is for example difficult not to define as totalizing a *Siedlung* in the modern movement before considering what kind of furniture each home is furnished with.
2 __ P. Altenberg, "Der Freund," in idem, *Was der Tag mir zuträgt. Fünfundfünfzig neue Studien* (Berlin: Fischer, 1901).
3 __ A. Loos, "Voneinen armen reichen Mann," *Neues Wiener Tagblatt* (26 April 1900), then published in idem, *Ins Leere gesprochen* (Paris: Crès, 1921).
4 __ Ibid.
5 __ Ibid.
6 __ Needless to say, the annihilated *parvenu* is merely an instrument of the anti-Secessionist polemic and the attribution of this quality to Loos's writing means that in its place must be intended a culturally open-minded bourgeois in agreement with the system of forms borne by the architect and with whom he intends to participate in a certain élite taste.
7 __ A. Loos, "Die Abschaffung der Mobel" (1924), in idem, *Trotzdem* (Innsbruck: Brenner, 1931). The furniture that Loos suggests should be abolished here is that built into the walls. It must also be pointed out that almost the whole lack of evolutionary dynamics within Loos's theoretic system justifies the absence of clarification in taking elements on the same theme from a writing of 1900, and at the same time from one of 1924.
8 __ From the Secession to the Bauhaus, architects and movements, in respect of all these the sequence of Loosian writings poses a unitary contrast.
9 __ Compositionally translated by putting in the immediate foreground the smaller element, which is obviously the automobile.
10 __ Naturally, as regards the photographs and film, and the writings by Loos considered here, those qualities not directly implied by the matter in question are neglected. Concerning the lack of a hierarchy within the photographs of Villa Stein, however, an observation by Stanislaus von Moos may be noted here. He affirms that it is not clear from those images which element between the automobile and the house provides the context for a promotion of the "good contemporary life." See S. von Moos, and Le Corbusier, *Elemente einer Synthese* (Frauenfeld-Stuttgart: Huber, 1968); Eng. trans., *Le Corbusier. Elements of a Synthesis* (Cambridge, Mass.: MIT Press, 1979), p. 84.
11 __ J. Shulman, *Architecture and Its Photography* (Cologne: Taschen, 1998), pp. 193-194.

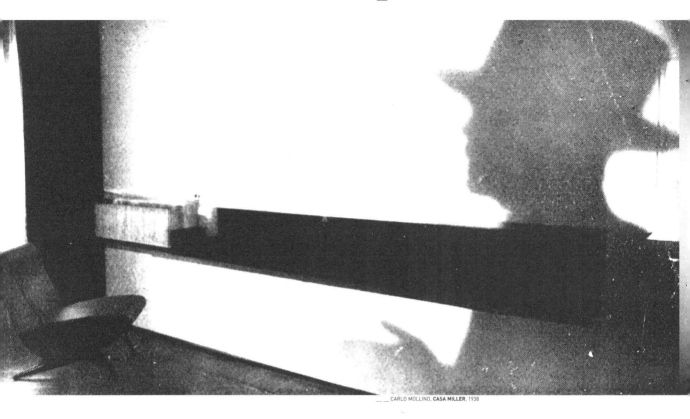

__ __ CARLO MOLLINO, **CASA MILLER**, 1938

__ __ TOMASO BUZZI, **TEATRO DELLA COMETA FOR THE PECCI BLUNT COUNTS**, ROME, 1956

In the beginning was divination; just as the guises, nests, dens and shells of animals were born, so were the ceremonies and laws, the homes, garments, weapons of man, and every device for communicating, building and transport: *the extension of the self* to live and thrive and still rejoice in this success.
Carlo Mollino, "Utopia e ambientazione," *Domus*, no. 237, 1949

___ CARLO MOLLINO, "VEDERE L'ARCHITETTURA," *AGORÀ*, 1946

___ TOMASO BUZZI, **STUDY FOR SCARZUOLA**, C.1965

Many aptitudes, many parallel activities form the personality of Carlo Mollino – architect, photographer, auto racing enthusiast, inventor, acrobatic aviator, skier, college professor, designer of furniture and installations, writer and experimenter with a taste for precision.

As an architect Mollino adhered to the modern, combining lofty formal and stylistic definitions with declarations of independence and creative freedom, and with a taste for rigorous technical and design control. Mollino saw the modern as the fallout from epochal changes and new lifestyles that multiplied rather than reduced possibilities for action.

Thus from the second half of the thirties Mollino was involved in a concrete attempt to invert that process triggered by the modern, which had abandoned decoration and the seduction of the senses, exalting nudity and visual harmony of proportions, and avoiding the sensual in favor of the cerebral, the tactile in favor of the visual.

On the socially committed architecture scene, the painful experience of the minimum housing unit was underway, with the "complete negation of the human dwelling," to use the words of Tristan Tzara. Mollino delved into the theme of the home as the scenario where our days are spent, the home as mirror and sustenance of its occupant's psyche. In other words, the Turinese architect explored the areas from which architectural culture was retreating, examining the connection between the inner life of the inhabitant and the world of objects and decor that form the landscape of an interior. While modernism spoke of the decline of the *interieur*, Mollino was busy rediscovering it, but without any nostalgia for lost values. Instead, he developed strategies with which to assert a complex, multifaceted inner world, suitable for modern lifestyles.

Mollino seemed to counter with an idea of living shrouded in shadow, nestled in a sensory and psychological den, a claustrophiliac cave in which to perform the propitiatory rites of reinforcement, where it was possible to achieve some sense of security.

In this Mollino approached the "closet" atmospheres indicated by Aaron Betsky in his interpretations of the forms of architectural space. The closet is the ultimate interior: a dark space at the heart of the house in which to store everything required for the construction of the self, one's appearance, clothing to be worn, but also clothing already worn out. It is that dark place where you can understand yourself, the opposite of the orderly place of appearances.

When he designed interiors with padded walls, sinuous lines, alcoves and red sofas in the form of lips, places that exalted dusky, tactile atmospheres, he seemed to share the disappointment of the surrealists and Tristan Tzara regarding "the aesthetic of castration" practiced by the new modernist orthodoxy.

Mollino is a rare case, an architect who grappled with the theme of the home as self-portrait. But how did he do this, how did he translate it into an architectural theme?

The connections between the inner life of the inhabitant and the world of objects and decorations of an interior have really been taken into consideration only in literature. In architectural culture only Adolf Loos addressed this problem, clearly declaring it extraneous to the act of design. In fact, he viewed the inhabitant, not the architect, as the one who constructs the home as self-portrait. And not as a building or an object: as an experience.

Nevertheless, Mollino tried to activate communication channels between these two spheres. He chose the path of confrontation with the inner world, with that potential separated from the architectural discipline. In Mollino's notion of the home as self-portrait this operation was conducted through a series of characters. They always possessed a degree of permanence that also made them recognizable as alter egos of the architect, though perhaps this is of little importance. What is important is that Mollino's interior architecture always appears as a narrative and a description of characters.

The character might be the editor of a magazine, uprooted, mobile, light, swept away by the pace of modern publishing. His dwelling is minimal, a temporary landscape, a study more than a bedroom. A floor-to-ceiling bookcase at the center of the room looks like some kind of exercise equipment. On the table, a typewriter. One enters the bedroom through a submarine hatch door, padded, quilted to protect his loved one from the noise of the typewriter. There are photo blow-ups on the walls. The character races cars. He feels a need to fill spaces up, transforming them into ideal stages for hermetic rituals. Celebrated alone or with friends. He wants to be everything. Flipping through fashion magazines, he exercises his gaze in sudden passages that caress the surfaces of the constructed, reconstructed, modeled bodies, investigating the play of appearances and the ritual of disguise. He inhabits obsessively concentrated spaces, broken down by means of mirrors, illusions, infinite ricochets and suggestions. Deceptions and doublings, precisely calculated evanescence, circuitous paths. Glass isn't used for transparency, but to trigger claustrophilia.

Now the character declares that his ideal house is a trunk-house, with the windows closed, although he could enjoy the view of the city. Or a trussed house, from which to descend only on skis. Or a hangar-house, from which to fly away with an airplane parked like a car in the garage. Or a house on high ground, part monastery, part tent.

The character is celibate, the last representative of a free race, "the last of the Mohicans!" The character in his situation. The bachelor in the garçonnière. Space dominated by a heightened sexuality, governed by oppositions: soft/hard, supported/supporting, flesh/bone. The perfection and ingeniousness of a contemporary invention coexist with the sensuality of a fabric that covers it. A slide projects a decoration on the ceiling. The drapes hang like red or dark green theater curtains: classical, petrified folds, velvet architecture. Dark curtains around the canopy bed, sumptuous drapes bordering zones of nightmare and pleasure. Transparent curtains, light veils that form a cloud of love, with dissolve effects.

The character surveys a closed world where all possible spaces must coexist: those of childhood and old age, the present and memory, exposure and modesty. But all this cannot be expressed with a hierarchical order, because "all things are equally close, and each implies an infinity of others, they jostle in the throng to avoid being overlooked." The illusions created by the mirrors and sudden alterations of size are means with which to break up the perspective views, to shift elsewhere, to slip out of the correct use of a technique, toward the false. "We are men precisely because we have shifted toward material uselessness, otherwise we would be reduced to the biologically perfect state of the most organized colony of insects, where nothing happens that is not useful for material life."

In a conscious intellectual game, Mollino slips into the realm where "form follows fiction" (we might say, in a retrospective use of Jeffrey Deitch's intuition). While modern architecture tends to be based on the simplification of a reality – material reality – the model of reality favored by Mollino is full of layers and composed of imaginary aspects. The interpreter of this reality is always the character, who spends time on the borderline between reality and fiction.

Moreover, the true/artificial short circuit is enriched thanks to the device of photography, and a vast production of images that follow the tracks of the character's rapid passages, rapid because he also lives elsewhere.

All this is not whimsical oddness, but the result of a titanic attempt to bring the tensions of the *interieur* back into architecture. Mollino himself didn't want his work to be considered as genre, neutralized as eccentric, extravagant production for luxury clients. He wanted to assign theoretical force to his expressions, the absolute value of his research, through a dual movement – nocturnal and diurnal – managed with awareness and the precision of a sophisticated weapon. He struck and penetrated the flesh of architectural culture and its convictions that had been immune too long to even fleeting relations with the impulses of life and its excesses, sexuality and the roar of the engine of a nose-diving airplane.

This exceptional theoretical tension perceptible in Mollino's work didn't cancel out certain relations with another universe of hyperdecoration that was very much alive in Paris, the fashion center, in the years between the two world wars and later. This was the culture of the *architectes décorateurs* and the *couturiers*, which produced sumptuous interiors where the elements of classical tradition were subjected to showy deformations, leading to the fashion of the baroque, all shot through with surrealist taste.

The houses of Charles de Beistegui were among the most famous examples of this pleasure of disorientation. Full of theaters and theatrical effects, one was designed by Le Corbusier – an apartment where the fireplace, the emblem of domestic life, is literally taken outside, on the roof terrace, and placed against the Paris skyline. The apotheosis of this world was a costume ball at Palazzo Labia in Venice, where the furniture, walls and clothing melded in a display of sensual atmosphere and light.

Charles de Beistegui's balls were attended by Tomaso Buzzi, an erudite, refined architect, pursued by all of Italian high society, both old and new. His story begins in the twenties in Milan, in a group of young architects with a neoclassical orientation, and in a particular relationship with Gio Ponti. Together they experienced a return to order, pursuing humanistic and classicist ideals, including an interest in the figurative arts, literature and music.

At times Buzzi's interventions were conducted in a domestic key (the architecture of villas), at times in a decorative key (primarily through sixteenth-century grotesque motifs). He quickly arrived at a stylistic and hyperdecorative hedonism, to the point of using a personal, imaginative and bizarre "alphabet" that recurred in furniture, fabrics, lace, ceramics and glass. His research on domestic comfort rapidly moved toward extreme forms, bordering on an idea of "prenatal comfort." This was possible by crossing the realms of *luxe, calme et volupté*. When playing the role of the *artiste décorateur*, he embraced elite private commissions, and was thus able to fully indulge his penchant for the bizarre and the extravagant.

The turning point in this direction can be dated to 1934, when he handled the remodeling of the Palladian Villa Barbaro at Maser. Buzzi's excellent results in Marina Volpi's luxurious home introduced him to the circles of Italian high society and aristocracy. The news of Buzzi's verve and genius – a man of impeccable taste and refinement – spread by word of mouth, and soon he was working for new noble clients.

From that point on, Buzzi's design orientation tended to favor sensitivity to the cycles of fashion. But there was a price to pay: he was excluded from architectural culture and ignored by specialized publications. In the meantime his professional life became intertwined with his social life, marked by an increasingly intense schedule of encounters, art events, theater, music, dinners and parties, which he could not and would not avoid. Buzzi chose the international horizon of *Vogue* and *Harper's Bazaar* instead of the petit bourgeois modern taste of their Italian surrogates, directed by his former friend Gio Ponti.

At this point, Buzzi's career achieved consecrated heights of success, and the distance from a figure like Mollino seems particularly evident. Nevertheless, the two architects began to share an approach to designing spaces full of artifice, utilizing theatrical techniques, manifesting the claustrophiliac taste for the nest, and being sucked into the undertow of the home as self-portrait. In the mid-fifties, when the link with the world of the *dolce vita* became so important for Tomaso Buzzi that he lost all self-awareness, the project for an "other" dwelling took shape. The architect purchased a former convent in the Umbrian countryside, and began to construct a private retreat where long-repressed tensions could finally be revived. It was a place to practice the most bewildering accumulation-collecting activities, and to launch the project of a pan-architectural delirium for the garden. "A carcass, an empty shell, a fossil seashell, a skeleton. My 'dinosaur,' a 'mold,' an empty form . . . a petrified shout." And further: "Autobiography in stone," "not the house of an architect, which reflects him, but the architect who becomes a house; not the house of life, but life that becomes a house."

What materialized was the vision of an architectural stage in the form of an infinite concatenation of theatrical situations that are difficult to decipher, wavering between the automatism of a marginal, hallucinatory practice and the erudite exercise of an architect dandy. It was an erotic, literary and neo-antiquarian composite that proceeded in successive impulses and grew with rhythms at times extroverted, at times dizzyingly imploded. It fed on refined citations, outlining a path in pursuit of some dream of love. And once again an odor of sex issued from a closed world. Private artificial paradises. Today, on the other hand, when "the form dissolves in illusion" (again Jeffrey Deitch), today when the industrial economy has been transformed into an economy of experience and aesthetics, today when we can easily invent a new identity for ourselves in a completely immaterial web, artifice has become a collective fact.

Maybe everyone is entitled to construct his own nest, as if he were installing a set for an imaginary character, for a role-playing game, to pursue fantasies of a perfect world. Maybe this is the death of the artificial paradise.

D/R INTERNATIONAL WINDOW
DISPLAY, NEW YORK

I was a teenage staple queen. I recommend this entry-level occupation for every new boy in town. Even if you're terribly shy, being a retail store display designer gives you a stage – the shop window – for performing your very own urban cabaret. And if your window has a prominent location, and the shop enjoys prestige, it feels a bit like playing the Palace.

The store I worked at no longer exists. Even the building that housed it is gone. It was located on the north side of 57th Street, between Madison and Park, where the Four Seasons Hotel rises today. The store was called Design Research – D/R for short – and it was one of the few retail emporiums of that time that possessed a cultural aura. D/R, legendarily, was the place where you could buy the objects on display in the Design Collection of the Museum of Modern Art. And since those objects had been created with the goal of commercial distribution, the store was arguably more faithful to their ethos than any museum could be, at least in the days before museums started to invest heavily in retail and commercial branding.

My life as a store display designer was brief. It only lasted for about a year and a half – little more than a year: 1968-69. Still, short as it was, this was the only time I ever got to do design, to play with shapes, textures, colors, spaces, entrances, images, processions and lights. Working with forms was very pleasing. But the best part was it didn't take place in a vacuum. The whole and entire purpose was, as we say, to "move the merch." To sell stuff. If store display is a cabaret, then the sound of a cash register is applause.

D/R had a great Bauhaus lineage, a more legitimate modern pedigree than the Modern's, in fact. The store was founded in 1962 by Benjamin Thompson, a member of a Cambridge-based firm called The Architects Collaborative. Walter Gropius established the firm after he'd emigrated from Nazi Germany to become head of Harvard's architecture school. In Germany, Gropius had dreamed of harnessing industrial technology toward enlightened social and cultural ends. In America, he entered into the center of the industry he wanted to harness.

To a degree, American industry responded. The Museum of Modern Art's Good Design shows, which often featured inexpensive products, did encourage and effect the design of common objects like dust pans, tea kettles, fabrics, chairs, typewriters, street lamps and even airplanes. They also helped define the esthetic of cultivated liberal taste. The Aspen Design Conference, an annual event in Colorado founded by a Chicago industrialist, reached out directly to manufacturers. Its mountaintop campus was a kind of Bauhaus Chautauqua, a religious revival meeting for progressive designers.

But if you wanted to buy the originals – the tables and chairs by Breuer, Mies van der Rohe, Le Corbusier and Aalto – you had to go to a decorator. Otherwise, your only option was Design Research. And D/R was the only public setting where you could mill around with shoppers of like-minded taste.

This gave the store a somewhat institutional aura. The salesgirls, all clad in Marimekko dresses, were notoriously indifferent to whether or not customers wanted to buy. Aware that the store was the only game in town, they seemed to see themselves more as curators than as shop assistants. Many had been chosen for their beauty. Others descended from impoverished branches of Scandinavian royalty. "Ja, I'm a princess, ja," I remember a gal telling me over tuna fish sandwiches one day during lunch break in the building's tiny penthouse.

I was very fortunate to have a boss, Robin Drake, head of the display department, who became a kind of mentor. It was Robin who first helped me articulate my love for city streets. He too loved the street – we walked around a lot together – and helped me see things more analytically but without losing the profound emotional attachment. Robin had studied at Pratt with Sybil Moholy-Nagy, a distinguished urban historian and widow of the Bauhaus artist Laszlo Moholy-Nagy. Robin gave me a copy of Sybil's book, *Matrix of Man*, and this book influenced me quite a bit. I'd come to the city in part to find a mother substitute, and this was Sybil's view of the city also. But she brought to it a historical perspective, and this encouraged me to look beyond my personal experience – the joy of walking down streets – toward a more global sense of connection.

It was in the context of these discoveries that I decorated my window. The window was a hinge between the street and a self-selecting public. When Thompson remodeled the building (it had formerly been the showroom for Mr. John's hats), he turned the high-arched, two-story window into a proscenium for the store within. You could look beyond the window display to a small street-level display area ("the slate," named after its dark gray floor covering), the ground floor several steps below, a high-ceilinged mezzanine above, and a landing for displays located atop a flight of stairs beyond that.

Five levels altogether were visible from the street, in other words, and the store's lighting emphasized the sectional emphasis of the design. This manipulation of interior space was in contrast to the stony facades and enclosed shop windows of other fancy emporiums. Rather, like a bazaar, it resembled a continuation of the sidewalk, set perpendicular to it. Or, in theatrical terms, it was like Palladio's permanent set for the Teatro Olimpico: an illusion of the ideal street.

Working alone after hours was best, especially on Friday nights. I would lose all track of time, completely absorbed in hanging a different fabric, repositioning the lights. People would stop to look. And this was a performance, a local enactment of the ritual of possibility for which all of New York stands. Sometimes I would come back the next afternoon, just to see how business was going. It was great to see the place packed, with the displays in disarray.

I must tell you about the Niederlander bells. We carried glassware by the famous Swiss designer Robert Niederlander. It didn't sell brilliantly, but it sold. But Neiderlander had designed these glass bells that had never sold. The blown glass ornaments were quite beautiful. Each was about three feet long, made of thin bubbles connected by thin tubes. And when they glanced off each other, they made a bright bell sound.

The problem with the bells was that they were expensive and, of course, you had to buy at least two them. But two of them looked rather sad just dangling there together. One of them looked ridiculous. The only way to move them was to present them in multiple. So I decided that for

Christmas we would take everything out of the window and dress it with all the bells we had in stock, the whole lot. Even if none of them sold, they'd make a great window, and they would chime when customers came through the door. So I had the girls get these dusty old bells out of the basement and clean them up.

Then I hung them with fish wire in one great diagonal strip the full height and length of the window, and lit them from above with white and pale blue lights. They looked like the aurora borealis and sounded like Christmas morning. And when the store opened on Saturday morning a lady came and bought the entire lot. Immediately. She must have cruised them the night before after I'd gone home. Of course, I had to do a new Christmas window, but it was worth it. The bells were gone. I derived confidence from their disappearance.

Just because you're in the business of selling things that doesn't mean that the sales pitch should be uppermost in mind. The best thing is to forget about it and please yourself. I assume that many people walking by the window didn't even suspect that the bells were for sale. They could have been just a nice abstract "Good Design" Christmas window. Which, in fact, it was. Meaning: a display designer's power to communicate rests on the capacity of his or her personality structure to connect with the organization of the viewer's fantasy life. In this, display resembles any other art form. It is driven by instinct, not science or reason. If you're doing a window, you're basically a song stylist. The melody and lyrics are givens, but you can perform them any way the mood strikes. A song stylist must never be cynical or bored. I'm utopian enough to believe that if you please yourself in a commercial context, people will want to buy. On some level, they'll understand that the work is basically about the freedom to be who you are. I'm a sucker for that kind of entertainment, myself.

The period I worked there happened to be an interesting time in the company's history. Thompson had decided to cash in and sell a controlling share to a Texas-based merchandising genius who had plans to open D/R shops in cities across the country and to expand greatly its catalog sales. Most of the New York employees resented this development. As infuriating and high-handed as Thompson could be, the store that we loved was, after all, his creation. He'd created a refuge for an interesting group of people. Under the Texans, the refuge couldn't last. Since I knew I'd be heading back to school eventually, I wasn't any more worried about my future than I was before the sale. But everyone who worked there felt a personal attachment to what D/R represented.

But the sale represented something in itself, a meaning that transcended the fate of a particular institution. It signified the absorption of production into the ethos of consumption. In its Bauhaus originals, the Good Design esthetic was based on the model of production. Like the buildings that Breuer Bauhaus designed for the Bauhaus, it was a machine esthetic. It even went by the name "Industrial Design."

In the immediate post-war decades, the United States was still based on an economy of industrial production. We had steel. We had Ford, General Motors, and Chrysler. And the products of these and other industrial giants were substantially manufactured at home. By the end of the sixties, this era had receded into the past. Late capitalism had decisively shifted toward investment in consumption. From its inception, D/R had been part of this shift. The sale of the enterprise was in this sense a natural progression. The store had always been a distribution system. The Texans planned to expand the system.

It happened that Thompson himself had already embarked on a series of projects that would come to epitomize the transformation of older urban centers from places of production to zones of consumption. The festival marketplace, a concept that swept the U.S. in the seventies and early eighties, was essentially Thompson's invention. Though financed by James Rouse, a developer and entrepreneur, the concept had long been part of what Thompson called "the D/R Idea."

I'm not going to go into the whole history of festival marketplaces. The entire genre turned out to be deeply flawed. In origin, however, Thompson's idea had been remarkably idealistic. The concept was one of programming rather than design. How do you get people back on city streets after office hours, when middle-class workers flee to the suburbs? Modern architecture had been accused of creating an emptiness for which cars were largely responsible. I still respect Thompson, himself a modern architect, for attempting to fill the void.

Hybrid crowds gather at the entrance to two large stores in Oxford Circus, in the heart of London: mass-market sportswear trademarks, one Italian, one American, large, very old buildings with new logos, in a very traditional commercial district full of public venues. There are no rules for shopping districts, just as there is no public plan for commerce. The imperative is to sell, to keep the brand circulating. Permanent unknown: the profile of the possible customer, and where to find him. All the rest is thoroughly variable: the position of the shop, its size, its vicinity to or isolation from other shops, in new or traditional territory, for one stratum of consumers or another.

"Shopping district" is an expression that applies to very different types of shopping. The area of shops in a small town or an outlying suburb, or the shopping center of a new Asian city. The shopping drag off the campus of the University of Berkeley, or a traditional zone of shops and department stores in the city. A famous street renowned for its luxury goods, or the modern extension of an old commercial area. An entire historical center that wants to fill itself with prestigious boutiques, or a new, completely invented "shopping strip" to boost property values, adding pedestrian zones in the name of ecology. An old produce market converted for luxury brands, or a crowded, traditional, popular place of mass consumption. A suburban shopping center of any size, or a mall anywhere, large or small, open-air or enclosed, luxurious or pop, isolated or part of a system of other contiguous malls, reached by means of clearly marked routes.

The major luxury trademarks are a presence on the market in many different ways: as small, exclusive, traditional boutiques; as larger, more isolated shops with minimalist furnishings; as trademark megastores in cities like Tokyo, Milan, New York, San Francisco; as sales outlets in shopping centers; or as specialized multi-brand shops in cities, suburbs or smaller towns. If an area is large, compact and entirely dedicated to luxury products, it undoubtedly fills visitors with a sort of excitement; the potential consumer of merchandise becomes a real consumer of this exciting sensation. Skillful marketing strategies regarding the choice of the site must combine with those regarding the type of product and the type of consumer. The strategist is faced with the same, age-old problems: where, who, when, how much, how.

The concept of totality comes to the rescue in the society and culture of consumption: to cover the total range of products and desires, reach all potential consumers, cover the entire useful area of the city with long paths. Major clothing brands also produce accessories and furnishings; outside and inside their megastores they widen the sales concept from products to lifestyle and free time; they focus on differentiating products in order to conserve luxury objects alongside (but also separated from) products everyone can afford. The traditional department stores in Paris and Berlin set aside several floors for a grouping of luxury booths, but without alienating their traditional mass-market customers. The great creative talents know they have to concentrate on everything: products, image, marketing, the look of retail outlets.[1] The true shopping malls try to subdivide consumers in strata, offering each group – known in the United States as "achievers," "emulators," humble and loyal "sustainers," conformist "belongers"[2] –

GIORGIO ARMANI OCCHIALI BILLBOARD, STAZIONE CENTRALE, MILAN

the most appropriate wares. Loyal customers in America are sold or given the background music of the shop: they can also listen to it at home, informing their guests of their faithful condition of belonging. Often the complex, diversified offering includes forms of entertainment, not just commercial transactions but also "experiences."[3] Therefore the mall of the future will be called a "destination entertainment center."[4] Thus the entire city is impacted by the completely commercial vision that was born in America's extra-urban or suburban malls. The mall begins by simulating the city, and in the end the city winds up being an imitation of the mall (which, in turn, simulates a historical or Mediterranean center, offering "reminders" or illusions, as in the projects of the International Gateway of the Americas). Contributing causal factors: the cultural and entertainment totality that makes commerce equivalent to any other form of popular or cultural attraction, such as the museum, the exhibition, the event, the installation, even the most artful spaces, or the fair, the amusement park; and the spread of shopping districts in every corner of quality urban areas. The mall becomes the metaphor – if not the allegory, or the substitute – for the home, life, the city, which in its own right has also always been seen as a theater, a stage. Those who stroll or buy can become generic spectators in the general aestheticizing and performance of life, beyond the traditional pleasure of spending time in the Grand Bazaar. In the metropolis the spectator may be a motorist; or perhaps he will go beyond this passive role, becoming an active person in the society of the enlarged space.

In every shopping district the sparkle of the merchandise and the crowds of people are the object of ecstatic contemplation on the part of scholars of social phenomena. This is an object that has always existed. In the modern era it exists at least since the department store in a famous nineteenth-century novel was seen as the paradise of ladies – just as it is today[5] – and its director dreamt of bringing the street into the store; or since, several decades later, the American Lyman Frank Baum, playwright and authoritative expert on shop windows, consultant "in the art of decoration and display," described the Emerald City in the *Wizard of Oz*;[6] or since the Futurist Depero, in the thirties, promised sparkling palaces for great commerce. The amazed observation of commerce today also includes a certain wrinkle of perplexity: the places of consumption imply significant social problems, and "in the future it will be necessary to develop an adequate critical vision."[7] Today the places of purchasing and those of being seen are the same. Multiple characteristics are combined: the parading of the *bel mondo* in the days of Stendhal's strolls in Milan or Baron Miccichè's by the marina in Naples or Palermo; the rushed – and often inattentive – gathering of crowds around shops, as on Corso Buenos Aires in Milan; the vain ecstasy a famous poet noticed on a Saturday provokes in the ingenuous youth who "gazes and is gazed at." The extension of the shopping and medium-luxury phenomenon to mass dimensions (though authentic cashmere is still rare) undoubtedly makes it a form of democracy associated with money, just as playing the stock market on the Internet or having a single-family house can be seen as a sign of democracy. The situation leads to contradictions and problems of strategy when we consider the strata of products or clients: the prestigious brand doesn't abandon great luxury, but also panders to the masses; the curator of a famous museum conserves his lofty notion of art, but accepts crowd-pleasing events and popular forms of artistic output.

The transformation of the city into a complex of malls, or one big mall – which is still preferable to the flight from the city toward suburban malls – is a well-known phenomenon that has been described for some time now in all its particulars, premises and consequences,[8] just as for some time now we have been aware of – and often ignored – a number of critical views on the situation. Major indicated drawbacks include: the careful corporate programming of individual behavior;[9] and the monofunctional organization assumed by the city,[10] which by nature should be, as it has always been, an environment of multiple, overlapping functions and activities, not that thing sought by a designer of malls when he dreams of a small circular city, like the Baghdad of the Caliphs.[11]

There is one theme that connects, and powerfully dominates, all the phenomena of the post-modern condition, which with the places of shopping are redefining the entire city, now that even the soul is global:[12] the invasion of life by images. The theme of the image is pervasive in malls and urban shopping districts: life as appearance, city as simulacrum, theme parks, exhibitions and museums, the world of the media, Disney-like worlds, new American urbanism of artful town replicas. If only the image has value, then the simulacrum has value, as Baudrillard acknowledged with resigned enthusiasm.[13] And so do the copy and the fake.[14] Those who still demand authenticity are perplexed.[15] If shopping takes on "increasingly predatory forms" and colonizes or pushes aside every other aspect of urban life,[16] perhaps admirers of beauty, too, will be perplexed.

Those who sing the praises of the artistic mode of production, the culture of amusement, of aesthetics – elegance, taste, style – must know that this optimistic viewpoint has to come to terms with other important, enormous social issues.[17] Those who study the cultural extension of commerce believe that a political problem is imminent: the cultural economy, of which the entertainment of malls is one example, will increasingly evolve in terms of the theme of inclusion/exclusion of many subjects.[18] And some anthropologists also chime in, indicating the mall as a simulacrum and a flight from freedom.[19]

Many believe that globalization cannot and should not be controlled. Attempts to govern it may only strengthen it further. Perhaps it is ineffective still to inject culture into contexts that have already learned to display it: I find I am the only person admiring the drawings of Leonardo in a suburban mall. To create cultural diversification in the total system through contemporary art requires, as always, an assimilation based on the experience of the subjects.[20] When injected from outside, this sort of lofty, aestheticizing cultural "time-out" that suspends the everyday dimension must be interrelated with the current culture to have meaning for the society.[21] Intervention of provisional safeguarding of the rights of those most threatened by local phenomena is welcome.[22] In the world of commerce there are laws to protect traditional sectors threatened by "category killer" companies. For the rest, it may be wise to let the contradictions inherent in globalization work themselves out.

Many of these contradictions are inherent to the themes of the city and the civilization of image. For sector professionals, products are increasingly a matter of image and symbols – consumption is culture[23] – but if we are looking for new creativity its definition isn't provided. If malls are identical to places of tourism, tourism itself may suffer. If the audience for television decreases, the culture of consumption and passivity that television has nurtured in entire generations may become less important, although television tends to become a political system. If fashion and museums aim at simultaneous contact with a high-end, educated, wealthy audience and a medium mass public, while at the same time – thanks to the aesthetic of pop spontaneity[24] – they find their stimuli in the street and among the lower classes, just as television does when it attempts to mingle with real life, the balanced functioning of such a total approach will be difficult to achieve. The strategies of consumers are complex. Japanese consumers utilize luxury shops, but then, ignoring the media and major retailers, they look for current products in small, humble stores. When a young man conforms to advertising in his consumption, the marketing experts are surprised, as they imagined him to be the autonomous maker of his own individual look. Actually the young fellow is aiming at creating his own true sphere of autonomy, impervious to borrowings, both in terms of look and in terms of attitudes in general. He knows that money seems more important than image, but less important than the unachievable belonging to the luxury classes; therefore he will be elegant when he can, present when he can and wishes, homologous as demanded by advertising, but always at a certain distance if he believes that what counts is personality,[25] as has always been the case among those who don't follow fashion but make it. When culture is commercialized and commerce opens to cultural occasions the result may not be so predictable. The magic of the Tate Modern isn't the museum but the lobby; one museum sells books but another sells clothes; the Palais de Tokyo in Paris and the Pulitzer Foundation in St. Louis prefer to display temporary events rather than art objects; a total megastore in San Francisco is subjected to fierce criticism, like its replica in Berlin; some big events turn out to be flops. If everything is stage and spectacle we need a director, but unreal life, constantly controlled from the outside, or the bureaucratic-corporate imposition of a fashionable philosophy are not everyone's cup of tea. In decades of debate on the culture industry and the culturization of leisure time[26] no consensus of solutions has emerged: the more a symbolic grip on everyday life is important for the subject, the more the subject risks losing autonomy and sense;[27] and the dream of the electronic designers of finding a transparent interface in media communications, to the point of making the medium vanish,[28] perhaps is still but a dream. In terms of image, though forecasts are premature at this point, after the tragic events of the recent past there have been reflections and reconsiderations: a more modest fashion for the future, a television we may ignore if it consumes itself in boring, arrogant productions, a development centered less on consumption and the ephemeral, a decrease in the exaltation of the image in itself. The worn-out icon. Ad-man Jelly Helm proposes operating toward "a more human world"; a female fashion designer realized that signature luxury "excludes those who are not rich."

And then there are the more general contradictions. The entire world is not engaged by aestheticization and consumption, in fact the great majority is excluded. And even within our world large parts of the population are touched only indirectly, or only in passing, by these phenomena, and at times don't seem to be interested, like the Ecuadorian women on the tram headed for the outskirts of the city, or the elderly gentleman who buys a sweater in the little shop downstairs. And there are also subjects – persons, groups, metropolitan tribes – who want to intentionally elude the major totalizing forces that are imposed. How to dress, where to go, what culture to "consume," which urban places to frequent, whether to go to the pub or to Dracula Park or to the imitation of the Hermitage in Las Vegas or a fake indoor beach in Japan, what film to see, in a fluorescent extra-urban multiplex or in an old downtown movie theater, which video cameras to avoid, which philosophy to believe in: perhaps these things are easier to control than economic totalization or planetary dynamics. And they are more important than the current consumption in which we may indulge, where the brand name is not always as important as its creators imagine, nor is the organized scenario as decisive as it's supposed to be. Those who fall prey to what one urban sociologist calls the TINA syndrome (There Is No Alternative)[29] may perhaps find solace by observing and appreciating the pure complexity and variety of urban and social dynamics.

1 __ Tom Ford, at the conference "Fashion 2001: The Business and the Brand," Paris, 28 November 2001.

2 __ J. Rifkin, *The Age of Access* (New York: J. P. Tarcher/Putnam, 2000), p. 156.

3 __ D. Hazel, "Mall Maestros," in *Shopping Centers Today*, December 2001, at the website of the International Council of Shopping Centers, www.icsc.org.

4 __ J. Rifkin, op. cit., p. 158.

5 __ P. Falk, and C. Campbell, ed., *The Shopping Experience* (London: Sage, 1998). On the fashion/authority relationship in the world of women see H. Radner, "Roaming the City: Proper Women in Improper Places," in *Spaces of Culture*, ed. M. Featherstone and S. Lash (London: Sage, 1999).

6 __ W. Leach, *Land of Desire* (New York: Vintage Books, 1993).

7 __ V. Codeluppi, *Lo spettacolo della merce: I luoghi del consumo dai Passages a Dissney World* (Milan: Bompiani, 2000), p. 4. Not future but present, some critiques in M. Sernini, "I centri commerciali dieci anni dopo," *Commercio* 631 (1998) and *La città disfatta* (1988) (Milan: Angeli, 1994). See also M. Torres, *Luoghi magnetici* (Milan: Angeli, 2000).

8 __ For example "Mallification and Disneyfication," and "Consumer Aestheticism and the Neo-Flaneur," in *The Urban Condition: Space, Community, and Self in the Contemporary Metropolis*, Ghent Urban Studies Team (GUST) (Rotterdam: 010, 1999).

9 __ J. Hannigan, *Fantasy City* (London: Routledge, 1999). On corporations and the market see L. Boltanski, and E. Chiappello, *Le nouvel esprit du capitalisme* (Paris: Gallimard, 1999); E. N. Luttwack, *La dittatura del capitalismo* (Milan: Mondadori, 1999); G. Ritzer, *The McDonaldization of Society* (Thousand Oaks, Calif.: Pine Forge Press, 1993), *The McDonaldization Thesis* (London: Sage, 1998), *Enchanting a Disenchanted World: Revolutionizing the Means of Consumption* (Thousand Oaks, Calif.: Pine Forge Press, 1999). Sociologists collaborate with marketing by studying the paths of visitors: M. Grosjean, and J-P. Thibaud, ed., *L'espace urbain en méthodes* (Marseille: Parenthèses, 2001).

10 __ C. Boyer, *The City of Collective Memory* (Cambridge, Mass.: MIT Press, 1996); N. Ellin, *Postmodern Urbanism*, 2d ed. (New York: Princeton Architectural Press, 1999); M. J. Dear, *The Postmodern Urban Condition* (Oxford: Blackwell, 2000); W. F. Lever, "The Post-Fordist City," in *Handbook of Urban Studies*, ed. R. Paddison (London: Sage, 2001); S. Graham, S. Martin, *Splintering Urbanism* (London: Routledge, 2001); T. Hall, P. Hubbard, ed., *The Entrepreneurial City: Geographies of Politics, Regime and Representation* (Chichester: Wiley, 1998); L. H. Lofland, *The Public Realm* (New York: Aldine de Gruyter, 1998); O. Bauman, "The Creation of a Public Sphere," *Archis* 5 (2001); R. Sennett, "Reflections on the Public Realm," in *A Companion to the City*, ed. G. Bridge and S. Watson (Oxford: Blackwell, 2000); C. Boyer, *Cybercities* (New York: Princeton Architectural Press, 1996); T. Vanderbilt, "It's a Mall World

After All," *Harvard Design Magazine* (fall 1999); D. R. Judd, "Constructing the Tourist Bubble," in *The Tourist City*, ed. D. R. Judd and S S. Feinstein (New Haven: Yale University Press, 1999).

11 __ The Jerde Partnership International, *You Are Here* (London: Phaidon, 1999). The essay by M. Crawford, "The Architect and the Mall," underlines a certain fatigue of the mall typology.

12 __ P. Iyer, *The Global Soul* (London: Bloomsbury, 2000).

13 __ J. Baudrillard, *Simulacres et simulation* (Paris: Galilée, 1981).

14 __ H. Schwartz, *The Culture of the Copy* (New York: Zone Books, 1996).

15 __ "Conclusion: What Will Be.com of Us?" in *Life Style Bruce Mau*, ed. K. Maclea and B. Testa (London: Phaidon, 2000); G. Brandstetter, H. Völchkers, ed., *ReMembering the Body* (Ostfildern Ruit: Hatje Cantz, 2000), with the essay on image by B. Mau, "Stress," republished abridged in *Anything*, ed. C. Davidson (Cambridge, Mass.: MIT Press, 2001): "A culture that pushes social, biological, ecological, intellectual, emotional and psychological capacities to the limit of any possible effort is a culture of stress."

16 __ R. Koolhaas, and Harvard Design School, *Guide to Shopping* (Cologne: Taschen, 2001).

17 __ S. Zukin, "How To Create a Culture Capital: Reflections on Urban Markets and Places," in *Century City: Art and Culture in the Modern Metropolis*, ed. I. Blazwick (London: Tate Gallery, 2001).

18 __ J. Rifkin, op. cit., p. 160. Political difficulties to be resolved by political means, according to B. Sterling, "La città virtuale" (1994), *Parco giochi con pena di morte*, ed. W. Gibson and B. Sterling (Milan: Mondadori, 2001).

19 __ M. King, "Malls," in *City A-Z*, ed. S. Pile and N. Thrift (London: Routledge, 2000).

20 __ J. Dewey, *Art as Experience* (New York: Minton, Balch & Co., 1934).

21 __ K. B. Jensen, *The Social Semiotics of Mass Communication* (London: Sage, 1995).

22 __ S. Veca in the "Dialogo su Impero e democrazia," *Micromega, almanacco di filosofia* 5 (2001).

23 __ O. Toscani, in the dialogue "Il mondo e la sua immaginazione," ibid.

24 __ J-M- Schaeffer, *Adieu à l'esthétique* (Paris: Puf, 2000). On the Japanese home see K. Tsuzuki, *Tokyo: A Certain Style* (San Francisco: Chronicle Books, 1999).

25 __ Major mass levels are predicted for the phenomenon: D. Pountain, D. Robins, *L'esprit "cool"* (Paris: Autrement, 2001). Also see J. Lopiano-Misdon, and J. De Luca, *Street Trends* (New York: HarperBusiness, 1998). On the cool VIP see J. Levin, ed., *GQ Cool* (London: Pavillon Books, 2000).

26 __ E. Morin, *L'industria culturale* (Bologna: Il Mulino, 1963).

27 __ S. Juan, *Les formes élémentaires de la vie quotidienne* (Paris: Puf, 1995), p. 254.

28 __ J. D. Bolter, R. Grusin, *Remediation* (Cambridge, Mass.: MIT Press, 1999).

29 __ P. Marcuse, R. van Kempen, *Globalizing Cities. A New Spatial Order?* (Oxford: Blackwell, 2000). For a viewpoint that instead sees the end of the possibility of critical theories see S. Lash, "Informationcritique," in *Cities in Transition*, ed. A. Graafland (Rotterdam: 010 2001).

__ __ **PHARMACY,** LONDON, 1998

In 1998 Damien Hirst[1] opened the Pharmacy restaurant-bar in the Notting Hill quarter in London, and it soon became one of the trendiest venues in the city. The central room is white, the windows bear the pharmacy symbol, the walls are covered with display cases containing drugs. The place is like an environmental extension of the display case of pharmaceuticals the artist made in the first of many different versions in 1989, whose title *Holidays/No Feelings* already suggested, at the time, a comment on the widespread use of drugs as a way to control the emotions.

The menus, the wallpaper with pills in all forms, sizes and colors, and the furnishings in the rooms and bathrooms contribute to the visitor's immersion in a clinical atmosphere, rather than that of a restaurant; so much so that shortly after the opening the Royal Pharmaceutical Society protested about the resulting confusion, and forced the addition of the words "restaurant + bar" on the exterior signage.

Though this operation has a pop character that has undoubtedly contributed to its success, Damien Hirst is also working on a subtler, harder level, manifesting the obsessions of the society of well-being when it comes to chemicals, which are often abused as if they were a magic wand. In an interview the artist talks about medicine as a widespread credo of contemporary society, with a growing number of adepts busily pursuing the dream of immortality.[2]

The disorientation of entering a place where medicine plays an all-encompassing role is even more disturbing here than in other works by the same artist, with their explicit focus on the representation of death, like his famous dead animals conserved in formaldehyde. Pharmacy plays with the absence of life in the living, with anesthesia as a survival technique, with the tendency to transform everything that pertains to the sphere of physical and emotional suffering into pathology (to be quickly, discreetly eliminated with chemicals). In the background ancient phantoms appear, evoked by the etymology of the word itself, *pharmakon*, which "in classical Greek means both the poison and the antidote, the ill and the remedy . . . the magical drug or ambiguous pharmaceutical, whose handling must be left by common men to . . . priests, wizards, shamans, physicians, etc."[3]

But Pharmacy is not an isolated case. There are many design episodes today whose aesthetic is based on this image of medicine and the recurring signs of purity, order, the predominance of white, a white that doesn't express the yearning for a superior order of things, as in the modernist ideology, but an utterly earthbound desire to give form to an artificial landscape.

These elements return in the Beauty Corners in Prada shops, designed by Kazuyo Sejima and Ryue Nishizawa. Once again we are plunged into spaces that look more like a pharmacy than a place where creams and beauty products are sold. The rigorous mono-dose packaging of the products resembles that of pills rather than cosmetics. No makeup, no perfume, only creams for the face and body. The decorations are reduced to a minimum, the space is clean, the light monochromatic, the display cases containing the products white. The only interruptions are the pastel tones of the signage indicating the products. The color white takes us into a world focused on purity, innocence, the desire for a renewed relationship with the surrounding environment and ourselves. But history is full of occasions in which this color has been used to convey ideas connected to the classical world, to a dimension of moral superiority. . . . And the words that accompany the image in the advertising campaign for the launch of the Beauty Corners (purity, power, individuality) suggest scenarios that are not completely reassuring.

White, purity and an aseptic atmosphere are also found in the Sephora Blanc space designed by Jean-Marie Massaud in Paris. A two-hundred-fifty-square-meter store for a brand that makes products for well-being, another immersion in a sort of space of initiation to harmony and inner contentment.

In definitive terms, all three of these spaces lead us into worlds where atmosphere counts more than function, where the promise of well-being goes hand in hand with the idea of separation from reality, or more precisely this promise is communicated through the construction of an uncontaminated parallel reality, where dirt is just a bad memory.

But while restaurants and personal care boutiques pose as pharmacies, perhaps it is no coincidence that pharmacies increasingly resemble supermarkets, where drugs are sold alongside all kinds of other products, and the real protagonists are the cosmetics and everything people think might help them achieve a state of well-being.

In short, on the one hand there is an attempt to conceal medicalization (even today illnesses are often kept hidden, just as hospitals are still places separated from the rest of society), while on the other, ailments that until a short time ago were not even considered pathological factors are now included in our lists of maladies.

The definition of "lifestyle drugs," which according to Glaxo are "drugs recommended for the treatment of risk factors resulting from improper lifestyles or conditions that limit the well-being of the individual, and not only for pathological conditions,"[4] speaks eloquently of a revolution that has already happened, not to mention the statistics on the sale of pharmaceuticals which, for example, report that in the United States three of the top ten drugs, in terms of sales, are mood enhancers. Obviously this family of "new ailments" also includes problems connected with affluent society, such as eating disorders, problems connected with the increase in life expectancy and the decline of sex drive. A good illustration of the dynamic can be found in the definition of Bruce Jennett, partner in a leading American law firm in the area of Life Science, Heller Hehrman White & McAuliffe, who claims that "the lifestyle drugs are those drugs that make you healthy, young, cute, sexy, with good self-esteem. People need that, and they are willing to pay for it."[5]

The redefinition of the idea of health and well-being as a practice to be applied not only in case of emergency, but also in everyday life, is undoubtedly a positive development, but what raises certain doubts is the spread of total faith in pharmaceuticals (precisely medicine as a belief system, as addressed by Damien Hirst), in a sort of magic wand effect that means you don't have to change your diet to reduce cholesterol – just take the right pill. You don't have to rethink your relations with the opposite sex – just take Viagra. And so on. The suspicion arises that people are looking for a magic wand with which to fight the most difficult of all battles: coming to grips with the human condition.

And if it is true that the danger of our time lies, no more and no less, in being human (mortal, fragile, kept alive by invisible threads that can suddenly snap), it is obvious that the desire is to eliminate that risk, an attempt that takes the form of total programming, whose most sophisticated version is the design of the human being itself, an immortal, indestructible human, immune to illness. A machine that can be kept functioning, if necessary, by replacing its parts with new ones. In spite of its declared ironic approach, there is little doubt that the latest Diesel advertising campaign in summer 2001, *Save Your Life*, occupies a significant place in this panorama. The photographer Jean-Pierre Khazem photographed male and female models wearing masks that give them a robotic, completely artificial look. They are all posed, and each performs a gesture, explained by a caption that is a sort of recommendation on the proper behavior in order to "save your life." Drinking one's own urine, eating seaweed, never laughing, inhaling pure oxygen, reincarnating or getting cloned: little by little a surreal list of instructions emerges. The age of each subject is indicated, and all of them are over the age of one hundred, proof of the efficacy of the precautions they have taken. The efficacy of the campaign, on the other hand, lies in the markedly surreal image of the protagonists, while actually outlining possible responses to absolutely real, common fears and desires. To confirm all this, it is no coincidence that the company decided to change the slogan of the campaign after the events of September 11. The images have remained the same, but instead of *Save Your Life* the message has become *Stay Young*. The young people wearing gas masks had become too timely and too painful (yet again) when connected with the idea of the fight for survival. Therefore the campaign took a step backward, returning to the universal dream of remaining generically young.

The emotion prompted by the latest cinema robot can be explained along the same lines. David, the protagonist of *A.I.* by Spielberg/Kubrick, is capable of feeling true sentiments of love for the couple that has taken him into their home as their son, or at least as a (temporary) replacement for their real son, who has been frozen as he risks dying. While E.T. loves the youngster who, unbeknownst to the adults, has fed him and sheltered him in his room, David is identical in appearance to a flesh-and-blood child, and at first glance it is impossible to think of him as the product of a laboratory.

The paradox is that the film tells us humans the story of a robot whose mission in life is to become human. His objective is to transform himself from *mecha* to *orga* in order to be able finally to convince the people he loves "forever" to love him in return.

If it is true that every era has its illnesses or, as Susan Sontag puts it, that every illness becomes a sort of metaphor for the society where it has found room to spread, there is no doubt that one of the most serious illnesses we must face today is precisely that of contamination from real or imaginary enemies, the arrival of pathogenic substances from elsewhere.

On this topic the situation described by Camus in *The Plague* is still very timely; in fact, many elements of the novel suggest meaningful keys for the interpretation of the present. As we know *The Plague* is a perfect metaphor for the irruption of the absurd in everyday life: the story takes place in the forties in Oran, Algeria, where a chronicler narrates in great detail the arrival and spread of an epidemic. Against this backdrop the personal stories of the inhabitants intertwine. Camus tells an imaginary tale, but one that is dense with historical references to the Nazi occupation and the French resistance.

Symptoms of the contemporary malaise include the uncertainty discussed by Zygmunt Bauman,[6] among others, the sensation of never really being out of danger, even when you are at home. Recommended therapies include the anxious pursuit of security, religious faith in science, the drive to design drugs capable of making us invulnerable (once again, immortality), the planning of increasingly sophisticated systems of military defense.

One of the most insidious side effects of such therapy is the reappearance, in new guises, of ancient phantoms we thought had been laid to rest, situations in which the totalitarian dimension prevails over individual concerns or rights. Camus describes these situations with precision when he narrates the advent of the plague and the reaction of the people in the moment in which they become aware of what is happening, and start to realize how it will change the pattern of everyday life, altering their freedom of movement, their relationships, but above all causing them to live as if they had no individual sentiments.

The twentieth century has taught us that the erasure of individuality, the reduction of the individual to a number or a particle of a mass without exceptions (and without the possibility of escape), when taken to extremes represent typical concentration camp conditions and, more generally, the very DNA of totalitarian rule.

While today we have sufficient historical knowledge to recognize and be horrified by conditions of total control, and to evoke history every time we are faced with anything that resembles them, it is strange how hard it seems to be for us to perceive, with the same horror, other apparently lighter forms that are actually oriented – with the excuse of defending us from the dangers of the world – toward depriving us of our individuality and putting us in the condition of reducing to a minimum, or possibly eliminating, opportunities for experience (and for risk).

In *The Truman Show* (1998) Peter Weir narrates the tale of a man in his thirties whose life has constantly been broadcast on television, under the careful guidance of the director Christof. The life of Truman Burbank from birth is the subject of a very popular program, and it happens in a fake world, a town-set where everyone is an actor and where everything that takes place is carefully scripted, including the unwitting protagonist's family traumas.

While the most immediately striking aspect of the story is the fact that Truman's life is constantly observed by the concealed video cameras, an oversized Big Brother, the choice of the actual set for the movie is equally disturbing. Seaside, which in the film is renamed Seahaven, is a tourist area that really exists in California, based on a project by Michael Duane and Elisabeth Platter-Zyberk in 1980. Here the life of the local community unfolds in harmony, everything is under control, clean, orderly, the inhabitants live in single-family houses, everything is on a human scale. A veritable earthly paradise: the city is planned in such a way that every detail perfectly satisfies desires for livability and security (though only for those who live there), a sensation of well-being no metropolis could ever guarantee. Seaside is a close relative of Disney's town Celebration, in Florida. Here the citizens can live as if they were in a small town; there is no need for burglar alarms because the entire city is fully isolated from the outside world. Here the personal freedom and the sense of community most city dwellers complain have vanished are recovered, but within an isolated, and therefore artificial, reality.[7]

The Truman Show hits home because, though in an extreme version, it portrays a widespread dream (the elimination of contamination, as discussed above), transforming it into a nightmare, and one that already exists to boot. Yet going to live in neighborhoods separated from the city, maybe with a bit of greenery, protected by private security services, being able to leave the windows of your house open and the keys on the dashboard of your car, are dreams shared by the better part of the metropolitan middle class.

If the fear that afflicts us is fear of contamination (the fear of illness, the obsessive desire for security, in definitive terms the fear of death which, as we have seen, means the fear of that which represents the essence of the human condition), the totalitarian response springs forth as a reaction to this fear, and coincides with the ultimate aim of the Disney dream: a soft universe, oriented toward anaesthetizing the individual, a universe from which factors of insecurity and risk have been banished, where suffering cannot enter, where the passage of time causes no wrinkles and there are no illnesses, where everything is visible, under control, orderly.

The Truman Show finishes with the image of the protagonist who decides to leave the set and go out to live in the world. We can do the same thing: we can decide to make believe nothing is happening and continue, day after day, episode upon episode, playing the game of self-defense, or we can walk out that door and reclaim our right and possibility to experience the world. And if today the greatest fear of the society of well-being is that of the definitive crisis of the option of living in a safe reality, we are standing at a crossroads that we can transform into an opportunity for growth. It is up to us to take advantage of this opportunity, although it comes from a painful situation, or to make believe nothing has happened and continue singing the praises, with greater gusto than ever, of the dream-nightmare of the perfectly trimmed gardens of Seahaven.

1 __ With the collaboration of Jasper Morrison and Jonathan Barnbrook

2 __ Marcelo Spinelli interviews Damien Hirst, http://dh.ryoshuu.com/ms_science.html

3 __ R. Girard, La violenza e il sacro (Milan: Feltrinelli, 1980), cited in Roberto Escobar, Metamorfosi della paura (Bologna: Il Mulino, 1997).

4 __ See A. Puato, "Siate sexy, fateci guadagnare," Corriere Economia, supplement to Corriere della Sera (4 December 2001) and M. T. Cometto, "Il baby boomer è triste. Che business," Corriere Economia, supplement to Corriere della Sera (4 December 2001).

5 __ A. Puato, Corriere della Sera, op. cit.

6 __ See Zygmunt Bauman, La società dell'incertezza (Bologna: Il Mulino, 1999), in particular chapter IV. A catalogue of postmodern fears; and for reflections on the relations between fear and danger in primitive societies and modern society cfr. Mary Douglas, Purity and Danger. An Analysis of Concepts of Pollution and Taboo (Harmondsworth: Penguin Books, 1970).

7 __ See the reflections of D. M. Steiner on the relations between the so-called New Urbanism and the film The Truman Show, in "The Truman Show," Domus 816 (June 1999), pp. 8-10.

___ **YVES SAINT LAURENT AND HIS MODELS,** PARIS, MARCH 1985. PHOTO ROXANNE LOWIT

Exterior by night.

A downtown street in a big city. A crowd of onlookers, the flicker of flashes and sequins as limousines unload guests in front of towering glass doors. They solemnly enter the shiny new temple, with its imposing walls, back-lit altars, a double row of guards dressed in black and armed with champagne flutes. Voices: "Where can I find the Designer? Can I be introduced to the Architect? Where's the rest of the court? I am here to pay homage to Fashion."

Interior by night.

A white room, chrome and black leather armchairs, a fur carpet. The scene of an improvised cocktail party, designer plates and glasses, logo-printed napkins, trays of fusion-sushi, copies of *Wallpaper** and *Vanity Fair*. Two men and a woman. The ultra-flat screen on the wall displays images and speaks: "I am the actress in the award-winning film and I'm wearing a dress by the Designer. I created the music for the movie and my encounter with Fashion has changed my life. I am the host of the new talk show and I believe in Fashion."

Interior by day.

An immense hall at the end of a colonnaded corridor, the latest stage by a great architect. A thousand or so people seated, many more standing. Darkness, light. The faces of film and television in the front row. Darkness. Slowly the Designer's creations emerge, illuminating the ground they tread on. Ambient music. Whispers: "How many people are going to want a look like this? How much will they be prepared to sacrifice? I hope I get invited again to the season ceremony! I want a life like this, a life of Fashion."

These sound like scenes from a movie, but they are not: they are images of real life today.

The downtown streets of New York and Florence, London and Milan are a succession of fashion stores, temples built by architects in the images of the designers whose logos they bear. The ritual of shopping is performed in them. Magazines all over the world reproduce the same fashion ad campaigns created by famous artists and photographers. Their covers announce the stories of the lives of fashion designers. Television and movie screens reflect images of the same celebrities dressed in the designers' latest fashions. Home and office, food and everyday objects, restaurants and hotels, architecture and art are all increasingly controlled and conditioned by Fashion and its Gods, the designers.

When did fashion rise to power? When did it become a new religion? How did it escalate from being a marginal industry, simply manufacturing clothes to become a dispenser of lifestyles, almost a spiritual guide? What have we gained and what have we lost forever? Would it be better to surrender to the nostalgia of the days when designers confined themselves to dressing a select few and the streets were lined with craft workshops, or cynically accept the new system?

For centuries, fashion's evolution has mirrored society, and in the process has served to reflect a multitude of complex social changes. Fashion is therefore the intersection where globalizing forces at work in society become easier to discern. Style's ability to communicate through images allows the development and establishment of fashion brands to appear to be a cultural crystal ball, within which one may read the present and forecast the future.

The creation of a fashion label begins when a designer puts his or her name on a product. The signature acts as instrument of a transformation. Without changing the physical nature of the object, it completely alters its social role. For this to happen the fashion designers (or rather, the business organizations behind them) must be able to create legitimacy for themselves as the dispenser of a style, of which the product is a part but not the essence.

To be elevated from mere fashion, linked to a specific product and a specific time, to style, or lifestyle, has always been the ultimate goal of the marketing process behind every big brand. And this is achieved through brand focusing: the creation of a unique and strong image, an iconography, with its own specific and recognizable language. Spotting the medium by which the brand identity is communicated is the key to success. This has become difficult, because never has the collective imagination been as crowded as it is today, and never have so many brands been in competition for control.

The fashion industry itself has transformed: its reinforcement and consolidation through an availability of immense capital and an opening of global markets have driven fashion designers to create ever stronger, more urgent and omnipresent images. To compete in a fast and sophisticated market, constantly changing concepts have to be imposed and disseminated worldwide, in increasingly creative, pervasive ways. In the end we find ourselves perpetually surrounded by fashion, in a world where every image and every object carries a logo. Fashion designers themselves are compelled to struggle more and more fiercely to stay original and relevant and to reinvent themselves continually, often without the necessary time to create a tradition of products and a lasting visual legacy. They are forever on the lookout for new ways of attracting attention and appearing different from the others: new buildings, new stores, new design. Everything is reduced to the simplicity of sheer novelty and the uninterrupted succession of trends jeopardizes the brand name's actual life. Once it was sufficient to identify for each season a range of iconic products with which to reach the target consumer. Today a fashion brand has to open itself to increasingly variegated markets and to test its value in ever wider circles, so as to become more then a logo: the symbol of a complete way of living. This necessitates using more and more abstract images and techniques steadily less linked to a specific product, while continuously widening its business and applications. Thus we see Armani creating Armani Casa, Versace opening a hotel, Gucci sponsoring Richard Serra at the Venice Biennale, Prada hiring Rem Koolhaas for its new stores, Donna Karan presenting artists' books and Tommy Hilfiger putting his colors on stage with the Rolling Stones. Home and office, sport and leisure, vacations and culture, museums and theaters are the new territories of conquest and confrontation. The fashion names have had to extend their frontiers beyond the previous limits in which their products had dictated how they were perceived, by buying or consolidating the relevance and legitimacy they need to survive and prosper.

As recently demonstrated by Yves Saint Laurent, there is no future for a fashion designer who still thinks that the essence of his job is to create perfect clothes in the vacuum of his atelier, or for one who refuses to renew his creativity at every season and fails to exert total control over his world image. The closing of Yves Saint Laurent Couture, ironically reported with the same media hype and celebrated in the Georges Pompidou museum, is the consequence of a professed independence from the fashion conglomerates (not though, from the state subsidies of Mitterand's governments), and of a licensing policy that had delegated and dispersed its identity to the lowest common denominator. The new owners of the YSL logo will need to work doggedly to recreate that lost legitimacy. A much easier path is an inverted one, being followed by a new generation of fashion designers, whose aesthetic outlook trespasses on the world of art and entertainment. Their clothes are presented as symbolic objects, conceptual works, open to interpretation rather than to use – with no nostalgia for the past world of couturiers and ateliers.

In theory, a designer's aesthetic vision can be applied to any context, endlessly. The contemporary world offers infinite possibilities: to the point where one logo or another may often even be associated with pure chance, and not with the result of an intentional campaign. A drive into the English countryside reminds us of an advertising page in a magazine; the work of an artist seems inspired by, or the inspiration for, a pair of shoes. To the eyes of a neophyte everyday life begins to resemble an infinite succession of advertising images, a long video full of innumerable product placements, where even the casual reference makes the signature more real and effective than ever. Walking down via Montenapoleone or Madison Avenue, every shop we encounter is a border to be crossed into an imaginary world, a movie directed by a fashion designer, where for a brief moment we are part of the cast. It is a democratic experience, open to all regardless of the price of a gown or of a handbag. Designers openly invite the world to dream about joining their club.

A logo or an image that becomes a symbol of a much wider world, which we would like to belong to, is no novelty. In politics, flags, crosses, stars and stripes and hammer and sickle have long created a direct association with modes of behavior and philosophies of life. All we need is a sign to usher us into a whole world. Fashion communication has found in these precedents a perfect tool to use in the age of the globalization and concentration of names in the hands of a few mammoth groups. For few, since the idea of shopping replaced ideologies, fashion really has become the new religion, with its Gods and places of worship.

Through processes of association, appropriation and suggestion, the big names manage to communicate with the few and with the masses. On the one hand they satisfy the intellectual appetite of an elite, but at the same time they exploit easy symbolisms for the less sophisticated consumer. An exhibition in a famous museum, next to the handbag with its printed logo. Fashion as a contemporary discipline by definition has been the first to abolish all difference between high and low, between culture and business.

The most striking example is perhaps Gucci with its appropriation of the International Style: Gucci's precise aesthetic comprising clean lines, elegantly slick surfaces, rare materials, chrome, glass and leather has conquered the world thanks to an aggressive and sophisticated marketing campaign. To such an extent that when ordinary people see a precious ebony table, a chrome armchair in black leather or a house with glass walls, they are not reminded of Knoll, Mies van der

Rohe or Philip Johnson, but of something that ". . . is very Gucci." In the same way, Calvin Klein has modeled his minimalist image on the aesthetic visions of Donald Judd and John Pawson, so much that everything white, pure and empty ". . . looks really Calvin." Designers' names are now descriptive terms in their own right. So describing an urban and modern lifestyle, a monochromatic and faintly understated elegance, nothing is more effective than the "adjective" Armani. It conjures up instant visions of the polished beige marble surfaces of the stores and of the monochromatic clothes that people buy in them.

The designer in the United States who best illustrates the effectiveness and longevity of this system of cultural co-opting is Ralph Lauren. For decades the name has reigned supreme over all that is tweed and pinstriped flannel, equestrian tradition and the wasp life. Through its advertising campaigns – the first to narrate a lifestyle in cinematic detail – and the creation of a thematic store in an old-money residence on Madison Avenue, a riot of mahogany panels and hunting trophies, old books and deep leather armchairs, Ralph Lauren has succeeded in creating a historical inheritance for itself as the foundation of its legitimacy. For many American consumers, country houses in the English style and Ivy League colleges never existed until Ralph Lauren decorated and inhabited them with his models, the perfect stage-extras of this imaginary universe. Here is the prototype of the amusement arcade store and imaginary set; here is life as a movie. It is the brand as a pure lifestyle. The product is almost irrelevant, indifferent to ever changing trends – which doesn't mean immutable. Indeed, even the Ralph Lauren advertising campaigns and new shops have been moving in the direction of a more urban and less decorative modernity.

To succeed today, the fashion brand must take a global approach. Its aesthetic must be applied to every detail, from the shape of the perfume bottle to the interior of the store, from the method of advertising to the sponsored events. It must progress with an omnivorous appetite for constantly changing areas of influence, especially among those most sensitive to the image.

No one escapes this global image logic. Not even when a designer tries to buck the system or to stand aloof from it. Though silent and faceless, Maison Martin Margiela is now associated by more discriminating consumers with all that is whitewashed and authentic, Helmut Lang with all things conceptual and reduced to the essential, Paul Smith with all things eclectic and curious. With Rei Kawakubo who, for nearly twenty years now, has made Comme des Garçons the ever evolving symbol of something artistic, intelligent and uncompromising.

Such is the habit of this logic of thinking, where an image and a word sum up a lifestyle, that even magazines names are used as adjective when they express a totalizing point of view. The magazine Wallpaper* has been so precise in creating an aesthetic in which all the revivals of design in the sixties and seventies are brought together, that today the term "Wallpaper" is used to describe a host of fashionable spots, shops, clubs, hotels and the generation that frequents them. More recently the magazine nest managed with its distinctive aesthetic to unify everyone eclectic and obscure in interior design and architecture. Hence the nest style after the Wallpaper* style.

What arose from the necessity to grant legitimacy and longevity to fashion products has forever changed the nature of fashion branding and the world around it. From fringe presences they have risen to become the leaders of social and cultural life, invading the territories of art, design and architecture. It is no longer possible to establish exactly where their boundaries begin or end. In fact, these parallel systems, architecture and design, have rapidly and simultaneously learned the marketing and branding techniques typical of fashion, and have opened their doors to direct collaboration with fashion designers. So we have Emilio Pucci fabrics on Patrick Norguet's armchairs for Cappellini, Issey Miyake colors for objects by Karim Rashid and Paul Smith's stripes on Mini Morris cars. And a new star system with the names of new celebrities in lights, the high priests of style: Philippe Starck and Rem Koolhaas, Frank Gehry and Marc Newson. Co-branding is the new password in a contract where the architect and the fashion designer, the artist and the designer, promote each other under the eyes of a generation that has grown up in the world of Guggenheim Museums and Tate Modern Galleries, Conran stores and Ian Schrager hotels. A generation that no longer makes a distinction between fashion, architecture, design and lifestyle.

HiBYE® 7.0

Nomadic Worksphere Seeds
Basic units for nomadic working (in generic spaces such airports, airplanes, trains, hi-ways and MoMA) world wide.

Concentration
CONCENTRATION IS EVERYWHERE
Office is everywhere you are.
Non edible hard pill to play with and get
concentrated for work. You can also play with it
in your hand.

Chill out
RELAX IS EVERYWHERE
Non edible soft unit to play
with in your mouth and to get
relaxed.

PW
Breath Set-up / Pocket Window
Nomadic cultures are based on Oral communication.
Same as the nomadic worker's culture. It is a edible
ampule to get fresh breath.
Pocket window effect.
Fresh Swiss air as mode, you can be outside without
leaving generic closed spaces. For regenerating
yourself.

Orality Writing
WRITE ALL OVER
A unit that allows writing all over. You can eat it too.
You can use any surface and wipe it out easily.

DEO
APPROACH EVERYONE EVERYWHERE
A good nomadic worker talks information from the
rest, speaking with people everywhere, a way of
acquiring fresh useful 1st hand information.
Information is for nomadic work matter.
Deo patch, you take it to the mouth and then you
stick it on any part of your body. Saliva is used to
activate the stickier substance.

Sex appeal
Perfume patch, you take it to the mouth and then
you stick it on any part of your body. Saliva is
used to activate the stickier substance. Refers to
the private charge, defines the personal relation
between yourself and the rest of the people.

Sensory Redactors
ISOLATE YOURSELF EVERYWHERE
Edible "strpea", you take it to the mouth and then
it becomes soft. You introduce it in your ears or
nose or put it on your eyes. Saliva is used to get
different kind of softness. After using you can eat
them. A way of disconnecting yourself from
hearing or smelling or seeing the surrounding.

Dr. YOU
Portable doctor.
It is a multi-tablet construct that provides you
all you need to get healthy in any kind of light
illness. 100% natural !

GO Crazy switch
In work situations you need a kind of
reaction to refresh your mind. This
unit provides you with strong
sensation. It is made of Aluminum
that reacts with your teeth implants.
Non edible.

Food
BASIC POPS
Snacks made of basic nutrients elements from the world: wheat, corn, rice.

1 Corn nugget
2 Rice Ball
3 Bread

Culture Bridge
FEEL COMFORTABLE EVERYWHERE
A unit that provides you with specific regional or continental
natural flavors combined with digestive spices that you can put
over the generic food of airplanes and generic restaurants.

1 American spices
2 Asian spices
3 European spices
4 African spices

Drinks
POCKET DRINKS
Get water in generic spaces. This unit allows you to make tea or coffee with a glass of water. Whenever You put
the unit in your mouth and then you drink. You make the hint for the coffee in your mouth!

1 Green tea
2 Mint tea
3 Bat tea
4 Coffee

Thrill sweets
COLLECT EXPERIENCES
Experiences are necessary for life. Work travelers have no experiences in generic spaces. Full
flavored candies in the shape of own eyes (for example teddy bears) to combat dullness in generic
spaces.

1 Teddy bear eye
2 Teddy dog eye
3 Doll eye
4 Teddy Tiger eye

Communicator
Share!
Alcohol unit as a unmbalost for communication. Communication is a
tool for nomadic work = information.

Idea Ball
SPREAD IDEAS
Masanobu Fukuoka is a Japanese man that invented users ago
a very funny and rigorous functional system to release planet
earth. It consists in performing seed balls with earth. Sun Prize
is away in the landscape and they are there waiting for the ideal
conditions to germinate.
Idea ball is an energy amplifier to eat. Dry fruits with coffee glue
pastry mixture. An exemplar ball to germinate situations on the
way.

AURA
comes
SET AURA
The only reason to meet people personally is
to feel and to confront auras. The unit is an
Almond (Mandorla) unit. Mandorla is the name.
Marti Guixé goes in the aura in his formula.
Aura comes as the real time performance
effect.

Sock
In and Out Fits
Basic needs are fulfilled through units that you dissolve in
your mouth and you get link impact. Made of organic
material, they adjust to your body when you put them on.
Should be single use only. Designed are only "non look"
elements, the look clothes should change because of
fashion or situations or cultural reasons.

Breast Cover
IN and Out Fits

Adjustable underwear
IN and Out Fits

Peripheral
CARRY NOTHING
Don't transport matter, transport information, when there is no
possibility, have is the bag. Could be sponsored. It won't like
the underwear units and it is multi functional.

Patch system that allows to perform better
real time communication by establishing
(building) designed link areas in your face.
1 Business
2 Private
3 Travelling

Talking Object

Souvenir
Save a small object of the place where you experienced a good story and put
the piece into the capsule. Once you want to activate the memory take
capsule, put it in your mouth and start telling the story, the unit dissolves into
your mouth while you explain the story. Once finished you take the small
object and give it to the audience.

B HiBYE® COMPLETE CATALOGUE -7.0 PRODUCT CARD-

Worksphere at MoMA   HiBYE   www.guixe.com
© Marti Guixé (2000)

___ MARTÍ GUIXÉ, **INSTRUCTION CARD FOR HIBYE PROJECT**, 2001

There is an obvious codependency between food and life. They are intertwined. You cannot have one without the other. The same can be said of food and life*style*. Then what is the comfort food of the *Wallpaper** generation? What changes in your diet should you make to reflect the new consciousness brought on by the recent acquisition of six Morrison chairs for your dining table? What wine goes with your subscription to the *Economist*? As absurd as these questions might seem, especially in light of recent world events, they actually are legitimate. It is in these very hard times that taking stylistic charge of one's life carries a greater importance. Building one's own system of references can take a lot of conscious efforts and choices.

In the past, we knew what to do. Our mothers and grandmothers would teach us what to cook and how to behave, and fashion magazines would consistently tell us what to wear and how to look. But post-modern mentors like Rei Kawakubo, Madonna, and Pedro Almodóvar have taught us that elegance and beauty are all in the intention, the novelty, the composition and the attitude, certainly not in such reductive concepts as codes and homogeneity. Emancipation from the old-fashioned concept of "absolute style" was timely and unavoidable, and it is certainly one of the biggest achievements of the past century. Yet, for a while we lost our compass. As the world became more easily attainable thanks to increased mobility and better access to information, and as the binds that tied us to tradition loosened, the first period of free experimentation provoked some funny outcomes. In the realm of food, fusion cuisine – a portion of tuna sushi made with *risotto alla Milanese*, for instance, as offered by the restaurant Nobu in New York – was perhaps born out of this initial disorientation. Lately, however, a resurgence of regional and national cuisine has led the public to appreciate local authenticity and to seek it as a way to acquire knowledge and experience the world.

Style has become a matter of personality in urban music, fashion, design, and food alike. Take, for example, hip-hop music. Based on sampling and composing new and pre-existing tracks and giving them a finishing varnish of surprising novelty, it is the recipe for contemporary style. In fashion, after a few last attempts to revive first the sixties, then the seventies, and finally the eighties, all of a sudden anything goes, so long as the ensemble is meaningful and full of character. What matters today is not strictly the provenance, but rather the authenticity and success of the composition. Individuals have been upgraded to the role of authors and arbiters and are exhorted to pick and choose and affirm their personal taste. This shift of balance has engendered obsessiveness about style, which reflects on the whole spectrum of daily activities. Eating does not escape this tyranny.

Eating habits have been closely connected to the vagaries of fashion for a long time, especially with the ideal body-type shifts of each historical period and their meaning in the class system. Back at the end of the twentieth century, Tom Wolfe, in his novel *The Bonfire of the Vanities*, first published in 1987, called the elegant, ethereal Upper East Side ladies the "X-rays." Ten years later, their daughters were known as the victims of Heroin Chic. Both terms caricature *anorexia nervosa* as a beauty type, but in the late eighties the aberration went beyond the printed page and into the kitchens of restaurants. That was the unfortunate time of *nouvelle cuisine*, of the mighty lonely shrimp on three delicate leaves of arugula. In between came the athletic bodies of the early nineties and their bottled non-carbonated water, protein bars, and gourmet olive oil. We have to thank the powers that be for the recent relaxation in waistline regulations. Yet, all these thoughts are limited to food trends as byproducts of visual and aesthetic trends. They concern what food we eat and how much, and not who prepares it or how. Moved both by design concerns and by the recent disturbances in world affairs, many categories of thinkers are turning to food for comfort from unexpected angles. The outcome is sometimes surreal. The February 2002 issue of American *Harper's Bazaar*, as a matter of fact, features a curious article entitled "Is Cooking the New Shopping?" Next to a full-page image of female forearms and their heavily-bejeweled hands energetically kneading bread dough, the intro reads: "The latest trend is taking place in the kitchen. Amanda Vaill on why members of the social brigade now think cooking is cool." It might be that sultry Nigella Lawson's beloved British TV show is about to be launched also in the United States. Or it might be the post-traumatic effects of September 11, leading even the trendiest of people to curl up at home with friends around a fireplace. Or maybe fashion editors, after spending the last two years wondering whether design is the new fashion (sic) and feeling that they've run out of prophetic headlines, have to find a novelty paradigm. After Rem Koolhaas' *Harvard Graduate School of Design Guide to Shopping* that sparked the new Prada store in New York, are we going to see a *Harvard Graduate School of Design Guide to Cooking and Eating*?

It is true that in the United States chefs have been treated as celebrities for a long time. Signatures/*griffes* are a European invention, but Americans have brought them to more effective fruition by offering them to the lowbrow end of the market. Whole brands have been built around the proven skills of Wolfgang Puck, Emeril, and Mario Batali, to name just a few. Yet, be it in the form of frozen lasagna or a TV show, until recently these personalities were doing the trendy cooking, while buying their precooked TV dinners and watching the Food Channel were occupations of the lower-middle classes. Those in the know would rather leisurely go to the signature restaurants. But it was just an illusion to think that cooking could be the last corner of the world to be free from trend and fashion obsessions. Getting elbow-deep in dough has become an affirmation of social status.

In many regions of the world, food is a straightforward matter of life or death. In others, where food and wealth are more abundant, it becomes part of the ensemble of symbols that enable recognition of social status. Food is the deepest form of expression, both in an introspective and an extroverted fashion, for individuals and nations alike. It can be a sure way to highlight class differences. There are some obvious circumstances, for instance on a flight: First Class gets caviar and porcelain, Business gets Canadian salmon and ceramic, Coach gets overcooked pasta and plastic. But food becomes a communication tool mostly on the occasion of social gatherings. There is no culture in the world where a banquet isn't considered the most appropriate way for the host to celebrate his guests, the occasion, and himself. The chapters devoted to entertaining in such classic studies of social climbing as Thorstein Veblen's *Theory of the Leisure Class: An Economic Study of Institutions* (1899) or Paul Fussell's *Class: A Guide Through the American Status System* (1983) make for highly entertaining and informative reading. In the United States, the noun "lifestyle" addresses quality of life in a very visible, tangible way. Inaccessible class landings do not stifle upward mobility in status as they do in Europe; it is a free climb marked by landmark possessions. In understated and inhibited Europe a better lifestyle signifies, beyond a better car and better tailored clothes, first and foremost more time to cook with friends, better wine, and maybe better furniture in the same old family house, while in the United States it easily manifests itself in costly accoutrements. As most candidly displayed by rap music videos, part of the American dream is to progress in society and buy a bigger house, a faster car, a big rock for the girlfriend, and a fur for mother. A fine bottle of balsamic vinegar perched on a Boffi kitchen shelf is the white urban equivalent of the rapper's heavy gold chain.

On both continents, lifestyle is a matter of design. This calls for a more in-depth analysis of the relationship between food and design. Food is an ode to human creativity applied to design and architecture. Many recipes, like those for a Chinese spring roll or a New Orleans gumbo, are naturally translated from generation to generation. Others, like *cotoletta alla milanese* and its Austrian version *Wiener Schnitzel*, are the subject of endless attribution diatribes. Much like the architectural scheme of a vernacular local dwelling, they are based on the composition of some immutable elements dictated by the region's material culture, and they can then be mutated by contemporary popular culture and innovation.

Some of the basic elements of gastronomical architecture, moreover, are archetypical designed objects. Some of them have been updated from crafts tradition and are now hand-produced in series, or even manufactured industrially, with advanced automated techniques. Pasta, for instance, passes all the tests of a good contemporary design object. The simple mixture of durum wheat flour and water, shaped or extruded by hand or machine, is a perfect reference for the design discourse and can be easily approached from all critical angles. Some examples of pasta's high design status: first of all, pasta is historically an outstanding case of direct balance of means – the scarce available resources in poor countries – and goals – the human need, nonetheless, for a somewhat diversified diet. It is such a simple and strong design idea that it has been able to generate an endless variety of derivative designs – the various types of pasta and the dishes made from them.

Moreover, it is a timeless design, in that its production tools have been updated across the centuries, but its basic form has remained the same. It is also a global design, easy to appropriate and adapt to local culture. It is a universal success among critics and the public, thus passing also the marketing-driven design test. It exemplifies the zero degree of the design discourse, because it is an example of form coinciding with function. Its is nonetheless somewhat resistant to merely formal manipulation, as demonstrated by the several unfortunate attempts made by renowned designers all over the world, among them Philippe Starck, Giorgetto Giugiaro, and Luigi Colani. They all failed. It is a design born out of necessity and resistant to unnecessary stylistic manipulation.

The quintessential design nature of food can begin to be manipulated only when the basic units get assembled in plates, those plates in meals, and those meals in occasions. Several artists currently working with food have understood this simple principle. Some, like Martí Guixé, have concentrated on the design of the single units. Others, like Lucy Orta and Orphic Studio, have dedicated themselves to the choreography of the communal meal. Their work is a commentary on current practices and future behaviors. Guixé, a Catalan living between Berlin and Barcelona who calls himself a Techno-gastrosof, Tapaist, and Designer, has concocted for instance the techno-tapas, compact appetizers small enough to be popped directly into the mouth and practical enough to be served at gallery openings and other crowded, standing-room-only gatherings. His are also the sponsored pizzas, on which corporations can inscribe their logo in mozzarella over tomato. The profits from the sale of pizza space go to sustain the livelihood of struggling artists.

Orphic, a.k.a. Mimi Oka and Doug Fitch, is based in New York and active both in the United States and in France. Their many projects include the poetic *Floating Island*, a banquet inspired by the well-known French dessert and actually consumed by a cheerful company sitting at a round table floating on a river in the South of France in the summertime. Waist-high in water on their floating circular bench, dressed up for a banquet, they receive their several elaborate courses either by boat, or from a bridge above.

Lucy Orta, British by birth, Parisian by adoption, is interested in social engineering. Food for her provides one more means to discuss the same political issues that she has often tackled with garments and architectural installations. Her performances, such as the lunch for four hundred people on one unique, long table that she organized on the occasion of the 51st International Design Conference in Aspen (2001), create occasions for people to come together in new ways and take a fresh new look at meaningful rituals.

The ways these four designers/artists consider our relationship with food transcend style considerations without discounting them as futile. Their thoughtful ideas reflect a new attitude that is less self-centered and more geared toward our fellow humans in the changed world. It is an attitude that is a quintessential tenet of design. The truth is, style is not the motor, and it is nothing without heart. There is no better personal style than that which comes from sensitivity and kindness, generosity, awareness of one's surroundings, knowledge of one's limits, and self-assuredness within, in shopping and cooking alike. Just what our grandmothers would say.

__ __ FABIEN BARON,
PHOTO FROM **"FREEZE FRAME,"** *W,*
FEBRUARY 2001

Karl Marx, in his *German Ideology*, wrote, "If men and their condition in every ideology appear in reverse, as in a *camera obscura*, this phenomenon stems from their vital historical process, just as the reversal of objects on the retina stems from their directly physical process." We, too, can adopt this image, accustomed as we are by the language of fashion, to reverse concepts continually. Fashion, in fact, writes Roland Barthes, "tends to turn the reason of signs into the exact opposite of their physical arrangement." Thus a starched necktie suddenly becomes a symbol of comfort or a latex corset a symbol of elegance. If, moreover, we admit that September 11, 2001 was for our epoch a date that reversed a great many certainties, then a number of concepts of "living well and totally," meaning the quality of life, now likewise need to be seriously reconsidered. Maybe also with the help of a Marxist reversal. Given its invasive importance, both in ideological terms and in its everyday practical aspects, one of these concepts is undoubtedly that of luxury.

The word luxury, as we pronounce and perceive it, says a lot but explains nothing. This, it may as well be said at once, is its chief drawback, the cause of all its troubles and the source of all its self-inflicted misunderstandings. "Excessive and superfluous, not necessary, the display of wealth, splendor, magnificence, pomp." Moralistic and totalitarian, if not downright fundamentalist, dictionaries and encyclopedias define luxury thus, as if it were the root of all evil, the influenza virus that blunts human intelligence, the worst expression of a uselessness that appeases our sluggish consciences. Disliked by many without ideological distinctions, its revenge is all contained in that inexplicable fascination that makes it everybody's aspiration. Execrated, contested, humiliated even, but always held up as a symbol, it is mythicized and almost deified. In the best of cases it may be claimed to have a highly controversial destiny. Alas, poor luxury, the cause of its own ills, it is incapable of weeping over itself, yet it survives itself. It is self-nurtured and self-regenerated.

Dramatic, and even melodramatic when it sought to associate with fashion, the expression of modernity whenever the latter somehow springs from a traumatic birth of thought or history, without the blindness inflicted by moralistic preconception and without the guilt feeling induced by its apparent futility borrowed from fashion, luxury is instead an inevitable element of refinement. It is a necessary expression of a culture asserting itself, a striving that cannot be confused either with wealth or with ready cash. Nor can it be enclosed by a particular expression of human endeavor. Luxury cannot just be an expression of products, nor simply behavior, nor still less, a rhetorical figure reserved for the phenomena of custom.

LUXURY IS INEVITABLE __ Seen in the *camera obscura* of history, and therefore in its reversed form, luxury is a thought which can at times be expressed in a gesture, very often in a philosophy, always in a provocation. For this reason it is thwarted and loved, loathed and cultivated. In this respect it is inevitable. Every culture anxious to be worthy of the name is compelled to face up to its own concept of luxury. That is why it invents its own variant of expression and ethics, but also, like an urge for self-destruction, its own form of struggle. Every period of history, but also every political era, invents its own aesthetic and its own luxury. But while the evolution and consolidation of aesthetics have always found a justification (and art, architecture, literature et cetera serve that purpose), luxury has always been confronted by the wall of contrast. So once the idea of luxury is born, so also is its disputation: poison and antidote. Culture, in fact, could not bear luxury to gain the upper hand over aesthetics, with the pretext that aesthetics is useful to all (those who use it) and luxury only to the élite (who misuse it). The naive reason for this is that whereas in the aesthetic idea histories transfer the justification to their own Weltanschauung, in luxury they transport excess. Without calculating that the excess, which is bound to assume the function of an exception to the rule, is capable of admitting more meanings than normally allowed.

It does so to its own detriment, because luxury starts life with an original sin: it is reserved for the few. That in itself may not exactly constitute sin, but it does when the few happen to come from privileged classes, not when the few perform the difficult role of an avant-garde.

LUXURY AND CAPITALISM __ The greatest confusion, however, arrived late, when bourgeois capitalism gained the upper hand over all other philosophies (or should we say, over all other rules of social coexistence?), when luxury became the synonym for extreme wealth. Among the many faults that may be ascribed to a system so all-engulfing and un-liberal as to remain the only viable one, is also that of having made the idea of luxury disagreeable, classist and even deeply unjust. Guilty and guilt inflicting, this luxury that allows itself to be used and enjoyed only by people who are rich in money but hardly ever in ideas, begets monsters. And the monsters, contrary to what might be thought, are those who exploit for their own greater convenience this false idea of luxury, and not those who stay aloof from it.

However, because throughout the history of humankind it has been the expression of so many different realities as to have been frequently at loggerheads, luxury cannot be related only to the wealth of those who produce and consume it. We won't go into all the many examples here. Let us just consider the one that best illustrates our point. The ruling classes keep in their safes the greater part of the world's wealth; they consume all the expensive products that their system produces, but which "are luxury goods" only because the dictionaries that they themselves have compiled define them as luxurious and superfluous. In actual fact they have always confused luxury with wealth. Instead, the concept belongs to a different sphere of thought, where money counts (because it is necessary), but is not defining.

It is due to this very idea of luxury being dependent on money that the biggest misunderstanding that could possibly have arisen did occur. Indeed the misunderstanding verges on the delirious. Luxury finished up in clothes: a part for the whole, which also includes shoes, handbags, jewelry and other luxury commodities. And clothes are the easy vehicles of a platitude induced by the habit of turning luxury into a showy, loud, gross and ill-mannered expression of wealth.

LUXURY IS NOT GLAMOUR ___ The idea of luxury transferred into clothing brings us right back to the luxury-fashion link. True, fashion is a luxury too. But then so is design in its entirety, or so can any materialization of an idea be, when it requires costly elements to make it real. In the utter confusion created by abuse of the term, luxury and fashion have merged, as if one could not exist without the other; or as if to define one the other were necessary too. The fact is that fashion, especially in recent years, has been exploited as an easy means of extending the enjoyment of luxury. The passage from haute couture –reserved for those few among the few who are rich but also possess taste – to prêt-à-porter, mass-produced industrial taste, was meant to have rendered it more accessible. In reality that has never been the case. True, the fashion industry has produced and continues to produce beautiful and expensive things, which do not thereby necessarily also embody the idea of luxury. An expensive coat, for example, if it can be repeated in series and if, most of all, it does not in itself represent the idea of uniqueness, is unlikely to be perceived as a luxury commodity. Indeed, periodically there is a continual move forward in pursuit of exclusivity: one time it may be a precious fiber, another time a processing method, or another time again a limitation of numbers manufactured. Nor can we label as luxury that indefinable sense of elegance which for just under a century has been called glamour. According to the creators of the term (couturiers and fashion designers), by their own admission glamour is an unexplainable attitude that can cohabit with luxury. But it neither defines it nor is it necessary to its existence. They can live together, to be sure: glamour can also be found in jeans and a white shirt; and there in itself luxury can exist, but not necessarily. However, there is luxury in a Carrara marble floor in the Moscow subway, though that location would be hard to define as glamorous. Unless perhaps . . .

LUXURY AND REVOLUTION ___ Unless glamour may just happen, at times, to come to the aid of a truly bold definition. For example, to demonstrate that luxury is not a category of capitalism, it is easy to refer to the enormous fascination (glamour) exerted by the Red Army uniform.
In the months following the October Revolution, the Red Army used up the supplies left by the Tsarist armed forces. But clearly the new revolutionary army had to have a new uniform. Just as it was also absolutely clear that the common people had to change their style of dress. To deal with the first matter, in 1918 a temporary committee was set up to create uniforms, and shortly afterwards a competition for the best models was announced. Although the brief specified lightness, functionality and simplicity (no frills!), the designers turned toward the more distinctive and symbolic aspects of the uniform. A heroic epoch would be equivalent to heroic images. After more than a year the uniform, a collective effort, consisted of: a pointed woolen cap with earflaps, which substantially reproduced the steel helmet worn by fifteenth-century Russian warriors; a greatcoat manifestly influenced by the caftan, as was the tight-fitting jacket and the double fastening; while the decorative elements such as the red star on the beret and the red border of the buttonholes, chosen with extreme care, served to emphasize the details.

The next year the first greatcoats with braid on their left hem were introduced, and in the summer of that year the summer uniform appeared, with a shirt trimmed at the neck and chest. In giving precedence to the heroic aspect of the uniform, its creators had thus not only borne in mind its practical purpose, but had paid much more attention to necessities of form, to emotional and decorative features. In this way they stated an expression of luxury which, perhaps for the first time, used an element of exclusiveness that referred to the avant-garde and not to the élite. The Revolutionary Military Council gave its approval, aware perhaps that even such a luxury uniform might offer a sharp aesthetic definition of the period.

More or less the same thing happened with the birth of new fashion. Vera Mùchina, Jevgènija Pribylskaja, Aleksander Èkster, Nadèzka Makarova and others worked, together or separately, in the same year and in different ones, and before the advent of constructivism, on the definition of revolutionary fashion. And it had to last a long time. In fact the established criteria also considered their subsequent development. Meanwhile it was necessary to start from a concept, namely that fashion must be for all. But that didn't mean it had to be standard. As the Pribylskaja report reads: "The structure of the clothing is based on the breaking-down of the human figure and on an essentially mobile model. . . . The task of the clothes maker is not to seek a standard model, but rather to work out exact data on the basis of which to make the apparel and to define its outer look." Convinced that "embroidery creates the apparel together with its fabric," and taking up the whole Russian craft and peasant tradition, the women fashion designers of the Revolution eventually gave birth to this idea: "The structure of the dress consists of a straight and loose shirt, with wide sleeves and an open neck. Three ornamental stripes are set on the front; while two others at the sides pass over the shoulders and down the length of the back. . . ." Can we envisage a luxury so luxurious that it can afford not to appear so, so stylish as not to offend the eye and sensibility, that does not represent a superstructure but only a necessary definition of an aesthetic without moralism? Yes we can, and here it is. It is the same as that to be found in the immense, extraordinary, dazzling Moscow subway (at least as long as the trains continued to run on time . . .), where the stations are ballrooms with marble floors and glass chandeliers, bronze statues and gilded sculptures. Millions of passengers every day, and the marble always polished and clean, the lamps always on and sparkling, the escalators with their wooden steps and not a scrap of paper to be seen on the floor: a useful luxury available to many, a great many. Could this be a contradiction in terms?

The process can be repeated for the architecture of the period (can Stalin's seven palaces be a luxury aesthetic?) and for the theaters (can the luxury of velvet mix with communism? The fact remains that when communism finally collapsed, many historic theaters in all the countries of the Soviet bloc were closed down . . .). And the same thing, in different ways, has happened in China. What, after all, is that portrait of Mao Zedong in uniform if not the certification of an idea of luxury? Ah, how the communists loved luxury . . . (and we are sorry to use the past tense).

LUXURY AND ECCENTRICITY __ They loved it at least as much as the eccentrics have always loved it. And the latter, belonging by definition to an avant-garde, have nothing at all to reproach themselves for as far as the use, and also the abuse, of luxury is concerned. Solitary on the street where all is permitted ("the world dresses up in the gown of penitence and with plastic bags: it is up to us to wear a magnificent feathered cap," says Sting), the eccentrics do not ascribe a monetary value to luxury. Very often their "feathered cap" is falling apart and inhabited by colonies of moths. But their *train de vie* is a magnificent locomotive, even when there is no fuel to move it. Their luxury gains significance and is nurtured by their attitude toward life. Born to break the rules, to be far from the hub, their very existence is a luxury.

Barbara Hutton, having arrived in Tangiers in the wake of the great intellectual nomads who had gone to live on the Moroccan shores, with the exotic on their doorstep (a few hours by sea from the western Spanish coast), bought a house in the old Arab quarter of the city. She painted it all white, outside and in, and to furnish it she ransacked the stalls of the local souk. She collected a vast assortment of kilim, vases and trays in silvered metal, old doors converted into splendid tables, cushions made out of old sheepskin saddles, lamp-stands based on lanterns used to light Bedouin goat's-wool tents. On her terrace, periodically and by appointment, she gave sumptuous parties at which her numerous flunkies, recruited among the boys of the souk, would serve mint tea in gilded glasses. In the small hours the American millionaire would take leave of her friends with some small gift: a precious stone, a piece of amber, an embroidered cloth. In short, she lived in the lap of unbridled luxury while managing to spend very little money. On her death, her heirs sold the house (which is in reality composed of two distinct riads joined by a small bridge between the two terraces) to a rich French gentleman who did not like that ethnic furniture, the artistic lamps and all the rest. To visitors today, if they manage to corrupt the custodian with a few dirams, the former Hutton House looks authentically rich. It is full of antique furniture, designer lamps, precious porcelain and crystal glasses. But the luxury has gone. In its place is the impudent evidence of wealth. When Barbara died penniless, the luxury went with her.

For the luxury of eccentrics, we were saying, has nothing to do with money. Such figures, whose brains turn faster, may belong to various social classes but they have a motor inside them that drives them toward the same outlook on life. Peggy Guggenheim, for instance, was a rich lady who, after the various vicissitudes of her life, found herself one day even having to worry about money problems. She was surely an eccentric and she thought of luxury not so much as the collecting of art as the possessing of artists. Compared to her love affairs (from the young Samuel Beckett to Laurence Vail and Max Ernst), her Venetian palace with its inlaid mother-of-pearl floors, her dresses by Poiret and Fortuny, precious but worn out by the holes of time, her butterfly glasses designed by Jean Arp, and her mobiles by Calder, were worth precious little. The luxury of "Henry James's last transatlantic heroine," as Gore Vidal has described her, was to live with a keen awareness of the historical value of what she did.

CONCLUSIONS __ Seen thus, which might indeed be a good way of seeing it in these opening years of a new millennium, luxury may appear to be positively revolutionary, a source of drastic social and cultural changes. But the confusion is too much beneath the sky, as a certain Chinese helmsman would have said, whereby in our epoch it takes a great deal of effort to hack out a path for oneself through the jungle; where "luxury" is used to define Cretan jewels and Pashtun headgear (that of the Mujaheddin which has become a luxury article since the Afghan conflict); where luxury is confused with snobbery (whereas it is plainly the latter that feeds on the former and not the other way round); and where it is believed that to consume is in itself a luxury. But precisely the subject of consumer spending and richness clearly demonstrates that true luxury has no time for price tags. Luxury, in short, cannot be bought: it is *"nu' piezzo e' core,"* as Filomena Marturano, the refined thinker fashioned by Eduardo De Filippo's luxurious pen, would have said (in Neapolitan dialect). In other words, it is the inevitable necessity of a human thought.

__ __ **PORCELAIN CRUCIFIX**,
NYMPHENBURG MANUFACTORY, BAVARIA.
PHOTO DAVIS + STARR

There are very few occasions when you can walk into a place and feel you've just met the most interesting person on the planet. For me, this is what happens when I step into Moss in downtown New York. There, past the threshold of the store's cast iron façade and away from the fashionistas who now lord over the streets of SoHo, I've instantly engaged in a conversation, a curiosity, an education with the objects in that store and, by extension, with the person who put them there. In a sense, the conversation galls me: how is it that Murray Moss – who selects, installs, art directs and relentlessly Windexes everything in that place – how is it that he conveys so much about the subject of design, which is his passion and mine, without having to say a word? The objects speak for themselves. His extraordinarily specific, sometimes eccentric sensibility and worldly curatorial taste are there to read like a book. A very large book with about 80-point type.

So, I decided not to let Murray Moss get away with it any more. Instead of showcasing his amazing finds while remaining mute behind the counter, it was time for the mastermind behind his eponymous store to speak. Over breakfast on New Year's Eve, one of the few days of the year when he isn't at work, we discussed a number of philosophical and frivolous issues having to do with, well, subjects both philosophical and frivolous. But mostly we discussed design and all the layers, sometimes deep, sometimes shallow, that are there, in that subject, and in the Moss store, to behold.

Chee Pearlman: As an entrepreneur you've made the leap from founding a serious fashion label to becoming America's leading design retail pioneer. I'd like to go back a bit to talk about your former life . . .

Murray Moss: As a ballet dancer? (Laughter) You mean former lives! (Laughter)

CP: Well, the ballet part is news to me! But I wonder if your twelve-year career in the fashion world has had some influence on what you do now.

MM: When I started the company Moss Shamask in 1978, I was interested in what the Dutch designer Ronaldus Shamask was thinking about – even though he was not a fashion student and didn't know how to make clothes. It was the first time, believe it or not, that anyone looked at fashion from a different discipline – which in our case was architecture. Ron did flat architectural drawings for a kind of clothing loosely based on traditional Japanese clothing. So you work with the full width of the fabric and you fold, fold, seam, seam, and create almost a kind of origami clothes.

CP: Origami as architectonic fashion.

MM: Yes. It was about making a structure to house and adorn a body. It was a conscious effort to step away from traditional decoration, in the sense of pattern, or decorative elements. The structure was intended to be the only decoration. The work was influenced by earlier designers, namely, Charles James, Cristobal Balenciaga, and Madame Grey, and in particular by traditional Japanese kimono and the garments in the paintings of the Spanish painter Zurbarán. The garments were created sort of like edifices. Now it's a very common thing, but it wasn't at the time.

CP: Coming in with an uninformed outsider's view is often a position of strength. There is no way you can do what's "right" because you don't know any better. So you end up inventing.

MM: Yes, well we couldn't compete by attempting to do what others were already doing well. What interested us was inventing structure, exploring the properties of the materials, and the possibility of taking solutions from other disciplines and applying them to garments. So people looked at it as a kind of "intelligent" – not our word, their word – approach. In other words, it was made clear that to understand our clothing it helped to have a certain amount of information. That, by the way, is what's most interesting to me about product design now.

CP: That could be considered an elitist attitude.

MM: We took the position then, and it's the same position that I take at the Moss store now, that art and ideas are necessary, but privileged. In other words, we are not pretending to be involved with food, clothing and shelter in the sense of survival. We're starting with the assumption that one's basic human survival needs have been addressed. Unfortunately for much of the world, for a great number of people, this is not the case, so, regrettably, we're still talking about true luxuries. But a luxury that I believe is an important part of life.

CP: Luxury is a tricky concept, especially at the moment, because the word has become so debased . . .

MM: Yes. It has. But we are very fortunate to be able to consider and include it in our lives. If you're talking about an object as a means of expression – whether it be a jacket, or whether it be a fruit bowl – then already the conversation is going in an extremely luxurious direction, which I don't take for granted.

CP: When you were in the fashion business, did it surprise you that even after so much work, in the end everything was ephemeral?

MM: No. One of the things I liked about fashion as an industrial discipline is that it's evolved over such a long period of time, and it's so welcomed now in our culture, that we long ago abandoned the idea of clothing as purely a functional industrial product. It has always been used as a means of personal expression. We do buy clothing for so-called functional reasons – we use it to cover our nakedness, which is the law. And we use it to a certain degree to make ourselves comfortable in variable climates. But we do that in almost a secondary way.

CP: One of clothing's acknowledged functions is for it to tell us something about the wearer.

MM: Which is why we have multiple clothes. Because it's understood that if you associate yourself by wearing something one moment, you'll probably wear something else the next moment, and there will be a reason why you've made that choice.

CP: Or you play against type, and wear something casual when you're supposed to be formal.

MM: Yes. But part of mixing it all up is to show how much you know. A wardrobe is like a really good bookcase. You glance at it, and you understand what the person reads, how they think, what their interests are. And again, we're talking about the privileged, which is the Western world, to a great extent.

CP: Many fashion designers have grandly gone forward to say that they can design a "total life" and are putting their labels on extensive lines of housewares and home furnishings. I wonder if you believe that fashion skills and sensibilities are transferable?

MM: Okay, the problem with some of the home collections is a kind of a presumption on the part of certain designers. Look, here's the closest parallel I can think of: it's the same as when people think that they can go from America to England, and it's going to be the same, because we all speak the same language. You know? But I feel more foreign in England than I do in Italy! Part of the problem is that those two disciplines, if you call them that – product design, objects, home collections – and fashion, garments used to cover the body – are two dramatically different processes. They involve different skills and they each have long, diverse histories that are rich in their development. And the presumption – and it is presumptuous! – that because certain words apply to both disciplines, words like balance, color, proportion, texture, form, means that if you get one, you get the other. That is just uninformed.

CP: Okay, so Ralph Lauren, Giorgio Armani, even a mass-market store like Banana Republic, are all in business selling home "collections." Have they been able to educate themselves? Have they been able to make those leaps?

MM: It depends on what you mean by "leap." If you establish a company and make things in another discipline, I suppose you could say you've made the leap. In my opinion, those are not informed products. My feeling is this: if a person is a brilliant pianist, it's an extraordinary person who can also play the violin. What I find audacious is if a violinist says, "notes are notes" so I could play the piano. (Laughter) You know? Because the instruments and skills are different.

CP: But then I wonder, Murray, if that isn't a sad commentary on the consumer, because if they shop at Armani or Lauren or Banana, are they so label-smitten that they believe "notes are notes?"

MM: No, it's not so terrible, because here's what I think is happening: just as fashion is an extremely developed art, and it's taught us through our daily participation in it, our appetite has become whet for that same kind of expression in other things we have even more intimate contact with – like our forks and spoons, our chairs and drinking glasses and beds and toothbrushes. So that's the good news. People are starting to say, "I know things. I understand how to look at things. I know things are made in particular ways, and facilitate different experiences," and that we can use functional products for many different reasons.

CP: And have relationships to them. I mean, how could there be a more intimate relationship than the one between a person and a spoon!

MM: Exactly.

CP: You've always had a sense of theater about the store, from the way objects are installed to the events, like your exhibition of porcelain figurines created by the ancient Bavarian porcelain manufactory, Nymphenburg.

MM: My job isn't to show you how to incorporate something into your daily life, or even to presume what your daily life is. How would I know that? My idea is in fact to "theatricalize" – if that's the word! – to "magnify," to "illuminate" an object, to present it to you in such a heightened way, that it can reveal everything that it wants to be, tries to be, is intended to be, and can be seen so that you can understand it fully, or at least understand that there is information given there, an idea, a point of view, whether about sociological or economical or political issues, as well as a practical solution to a particular need. The products I am interested in are usually "utopian" to a degree, in as much as they are an intelligent person's personal proposal for a more perfect world. If we acknowledge that product design, like fashion design, is one of the communicative arts, then there is the need for a director to create a scenario in which that communication flows freely and clearly. That's what I think a retail shop is. As far as how you use this product in your life, I can make a proposal, but then you're really on your own. After all, I do give some credit to my "audience."

CP: I know how rigorous you are in selecting and curating your collection – these objects must meet your own personal, very high, sometimes eccentric, standard. When you choose a product, what are you looking for?

MM: Objects are tangible evidence of ideas, so first I try to "read" them to find interesting ideas, interesting proposals, interesting, relevant questions being asked. My job, I believe, is to try to discover, and then to present the idea an object was created to communicate. In product design, that happens much less often than you would think, and so I'm quite happy to take what I can get. It's rare to find an object where the idea is well communicated, and is perfectly realized in its execution, and is made at such a price that most people can afford it. And why should that be a given? We don't presume that in fashion. We don't assume that the jacket will be perfectly well made, conveniently available to you at your neighborhood store, and really cheap.

CP: I hear Bill Clinton has become a Moss customer. Does he have good taste?

MM: He has good intentions.

CP: A lot of designers like to justify their existence by saying that good design costs the same as bad design. Do you agree with that adage?

MM: No. It can cost more, it can cost less. What an object costs is just part of the design, part of the process, part of the decisions made by the manufacturer and designer. It is a choice, not a given, and is a kind of "window" to the particular circumstances of the individual players involved. Something costs what it does because of a long list of reasons that consumers don't necessarily like to think about, but that includes a lot of logistics like how many you're going to make, how much investment was made, how much will it cost to tool, types of materials, and how much money a manufacturer needs to earn in order to be interested in producing the object. Price is probably the most socially relevant part of the design. It sets parameters, such as to whom this product will be made available, and, indirectly, contextualizes the product based on monetary value comparisons. In others words, this chair has been given the same value as this particular coat, this particular amount of food, this particular amount of health care. But it's just another part of the design.

CP: You have a crucifix hanging in the store. What are you saying with that?

MM: It's an object. It's a Nymphenburg porcelain figure of Christ on the cross. It was designed by Franz Antoine Bustelli in 1756. And it's still in production.

CP: Christ has a way of being continually in production. It's an evergreen, as they say. (Laughter)

MM: I hope so! I know as a retailer, religion is not something you are supposed to go near, which why it's interesting. But a religious object, any object that's part of a religious ritual, is still first and foremost an object. And it's something made out of a material, formed into something that we clearly have imbued with meaning. In the case of the crucifix, that same form has repeatedly been imbued for 2000 years with meaning, that we now find it impossible to look at and not be flooded with images. It's a good example of a very "enriched" object.

CP: So what is its meaning when it's in your store?

MM: My point is that that's one end of the scale. It's also possible to do that with a drinking glass. Not to confuse a drinking glass as a religious object, or to be sacrilegious in suggesting that, but to suggest that an object, a dead object, made by a person, can be infused with such richness that it causes us to expand. To enrich ourselves in the same way that religious objects do.

CP: Is there literally a drinking glass where you could say, given another 2000 years or so, is on its way to that level of significance?

MM: (Laughs) Well, look, people call it sentimental, or nostalgic, but how many people have glasses that they got from their parents, that they remember from childhood or from Thanksgiving, that have great meaning to them. All of that significance is brought to an object by our experience.

CP: Have you sold many crucifixes?

MM: Many? (Laughter) We've sold several.

CP: To go back to that other question about social relevance, how much does a Nymphenburg crucifix cost?

MM: The one you're speaking of costs roughly $4000.

CP: That buys you a lot of information!

MM: But also I like putting the crucifix in the same room with other objects that we're selling, like sofas. Because the crucifix also has its functional side as an object.

CP: Absolutely.

MM: You can choose to use the function or not. You can use the crucifix as a religious icon, or you could enjoy it, as a work of art, an extraordinary figural sculpture of the mid-eighteenth century. And at the risk of being extremely audacious, to a certain extent you could do the same thing with the sofa. You can buy the sofa because you need a place for three people to sit, or because you need something red to pick up the color in the wallpaper. Or you can buy that because you enjoy the work of Marco Zanuso.

The longevity an object has in your life – its usefulness to you – cannot be seen strictly in terms of how long will it last before it wears out, but in understanding that we change as people, and in seeing how the object will be able to accommodate our changes. If its usefulness to us, as a three-seater, becomes obsolete, because we no longer entertain at home, the fact that it's by Marco Zanuso may become more relevant to us at that moment, and therefore keep it current, because perhaps now we understand his work and newly appreciate it for that. I think we should expect that to happen. As we change, develop, grow as people, the relationship we have with our familiar objects will also change, develop, grow. And the "reasons" why we like them, why we continue to keep them, should be expected to change. Like they do with the people we love.

CP: There's something very mischievous, almost subversive about how you're mixing things up.

MM: But this changing of how we categorize things is what enables us to learn. Fashion garments used to be categorized generically by function. So you would have jackets in the jacket department, skirts, shoes and handbags, each in their own department. Then around 1970, things began to be grouped differently. So you would have the Giorgio Armani jackets and pants, and they wouldn't be in the pants and jacket departments, but they'd be in the Giorgio Armani department. And you'd say, well what does the jacket have to do with the pants? And the answer would be they're both by this person and the point of view supersedes the specific function of each of those things . . . because all of that helps you to understand this point of view, which is ultimately more important, or, I believe, at least more to the point.

CP: Crucifixes are traditionally in the crucifix department – or they used to be!

MM: Right, and sofas are in furniture stores, and glassware is in tabletop stores. When you put a glass in close proximity to a sofa, in close proximity to a crucifix, what we're doing is we're re-categorizing things in such a way that we're asking you to see an association between them that you perhaps didn't know existed. That is how we learn. And that is part of my job.

CP: So are you suggesting that it won't be long before we start to see Giorgio Armani designing crucifixes?

MM: (Laughs) Madonna!

__ __ **ARMANI/TEATRO**, MILAN, 2001.
DESIGN TADAO ANDO

Dear Mr. Ozu,

My name is Gladys Glover, and I am a great admirer of the things you do. I know it's ridiculous to write to you personally, but one of your mutant dresses does not quite fit me anymore. I have read that you personally created a living fabric, so perhaps only you can give me the advice I need.

Your affectionate,

Gladys Glover

___Dear Miss Glover,_

I am sorry to hear of your inconvenience, and am honored by your request. From a distance, however, I am unable to help you. It is therefore my pleasure to invite you as my guest for a weekend. My assistant, Miss Wu, will be getting in touch with you.

Yours,

Ozu

Miss Wu asked if she could come up. In a gray-black mutant jacket and lapis lazuli pants, she looked about thirty. Bright red nails and lips. She bowed. "Please excuse intrusion," she said, with a vaguely foreign accent. "Mr. Ozu likes to know exactly what sort of homes the admirers of his clothes live in, and would be grateful if he could look round your house . . . through me." "I'm afraid it's terribly untidy . . ." I began. But she was already in the living room saying something like, "People reveal themselves through little things." She bent down to stroke Fafnir, my big black cat. "Is it no problem for you to leave cat here? We can arrange . . ." "Oh no, a friend of mine, Leonie, comes in; she's our neighbor." Miss Wu poked around everywhere. She looked out the window and even asked to open the fridge. "Thank you," she said again, as if I had done her a great honor. "Pardon my curiosity," I asked her, "but how can Mr. Ozu actually see . . ." "By satellite," she replied but did not elaborate. Then she noticed my suitcase and said, "You don't need to bring anything. Mr. Ozu's hospitality is total." I must have looked amazed, for a half-smile flickered on her lips. "Never mind," she said, "bring it if you wish." The limousine dropped us opposite a kind of canyon carved into the hillside. The "Guest Path to the Baths," as the young lady had told me before saying goodbye, was a wooden pontoon bridge set between two black marble walls covered by a veil of rose-scented water. Eventually I came to a wall of green stones as thin as rock strata, where a revolving door swung open. Semi-darkness. Steam. Silence. Zigzag cracks of light in the ceiling. Corridors. A maze. Walls, floors and baths, all in green stone. Maybe I was in some kind of vast Jacuzzi, filled with fuming, gurgling and still waters. Was I supposed to take a bath? There was in fact a bathrobe in the changing room, plus a roll of white fabric and a pair of flat shoes. I undressed, got into the hot bath with flowers floating in it. Outside I could see another bath that looked very deep. I don't know how long I stayed in the water. When I got out my clothes and bag were gone. I unrolled the length of fabric, which . . . became a plain tunic. Miss Wu was expecting me. She too was wearing the same tunic. "Mr. Ozu," she said, "wishes all his guests to be able to release energy from their bodies." "Energy? Is there no heating?" She smiled. "*Sensorial energy*. Every room has its own conditioning system: it may be cold, warm, humid, exciting . . ." "Exciting?" "With more oxygen. It is our bodies that decide. This way please." A revolving door opened into a tunnel of pale cloth. The inside of an earthworm. Splashes of color walked along with us. I stopped, and so did the colors. "It is a fabric sensitive to our waves," said she, lifting one arm as a red flame darted across the curved wall. "What waves?" I asked. "The magnetic waves of our bodies," came her nonchalant reply. We had arrived at a roundabout beneath a cupola, with more tunnels left and right. She indicated one of these. "Mr. Ozu will meet you down there," she said as she vanished again.

I came to a ramp similar to that of a garage, winding its way around . . . I looked over the parapet . . . an enormous hollow tower. I glanced up. The bottom of a bath sent out pale blue waves onto the glazed walls of the tower. I looked down. Along the full walls were fans, portholes, screens turned on, reflectors, Virginia creeper. I felt a draught of warm air. Two or three floors below a . . . giant piston was rising and slowly filling the void. On that elevator as large as a building was a . . . roofless doll's house, with its chairs, a writing desk, a lamp, tables, carpets, and two white cupolas. And a person wearing a tunic identical to mine was watching me. The *thing* stopped silently in front of me. The parapet slid away and there the famous fashion designer Ozu, exactly like the photographs, was holding out his hand to me! There was no step, but I jumped nevertheless . . . and it was like falling into empty space: the floor was transparent. "Welcome on board," said Mr. Ozu. "Excuse my small hands, the baths, the tunic . . . they are part of a kind of . . . purification to put us all on the same level." "No . . . don't worry, that's fine by me . . ." I said without thinking. "I am glad you feel at ease, even if you have not been able to look at yourself in the mirror." In fact there was no mirror in the changing room. We sat down on two little revolving stools. At that moment a butterfly settled in my lap. I held my breath. "Is . . . is it really real?" I asked. "Of course, it is not a steel butterfly, if that is what you are thinking," said Mr. Ozu. "Some of them escape from the tropical greenhouse . . . they are flying flowers. . . . But please make yourself at home, and now let us do a guided tour."

"Down," he whispered.

And we began our descent. The butterfly hovered and then flew upwards. Who was flying? "You have already seen the outdoor swimming pool up there," began Mr. Ozu, turning the chair as if he were Captain Kirk on the bridge of the *Enterprise*. "At this moment you can see a few modern works around us." I didn't quite know where to look: those strange neon sculptures? Mr. Ozu noticed. "I always travel with my art collection, and a fine library. This . . . raft reminds me that immortality resides in everlasting change . . . but to get around, we need empty space, and only in emptiness can be found what is really essential." "Does one become immortal by traveling in an elevator?" I asked in amazement. "No, no, in Taoism it is . . . the quest for harmony in everything around us." Hmm. In effect, a whole lot of things were revolving around us - the spiral ramp, the glazed walls, continuous bookshelves, giant pictures, hanging fabrics, maps, monitors . . . "Try seeing it only for what it is," he told me, looking hard into my eyes. "The . . . service elevator of a spacecraft?" I answered. "If the architect Schindler heard that . . . well, a service elevator that now takes us in front of a window onto the world," resumed Mr. Ozu. We were moving inside a continuous panel that surrounded the interior of the tower like a ring. A cobweb of swirling lights, lightning flashes and colored waves.

"Slow," said Mr. Ozu.

Our descent grew slower. "On this virtual horizon every small flash represents in real time the sale of one of my products somewhere in the world," Mr. Ozu told me with a hint of pride. "Uncle Scrooge would like that," I said absent-mindedly, and bit my lip. "I'm sorry, I didn't mean to . . ." "Admirable sincerity. Business is business. But I am not miserly. I try to . . . *feel*. Those colored vibrations are climate and temperature plotted by satellite. The fixed lights are our street billboards, the flashing ones are the exhibitions put on by the Ozu-Art Foundation, and the streaks are contacts with Internet sites. Even if the market analysts don't get much out of it for us, I still like it. It is a work by the web-artist Otis, who interprets computer data. Applied art." The panel slid away vertically. Now we were descending faster. "Here we are at sea level, Captain Nemo's cave." We stopped. The ramp ended. Through the big windows we could see the coast, the sun setting, and a harbor with a sailboat in it. I looked up. I thought I could still see the butterfly. Dizziness in reverse. How long had passed? Mr. Ozu got up and gazed in silence at the sea. "It's beautiful here. I like the sea from close-up," said I. He nodded and said, "Once there was a lighthouse on this promontory that had been scheduled for demolition. We managed somehow to replace it." At that moment we started up again. "This time you didn't give it an order," I said. "Every now and again it does everything by itself. It evidently thought I wanted to go up." "It who?" "The computer, maybe," replied Mr. Ozu rather vaguely. "As you see, I am surrounded by all I need, and I can pitch camp wherever I like." And he started walking along his . . . raft. I followed him through a confusion of cushions, settees, magazines lying on the floor, screens, tables covered with cloths, computers, and a small radio switched on. Then a cupola and an awning of white cloth. It felt strange to be walking and ascending at the same time. "And isn't this . . . where the bathroom is?" I felt like asking. Mr. Ozu burst out laughing. "This toy costs millions of dollars but there is no bathroom! The bathrooms are not exactly here, it is true, but you only have to stop at one of the floors to reach them immediately." I felt acutely embarrassed. Never mind, we had already sunk far enough, hadn't we?

"Wait," said Mr. Ozu.

We stopped. "You see, there are corridors to the other parts of the house, and one can always use the ramp." The butterfly reappeared. Was it we who had returned or had it been waiting for us in mid-air? "It's fantastic, Mr. Ozu. Is this where you create all your beautiful things? But I don't see any clothes . . ." "Let us say that this space helps me to work and to rest. It took me many years to build, and it is not finished. It never will be. Famous architects have worked on it: Zurg & Debussy, Warmhaas, Thorm, O'Gear, Newell. And the artist Bauer changes it all the time. It is an eternal present. But my guests also change it . . ." and he bowed slightly toward me. "Do you mean that someone like you would take advice . . . from me?" "You'll see, my dear young lady, you'll see. This environment is capable of . . . feeling many things. It feels energy, force, and perhaps even dreams." Certainly this was strange, really strange. "Follow me. There may be no bathroom but there is a gas stove in the tea-house." We knelt down beneath an arch in the fabric of the cupola. "Humility," he said. A chrysalis of hazy light. "A wretched interpretation of what in Japan they call the Abode of Emptiness." Well, in effect there was almost nothing there, except a vase with a single flower in it. Mr. Ozu poured tea from a bulging kettle into a spiky teapot. My cup was light, his heavy. "Different forms avoid pointless repetitions . . ." he explained. " . . . Everything here is balanced, but it is a precarious balance." When we had come out of the cupola again I realized that we had moved still further up. Perhaps this was what he meant by precarious balance. At that moment there appeared on the ramp one of his assistants, dressed in the usual tunic, bringing him some sheets of paper. Mr. Ozu placed them on a wooden desk and switched on a green lamp. "So this must be your office then, not your living room," I ventured. "This room is a living, vital, open space, a bit of everything," he replied. "I see it as a workshop." "Excuse my asking . . . but do you sleep here too?" "No," he answered, lowering his voice, "my bedroom is somewhere else, and believe me, it is not much larger than a closet. I prefer to sleep there. You know, here I can't close the door . . ."

The young lady showed me to "my apartment" before dinner. From the tower we took another tunnel. Halfway down it was a children's rocking horse. Was it a work of art? I stopped for a moment to run my hand along the wood. The young lady left me in front of a door that looked just like the door of my own house, with a peephole and two locks. I went in. It *was* my house! The narrow entrance, the kitchen on the left with the black and white tiles, the living room with the carpeting. Except that it was . . . empty. Like before a move, or as if burglars had taken away nearly everything, except for an armchair and the bed. On the bed was a roll of black fabric: the evening tunic, naturally. My suitcase and the handbag were on the floor. Nice surprise I must say! The famous fashion designer invites me to his fantastic mansion and . . . here I am back home again! The walls were extremely thin, like rice paper. In the bathroom, no mirror. That's annoying; in my house there is a mirror. And from the windows . . . exactly the same view as the one from my own. Then I opened one and everything vanished. The wind hit me violently. The air conditioning went off.

Dinner was on the platform, under the awning. In the tower swathed in darkness the lights from the bay shone through the windows like stars in a galaxy. Mr. Ozu introduced me to the other guests: the video-architect couple, Dillinger & Scoglio, the painter Navarro, and the movie director Tatischeff. Set on a long thermal bench were Mr. Ozu's plate-trays, filled with food in weird shapes. Mr. Ozu invited us to choose, but without telling us what they were. During the meal he kept asking us what we thought of the various dishes: as far as I was concerned it was all very good, including the wine. But what were we eating? "Ozu-Food prototypes," revealed Mr. Ozu in the end, as he showed us a completely transparent pantry and refrigerator, with various packs of food in them similar to those of our supper. "If good things to eat are also nice to look at . . . why hide them?"

Feeling rather light-headed, I went back, alone, to "my apartment." I realized at once that something had changed. There were two armchairs now, a stool in the kitchen, and a coffee table. By this time nothing surprised me anymore. Not even the rocking horse that I found in the sitting room: the one I had seen in the tunnel. I could hear the hum of the air conditioning, was that "exciting?" I threw myself onto the bed. A new bedside lamp. And a book on the floor. The same Wilbur Smith that I read every evening. It was new.

In the morning something was tickling my nose. "Fafnir, stop it!" I grumbled. But I wasn't at home. I sat up. Was I dreaming of an electric cat? A large black cat at the bottom of the bed was staring at me with green eyes. It started mewing. I was well awake. It was not Fafnir, but it was real. I got up, and the cat went off toward the kitchen. A bowl and a can of food that weren't there last night. I gave the cat some food. In the bathroom, as in my own, was its litter. But still no mirror.

When I came out of "my apartment" later, instead of the tunnel there was a winding, very high corridor. Was this the artist Bauer's doing? In the end I came out into the tower. The platform had come to halt in front of me. As soon as I stepped onto it, it began to descend gently. When it reached the ground I headed for the beach exit. A door opened by itself and I bumped into Mr. Ozu who was jogging, dressed in a t-shirt and shorts. "Good morning, slept well?" "Oh yes, very well . . ." I wanted to ask him about the cat and all the rest, but I gave up. I asked him about his sporting apparel instead. "Is there no jogging tunic?" "You are making fun of me, my dear young lady," he said with a smile, "however your tunic keeps out the cold wind, if I'm not mistaken." This was true. His funny fabrics: were they not the reason for my invitation? "Have you had breakfast? Would you like anything particular?" asked Mr. Ozu. I had already had breakfast . . . in the kitchen of "my apartment." "Oh yes," I asked, "can you change the color of the sea? It's too gray in the morning!" "I'll do my best," he said with a very serious air. "Let me just change and I'll be with you at once." After a few minutes we walked up the ramp. I told him that the platform had moved as soon as I had stepped onto it. "It interpreted one of your wishes," explained Mr. Ozu. "Yesterday you said you liked to be by the seashore." Yes, but how . . ." "Oh, it's just a trick. Your tunic has a sensor in it." "I hadn't noticed," and instinctively I touched the material. Is it in the fabric?" "It *is* the fabric," he said imperiously. "Your famous fabric? And how does it work?" We had stopped in front of one of the windows. I didn't understand. The color of the glass began to change, to green, then pale blue . . . "Is that all right for you, the color of the sea?" he asked, very seriously. "Yes," I stammered. Then Mr. Ozu spread his arms. The whole window turned the same color right up to the top. "Your every wish is my command," he said, bowing. No messing around, with a man like this.

"Pity we can't see the artist Hollock's installation," continued Mr. Ozu. "He has put colored filters in the gutters, so the water paints the windows. A work of weather-art, it is called *Over the Rainbow-Window*." "And when can it be seen?" I asked foolishly. "Only when it rains, of course." "And was this the thing that inspired your striped models?" I continued, hoping the question might sound intelligent. Mr. Ozu looked at me in amusement. "Only the raincoats, naturally." The platform had followed us in silence. At the center of it was an empty space. "The rehearsal room," said Mr. Ozu as he led the way. "If you agree, I would like to cut out a dress for you . . . to measure. After all, every person is different." On the table were rolls and packets of fabric. "You choose them, or have them choose for you." When I touched them they changed color. "Live fabric, this is your secret, isn't it?" I asked excitedly. Mr. Ozu remained unruffled. "Some bio-fabrics don't have to be dyed: the cotton is born colored. The plantations are ours, and the graftings are done by scientists at Ozu Genetic Materials. The clothes cost very little, they fit everybody and all climates, and they are bio-degradable." "So it's true then what people say about . . ." "I'll tell you another thing," interrupted Mr. Ozu as he took a box out of the desk drawer, "this is a medicine for a rare disease, developed in the laboratories of the Ozu-Gen Non-Profit Foundation." He pulled out some phials containing an iridescent liquid. "After arguing with everyone I wanted to design the package, and to put these special effects into it, which obviously don't improve the efficacy of the drug. I have been accused of clinical vainglory, just think. From the point of view of the image it was only a risk. Some while ago a person being treated with this medicine wrote me, "If I really must die, let me die in style." "And then . . . did he die?" I asked, very struck. " . . . He went into a coma." "Oh, poor guy!" "But then he came out again, and now he is better; from apparent death to total life." "What a relief!" I sighed. In the meantime one of the fabrics that I had been holding had turned an odd mauve color. "You can try it on behind the screen," said Mr. Ozu. I put it on. There was, of course, no mirror. "How does it suit me?" "I don't know," answered the famous fashion designer. "That's for you to say. And don't ask me for a mirror. You will have understood that I am tyrant in here. No mirrors in the home of . . . a person who makes clothes. I find it annoying to look at a person and their portrait at the same time: which of the two is a fake?" When I opened the door of my house, or of my apartment I should say, the cat came up to me purring loudly. I tipped a few kibbles into its bowl. People reveal themselves in little things. Everything was as I had left it. Nothing had been moved. The usual view from the windows. The carpet was still the same, as were the kitchen tiles. The two armchairs and the coffee table were still there. The bed was still in the bedroom, where I put down the roll of living fabric. The bedside lamp and the book that I had left on the floor before going away were there. The cat followed me into every room. Its litter was in the bathroom, clean. But now there was a mirror on the wall. I didn't look at it. What had Mr. Ozu said? "Is what we imagine real?" No. "Does everything that is solid dissolve in the air?" I no longer knew. No air conditioning. I felt dead tired and sank onto the bed. Fafnir, my big black, yellow-eyed cat, curled up at my feet. At last I could dream.

With thanks to Kurt Vonnegut, Philip K. Dick, Andrei Tarkovski for the special effects, to Stanley Elkin, James G. Ballard and Stanislaw Lem for the condominium regulations, to Buster Keaton, Jacques Tati, Yasujiro Ozu for the interiors, and to Roald Dahl for the elevator.
Special thanks to Judy Holliday.

__ __ DETAIL FROM THE **VALENTINO ADVERTISING CAMPAIGN**, FALL/WINTER 2000-2001. PHOTO STEVEN MEISEL

I think I'd like to have a portable tape recorder to fill with my thoughts. To do what I've often seen people do in movies. Example. A woman alone in a car. Every so often she nervously grabs that small object, nearly always tossed on the seat beside her, brings it to her lips and whispers what is going through her mind. Thoughts, ideas, reflections, desires. In this talking that almost immediately becomes a dialogue one is inevitably guided by an internal rhythm. Then. To speak what comes to mind, charged by the euphoria of the drive, the music playing at top volume, solitude displayed like a flag of independence. And then to be inebriated by the rapid sequence of the different landscapes, like a continuous ribbon before the final cut, seen through the windows. Again, to watch yourself act. To see your lips moving and hear the grain of your voice. A different, porous voice that manages to absorb all the colors and emotions revolving around you. It's easy to be daring when you're protected by the metal shell of a car, with the doors safely locked. To finally feel like a man on the hunt. But not to act. There's no action in this film.

Again. "At the beginning of the dream I'm here inside," I'd like to say, imitating one of those recurring characters in the films of David Lynch who suddenly appear and short-circuit the narrative. I am here. To be precise, I am inside the aura projected by this marvelous image. Beauty isn't a single-purpose compact harmony, but the result of a tension constantly in the making, a conflict: a combined composite, you might say. A continuous present that questions more than it answers.

I am here. Standing on the border zone where the fantastic, the gothic, the imaginary and everyday comedy continuously interact, upsetting the static concept of genre.

Images and imagination run fast, run forward. What happened yesterday is used simply as entertainment, a postcard, a record of a search, the background for a new story. Another film. Another enchanting scene custom-made to suck me into one of the many possible worlds proposed by advertising.

Advertising, which more directly than cinema, more explicitly than TV, reflects the relationship between the spirit of the times (still incarnate within it: the civilization of consumption, the dynamic and dialectic between standardization and differentiation) and the portrayed matter of the world. But advertising also narrates our interaction with others and the outside world, projecting the results of the world's own splendor or dullness into the communicative values of products.

I'm standing by the window, the telephone glued to my ear, watching the lights of the city and the nearby houses. I stay there by the window for quite a while. I stand there to watch the glowing houses of my neighbors. As I am watching, a car enters the driveway of one of the houses. The porch light goes on. The door opens and someone stands waiting. I am distracted by the lyrics of an old song echoing in the silence. When I look back there are two figures on the porch. They hug and go into the house.

True. Plausible. False. Report. Recollection. Fantasy. Desire. I construct a story and I am the leading player. I am here, in my ordinary little apartment on the third floor of a serial building on the outskirts of the city leafing through one of those nice glossy magazines. This one is gorgeous, it might be the nicest one I've ever seen. I bought it because I needed to dream a bit, to go far away from here. To send myself elsewhere. To construct a film for myself. Every page offers an escape route from that disturbing desert of reality that awaited the protagonists of *Matrix* at the end of the continuous exchange of dimensions.

The pages of the fashion magazines, with the endless initial sequence of ad campaigns for the main fashion brands, supply a repertoire of images and stories for every season, for everyone. These printed advertisements are no longer the communication medium utilized by fashion designers to show the pieces in the latest collection and to promote sales. They have become the setting in which each designer stages a special world, the theme universe that is taking form in his or her work. A precise, complete, clean project where everything is based on and associated with a total, all-pervasive aesthetic. Definitively clarifying the connections that have always existed between merchandise and communication.

The lightning bolt of that incredible view from the Hollywood hills that stretches, without a moment of visual relief, to embrace the city of quartz, Los Angeles, has produced that icon-house (Case Study House # 22) of contemporary style that has become not only a set, a backdrop, but also a co-star for many of the most beautiful fashion images.

This work of architecture by Pierre Koenig is the perfect paradigm of the houses with pools that host the designer-labeled parties described by Bret Easton Ellis, the postmodern directors, the thousands of fragile girls willing to go to any lengths to become stars, the stars who love to surround themselves with fragile girls, the rich movie producers obsessed with sex . . . in short, the entire cast of special guests captured so perfectly in the latest film by David Lynch, *Mulholland Drive*.

A group of young people, male and female, on yet another sunny day in California. They loiter apathetically, indifferent to this special house. They are cute, rich, elegant. They are somber, self-absorbed, apparently without a care in the world other than the problem of displaying their "being there" then, in that moment, that precise instant. Steven Meisel, the American photographer-guru who created this ad campaign for Valentino, perfectly fulfills the task assigned, narrating with a wealth of means and formal perfection that "Planet Valentino" that is to enter the audience's image-bank, derailing them from the banality of the workaday world. Not only for those who can afford to buy the fantastic outfits, but also for the widest range of members of the social categories that inhabit the realm of global fashion entertainment, though perhaps all they buy is a designer belt.

Then. No longer just a figure placed against a backdrop. An elegant silhouette enhanced by the decoration of the surfaces. Instead, an icon captured in its natural habitat. Here's another special house – this time not stretching over the landscape, but looking inward – with opulent furnishings, famous paintings on the walls, statues worthy of a museum scattered around the rooms. Meisel, it's him again, this time showing us the poised and posed, almost classical figure of Amber Valletta, ravishing in her Versace. Perfectly at ease in that spectacular suite of bourgeois parlors we see spread out behind her.

It is necessary to construct another dimension in which to shift desires, to orient needs. What's being sold is no longer just clothing, it's everything that goes into the composition of life's variegated stage. To be effective the total project has to tell a fairytale: to evoke a special version of existence, carefully selecting a place, finding the right people to inhabit it. In short, the project has to put together the pieces of that puzzle which, in the end, will conjure up the image of *A Wonderful Time*. At this point the top model is, almost, no longer the protagonist, because she is too self-referential, with too many connotations. At best she can appear as a solo presence. But the script calls for dialogues and conversations. Multiple characters and multiple subplots. The cast is assigned the task of existing in that perfect world constructed especially for them. They shape the atmosphere of their surroundings and therefore interact in the development of the advertising sequence. The choice of the players, the casting, is done by looking for men and women with intense, glowing faces but without names, who can easily become a presence with which to identify. Long background shots, tight foreground, two-page spreads to permit a horizontal, film-like frame; these are the elements that declare the intent to assemble a brief cinematic sequence, a short, with the different images.

There's a house, a gaudy villa, positioned to overlook the entire city. Again, it's the spectacular Case Study House # 22. We see the city by night, with the lines of lights running like meridians and parallels across a black carpet toward the ocean. From up here the city is transformed into a prism of visions, filling up with emblematic figures.

In the darkness of the house, a modern house with glass walls so nothing will escape the comprehension of the gaze, a woman moves about, alone. Beautiful, slender, sexy, elegant, rich. She restlessly paces in the deserted but perfectly furnished house. Her white dress glows in the room, which is dimly lit to enhance the effect of the complex glow of the lights out there in the distance. She lives to be watched, desired, envied, imitated. We don't care if she is happy or not. In fact, that dusky melancholy that pervades the scene gives her a sort of heartrending emotional resonance. We want to be like her. And if we can't live in that dream, at least we want to have that fantastic Gucci dress, and slide it slowly over our perfectly toned, supple, soft body, scented with that oh-so-new oh-so-designer fragrance that will drive everyone mad with desire when it touches our skin.

Fashion photography borrows the structure of filmmaking (location, casting, script), dismantles its mechanisms and constructs images, narrative sequences that fully engage the viewer. This involvement in the story, as happens in films, soap operas, sitcoms, gives the spectator the sensation of entering a separate, parallel world where other lives are acted out. A catalogue of lifestyles from which each of us can draw to create his or her own character. To have the illusion of being different. Special. Thus the advertising image attempts to take the place of real imagery, forgetting that a difference always remains, which can be gauged by the ability to evoke spheres of life that take place outside the ad itself. An ad that, having abandoned the simplicity of pure presentation, increasingly becomes chronicle, story, creating a narrative plot. Or again, it presents itself as an antagonist. It slyly sheds its commercial character to become something else. Messages of pacifism, ecological pieties, ethical urgings. It reaches the point of denying itself, but always to achieve visibility on the market.

2001 International Year of Volunteers is the latest Benetton advertising campaign, which, after the shocking images (the dead soldier's bloody uniform, the patient dying of AIDS, the copulating horses) devised by Oliviero Toscani to astonish people and sell more sweaters, shifts the communicative focus, under the direction of the photographer James Mollinson, to the faces and bodies of the volunteers who, all over the world, make a commitment, based on the verbs to prevent, to help, to combat. The strong images, lifted from the reality of life, do not narrate perfect worlds of happy people, but poverty, squalor, addiction, war, despair. They force each of us to examine his or her conscience, under the aegis of the United Colors of Benetton. Perhaps the time has come to run a risk, to step forward and also propose a different concept of life. The nodes between communication and reality, nature and quality of media technologies and effects of social, cultural and political change, must emerge in a necessary plot: the same one involved in the meaning of images consumed while watching television.

In this unstoppable flow that mixes every type of image and message, Philip-Lorca diCorcia creates the sequence of the images for *A Perfect World*. His artist's gaze captures the pathos in the everyday actions of life, isolating the fragments of routine in the peaceful, uncanny houses of the American sprawl, cutting out the days shut up in the big offices of the skyscrapers of New York, arresting the river of pedestrians in the crowded streets of the metropolis. Or, as in the *Mani per Giorgio Armani* campaign, he photographs the suspended atmosphere of places of waiting and transit, turning it into an absolute metaphor.

He is interested in capturing the mystery that envelops every individual. He wants to capture the soul that echoes in the gazes of the citizens of the twenty-first century. In his narrative every fragment of banal existence is transfigured, assuming the contours of a revelation. His characters seem to live in a state of grace. Silhouettes, cutouts detached from their own reality. The chaos around us becomes a fresco. It takes on the features of the life of every one of us. Without rhetoric, without rancor or restlessness in the face of an ordinary existence.

* __ *Good Times on Our Street* is the book all American students once had to read. The novel narrates the joys of everyday life and good neighbors.

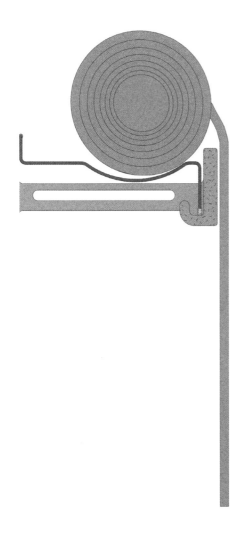

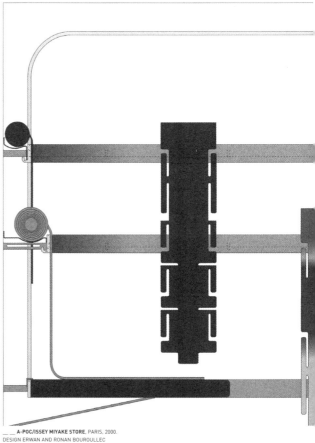

__ __ **A-POC/ISSEY MIYAKE STORE**, PARIS, 2000.
DESIGN ERWAN AND RONAN BOUROULLEC

Architecture has been both fascinated by, and dismissive of, fashion for at least three generations. It has, until very recently, been a very one-sided, unrequited fascination. Le Corbusier, whose wife Yvonne was actually once a model, put the sense of barely concealed antagonism between them into words when he suggested that style in architecture was of no more significance than the feathers on a woman's hat, pretty enough, but of no real importance. Adolf Loos on the other hand, while he is so often caricatured as a stern moralist with a distaste for applied decoration who believed that ornament is crime, found the issue of clothes to be of a biding interest. He wrote a sophisticated series of essays in which he claimed to find in the restraint of English tailoring, the perfect expression of modernity. He actually designed a couple of gentlemen's outfitters himself, perhaps the earliest example of what has become an increasingly close, if occasionally tortured relationship between fashion and architecture that leads from late nineteenth-century Vienna to a stretch of Madison Avenue a century later where each major designer has an associated architect to create the look of their stores, from John Pawson and Calvin Klein, to David Chipperfield and Dolce & Gabbana. Japan was onto the idea earlier, with Shiro Kuramata's remarkable stores for Issey Miyake, and the extraordinary interiors of Comme des Garçons stores.

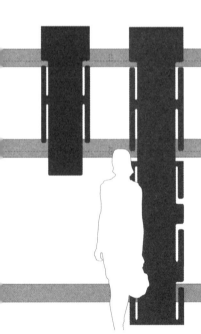

Architects like to see themselves as being somehow beyond fashion. They regard their work as being concerned with permanence and seriousness. But they have looked on jealously at fashion's strengthening grip on the popular imagination. Meanwhile fashion has secretly craved some of the cultural credibility that comes from the heavyweight baggage that architecture brings, even while it has struggled to find any kind of critical language with which to examine its own achievements. Partly the mismatch is to do with the different timescales. Three months is an eternity in the frenetic fashion year, while architecture is lucky not to look hopelessly out of date by the time it has negotiated the treacle-like speed of the construction process. And even when they are finished, most buildings – after a decade or so when they may, or may not, look more or less contemporary – must endure another quarter century in which they are regarded as hopelessly outmoded. Then, if they are lucky, the best of them may be understood for their intrinsic qualities rather than through the filter of any particular stylistic language.

Fashion has an entirely different pace. Yet fashion is about a whole range of issues that are anything but trivial. Fashion is about money; it's a huge industrial system, as well as a close reflection of power, status and sex. And architecture has come to matter a great deal to fashion. It can be used to create a setting for designers that distils the essence of what they are trying to say about their clothes. You could see it as a particularly elaborate form of packaging. Just as you find that high fashion shops wrap purchases in tissue paper, then put them in a box, and put that box in a cloth bag, then put the whole lot in a glossy carrier bag with rope handles, so the architectural wrapping of a store becomes equally elaborate through the adoption of heavyweight architectural firepower.

But architecture raises the stakes. It's a powerful tool for differentiating one brand from another. If you want to understand why Miuccia Prada hired Rem Koolhaas, Jacques Herzog and Pierre de

Meuron and Kazuyo Sejima to put their credibility at risk to work on what she has called "the reinvention of shopping," it's enough to flip through a recent issue of *Vogue*, all 794 pages of it, not to mention a 328-page supplement.

It's crammed with advertising whose sole purpose is to differentiate one fashion brand from another in the fraction of a second it takes to turn the page. There's no time for words, or even to show the clothes, just for a relentless and endless series of head-spinning images that can, however briefly, grab a jaded audience by the jugular. Inevitably the process is subject to the law of diminishing returns.

Pictures that would once have been arresting lose their power to engage very quickly. And fashion, despite turning into an industrial juggernaut, dominated by three or four multinationals, is basically parasitic. It depends on art, film, photography and architecture for its visual imagery, but it uses them so relentlessly that their themes are quickly stripped clean of meaning. One Helmut Newton or Robert Mapplethorpe in a fashion magazine, and you pay attention. A whole magazine full, and you start to glaze over. As a result sex in fashion is endless and even more explicit now. Almost every Italian label has explored loving recreations of seventies pornography or models carefully styled to look like hookers from the forties. Prada has stayed away from sex so far and is big on art – all those Andreas Gursky photographs – and is now going all out for architecture as its signature with a series of enormously expensive stores planned for New York, Los Angeles, San Francisco and Tokyo, only one of which has opened so far. The company has little choice if it is going to stand out from the crowd.

Such commissions would once have seemed as, at best, distractions for an architect who is the recipient of the Pritzker Prize, and in line to build museums and law courts. Some critics still see it as running the risk of compromising a reputation for seriousness. But it's not hard to see why Koolhaas got involved. He has spent his career as an architect scratching away at the uncomfortable scar tissue at the point where academic speculation meets popular culture. Fashion, art and architecture are converging with alarming speed and Koolhaas is no longer content with observing from the sidelines. He is trying to force the pace. Prada's new store in the downtown Guggenheim building in SoHo, New York has what Koolhaas calls a "Siamese twin relationship with the museum."

Koolhaas says he wants to see the New York Prada store blending seamlessly with the Guggenheim to offer after-hours culture. But a more jaundiced interpretation would be to see the Guggenheim getting even more commercially contaminated. It has, after all, already been heavily criticized for accepting a substantial donation from Giorgio Armani, and then putting on a show of his work seen by many as flawed in the cupola of its original Frank Lloyd Wright-designed building. But this was more than an architect designing a space in which to sell clothes. Koolhaas was being asked to talk about the nature of fashion, and Prada was prepared to listen to what he had to say. "Prada is a brand," says Koolhaas, "that has aura without obligation." It is also about luxury, and he goes on to define luxury in ever more gnomic ways: "Luxury," he says, "is stability"; "Luxury is waste"; "Luxury is intelligent, Luxury is rough, Luxury is attention." But then he gets it absolutely right: "Luxury," he says, "is not shopping."

The real question is not so much "Is fashion art?" but "What has fashion done to art, architecture and design?" Fashion has always been a parasitic form. In the days when Russian constructivists inspired the smocks worn on the collective farms, and Sonia Delaunay borrowed the colors of Fauvism for her textiles, fashion remained a minor footnote to high art. But fashion is something else now. It has entered the same phase of industrial consolidation that the car industry went through when Ford and Chrysler started to divide the world between them, sharing out all the lesser brands. But there is nothing minor about fashion now, which mainlines on sex status and celebrity. And that is a combination that has turned fashion from a craft into a major industry. In the process conferring a huge amount of clout both financial and cultural on those who control it. Put all that together and fashion becomes just too big and too powerful to be written off as a frivolous sideshow. Fashion has the ability to press all the buttons of contemporary life. And it is this convergence between high culture and popular art that gives fashion its power. It can address serious issues, and it has also got its eye on the mainstream, if not the main chance.

What else can engage the undivided attention of bankers and manufacturers and artists? Fashion for better or worse has become the dominant industry and the dominant cultural source. Fashion might not be art, but it is taking the place of art. Like an opera house in the nineteenth century, a contemporary fashion show has become the place for the smartest public life to take place. But unlike an opera, a fashion show lasts a mere twenty-one minutes rather than three hours: perfect for the diminished attention span of the MTV generation.

As if to underscore the point, Giorgio Armani has opened what he calls a theater in an old chocolate factory in Milan. His architect, Tadao Ando, has done nothing less than create the fashion world's equivalent of an opera house. It's the place for celebrities to disgorge from their limousines, to promenade along what feels like a triumphal route to their reserved seats.

The passage from the messy industrial suburbs outside to the world of Armani inside is marked by a stately march of austere concrete columns. This indoor avenue suddenly opens up into a great reception space in which giant doors open into the theater; and next to it is an austere, magnificently proportioned dining room, its low windows carefully positioned to frame the reflecting pool in the courtyard outside. Whatever the clothes are actually like, nobody can fail to come away convinced that they have taken part in an event. Ando's architecture has been turned into a magnificently crafted concrete picture frame.

The still unresolved question is about where the balance of power lies. Does architecture now need fashion more than fashion needs architecture? Are the architects who have been strip-mined of ideas by the fashion world about to be discarded when they run dry? The answer probably has at least something to do with the profitability of the new generation of architect designer stores.

Aaker, D. A. *Managing Brand Equity*. New York: The Free Press, 1991.

Aaker, D. A. *Building Strong Brands*. New York: The Free Press, 1995.

Aaker, D. A., and E. Joachmsthaler. *Brand Leadership*. New York: The Free Press, 2000.

Aarons, S. *A Wonderful Time: An Intimate Portrait of the Good Life*. New York: Harper & Row, 1974.

Ábalos, I. *The Good Life: A Guided Visit to the Houses of Modernity*. Barcelona: Gustavo Gili, 2001.

Abruzzese, A., and N. Barile. *Communifashion: Sulla moda, della comunicazione*. Rome: Sossella, 2001.

Agrest, D., P. Conway, and L. Kanes Weisman, ed. *The Sex of Architecture*. New York: Abrams, 1996.

Albrecht, D. et al. *The Work of Charles and Ray Eames: A Legacy of Invention*. New York: Abrams, 1997.

Albrecht, D., R. Schonfeld, and L. Stamm Shapiro. *Russel Wright: Creating American Lifestyle*. New York: Abrams, 2001.

Amendola, G. *La città postmoderna: Magia e paure della metropoli contemporanea*. Rome and Bari: Laterza, 1997.

Appadurai, A. *The Social Life of Things: Commodities in Cultural Perspectives*. Cambridge: Cambridge University Press, 1986.

Appadurai, A. *Modernity at Large: Cultural Dimensions of Globalization*. Minneapolis: University of Minnesota Press, 1996.

Ariès, P. *Les fils de McDo (La McDonaldisation du Monde)*. Paris: L'Harmattan, 1997.

Atelier van Lieshout: A Manual. Ex. cat. Cologneischer Kunstverein, Cologne; Museum Boijmans Van Beuningen, Rotterdam. Ostfildern: Cantz, 1997.

Augé, M. *L'impossible voyage: Le Tourisme et ses images*. Paris: Rivages Poche, 1997.

Ballard, J. G. *High-Rise*. London: Cape, 1975.

Banham, R. *Los Angeles: The Architecture of Four Ecologies*. Harmondsworth: Penguin, 1971.

Barber, B. *Jihad vs. McWorld: How Globalism and Tribalism Are Reshaping the World*. New York: Times, 1995.

Barthes, R. *Système de la Mode*. Paris: Seuil, 1967.

Barthes, R. *Mithologies*. Paris: Seuil, 1957.

Basilico, S. "Interview with Andrea Zittel." *Bomb Magazine* (March 2001).

Batchelor, D. "Less is More. John Pawson's Minimum." *Frieze* 31 (October 1996).

Baudrillard, J. "Design e Dasein." *Agalma* 1 (June 2000).

Baudrillard, J. *Simulacres et Simulations*. Paris: Galilée, 1981.

Bauman, O. "The Creation of a Public Sphere." *Archis* 5 (2001).

Bauman, Z. *Globalization: The Human Consequences*. New York: Columbia University Press, 1998.

Bauman, Z. *La società dell'incertezza*. Bologna: Il Mulino, 1999.

Beaumont, T. de. "Ora-ïto." *Interni* (April 2001).

Beck, U. *Risk Society*. London: Sage, 1992.

Beecroft, V. *VB 08 - 36: Vanessa Beecroft Performances*. Ostfildern-Ruit: Hatje Cantz, 2000.

Beirendonck, W. van, ed. *Mode 2001: Landed-Geland Part I*. Antwerp: n.p., 2002.

Beirendonck, W. van, ed. *Mode 2001: Landed-Geland Part II*. Antwerp: n.p., 2002.

Belcove, J. L. "Ruff Cut." *W* (July 2001).

Bertolino, G., and E. De Cecco. *Ottonella Mocellin: A Darkness Beyond the Reach of Vision*. Ex. cat. Turin: Galleria Luigi Franco Arte Contemporanea, 1999.

Bertolino, G. *Nicola Pellegrini: Sight- Specific*. Ex. Cat. Turin: Galleria Luigi Franco Arte Contemporanea, 2000.

Bertoni, F. *Claudio Silvestrin*. Boston: Birkhäuser, 2000.

Betsky, A. *Queer Space: Architecture and Same-Sex Desire*. New York: William Morrow and Company, 1997.

Bick, E. "I Shop Therefore I Am." *Frieze* 57 (March 2001).

Binet, H. *Peter Zumthor Works: Buildings and Projects 1979-1997*. Baden: Müller, 1998.

Birnbaum, D. "Art and Ikea Spirit." *Frieze* 31 (October 1996).

Birnbaum, D., A. Sharp, and J. Heiser. *Doug Aitken*. London: Phaidon, 2001.

Bluttal, S. *Halston*. London: Phaidon, 2001.

Boltanski, L., and E. Chiappello. *Le nouvel esprit du capitalisme*. Paris: Gallimard, 1999.

Bolter, J. D., and R. Grusin. *Remediation*. Cambridge, Mass.: MIT Press, 1999.

Bonomi, A. *Il distretto del piacere*. Turin: Bollati Boringhieri, 2000.

Bordieu, P. *La distinction: Critique sociale du jugement*. Paris: Minuit, 1979.

Bovone, L., ed. *Mode*. Milan: Franco Angeli, 1997.

Bovone, L. *Comunicazione: Pratiche, percorsi, soggetti*. Milan: Franco Angeli, 1999.

Bovone, L., and E. Mora, ed. *La moda della metropoli: Dove si incontrano i giovani milanesi*. Milan: Franco Angeli, 1997.

Boyer, M. C. *The City of Collective Memory: Its Historical Imagery and Architectural Entertainments*. Cambridge, Mass.: MIT Press, 1994.

Boyer, M. C. *Cybercities: Visual Perception in the Age of Electronic Communication*. New York: Princeton Architectural Press, 1996.

Braham, P. "Fashion: Unpacking a Cultural Production." In *Production of Culture, Cultures of Production*, ed. P. Du Gay. London: Sage/Open University, 1997.

Brandstetter, G., and H. Völchkers, ed. *ReMembering the Body*. Ostfildern-Ruit: Hatje Cantz, 2000.

Breidenbach, J., and I. Zukrigl. *Tanz der Kulturen: Kulturelle Identität in einer globalisierten Welt*. Munich: Kunstmann, 1998.

Briatore, V. "Renzo Rosso." *Interni* 480 (May 1998).

Briatore, V. "Li Edelkoort." *Interni* 497-498 (January-February 2000).

Bricchi, S. "A Chelsea, Comme des Garçons." *Interni* 493 (September 1999).

Brino, G. *Carlo Mollino. Architecture As Autobiography: Architecture, Furniture, Interior Design 1928-1973*. London: Thames and Hudson, 1987.

Browning, S., M. Mack, and S. Perkins, ed. *Surface: Contemporary Photographic Practice*. London: Booth-Clibborn, 1996.

Bruggen, C. van. *Frank O. Gehry. Guggenheim Museum Bilbao*. New York: The Solomon R. Guggenheim Museum, 1997.

Budd, L., and S. Whimster, ed. *Global Finance and Urban Living*. London: Routledge, 1992.

Bulloch, A. *Satellite*. Zürich: Museum für Gegenwartskunst, 1998.

Bulloch, A. *Rule Book*. London: Book Works, 2000.

Burks, S. "Intervista a Fabien Baron." *Interni* 514 (September 2001).

Buzzi, T. *Lettere pensieri appunti 1937-1979*. Ed. Enrico Fenzi. Cinisello Balsamo: Silvana, 2000.

Calefato, P., ed. *Moda & mondanità*. Bari: Palomar, 1992.

Calefato, P. *Moda, corpo, mito*. Rome: Castelvecchi, 1999.

Calloway, S. *Baroque: The Culture of Excess*. London: Phaidon, 1994.

Campbell-Lange, B.-A. *John Lautner*. Cologne: Taschen, 1999.

Canevacci, M. "Shopping mall, i nuovi contesti performativi del consumo." In *Attraversamenti: I nuovi territori dello spazio pubblico*, ed. P. Desideri and M. Ilardi. Milan: Costa & Nolan, 1997.

Caniglia, J. "Material World." *I. D. Magazine* (October 2000).

Canovari, I. "Anytown: Guida a Springfield, la città ovunque." Degree thesis, Caratteri dell'architettura contemporanea, Dams, Università di Bologna, 1999-2000.

Capella, J. "Cibo per designer di Guixé." *Domus* 828 (July-August 2000).

Capezzuto, R. "Il pane quotidiano." *Domus* 835 (March 2001).

Carmagnola, F. *Merci di culto: Dalla civiltà dei consumi alla venerazione della marca*. Rome: Castelvecchi, 1999.

Carmel-Arthur, J. *Philippe Starck*. London: Carlton, 1999.

Carrassan, F., ed. *La villa Noailles. Une aventure moderne*. Paris: Flammarion, 2001.

Casadio, M. "Art Down On the Ranch." *Casa Vogue* 256 (November 1993).

Casadio, M. "VBGDW: An Artwork." *Vogue Italia* 604 (December 2000).

Cascinai, S. "La moda, lo stile e il mercato." *Domus* 833 (January 2001).

Casotti, A., and C. Stami. "Dove alberga il nuovo." *Modo* (October 2000).

Castle, H., ed. *Fashion + Architecture*. A. D. Architectural Design, vol. 70, no. 6. Bognor Regis: Wiley-Academy, 2000. Essays by I. Borden, J. E. Markham, J. Merkel, M. Pawley, J. Rendell, K. Rhowbotham, D. M. Steiner; conversation between Ch. Jencks and R. Koolhaas; interviews with D. Chipperfield, R. Din, J. Kaplicky of Future Systems, and S. Mackereth.

Cattaneo, F., ed. *Roomscapes: The Decorative Architecture of Renzo Mongiardino*. New York: Rizzoli, 1993.

Celant, G., ed. *Louise Bourgeois*. Ex. cat. Milan: Fondazione Prada, 1997.

Celant, G. "Intervista - Miuccia Prada." *Interni* 479 (April 1998).

Celant, G., ed. *Sam Taylor-Wood*. Ex. cat. Milan: Fondazione Prada, 1998.

Celant, G., ed. *Marc Quinn*. Ex. cat. Milan: Fondazione Prada, 2000.

Celant, G., and H. Koda. *Giorgio Armani. New York*. Ex. cat.. New York: The Solomon R. Guggenheim Museum, 2000.

Chance, J., and T. Schmiedeknecht, ed. *Fame + Architecture*. A. D. Architectural Design, vol. 71, no. 6. Bognor Regis: Wiley-Academy, 2001.

Chaney, D. "Subtopia in Gateshead: The Metro Centre as a Cultural Form." *Theory, Culture and Society* 7 (1991).

Chaney, D. *Fictions of Collective Life: Public Drama in Late Modern Culture*. London: Routledge, 1993.

Ciotta, M., and M. Patrono. "Andrew Ross: Celebration la città ideale." *Alias*, supplement to *Manifesto* 52 (31 December 1999).

Chic Clicks: Creativity and Commerce in Contemporary Fashion Potography. Ex. cat. Boston: Institute of Contemporary Art; Ostfildern-Ruit: Hatje Cantz, 2002.

Clammer, J. *Contemporary Urban Japan: A Sociology of Consumption*. Oxford: Blackwell, 1997.

Clamp, L. *Fashion Marketing*. London: Routledge, 1994.

Clarke, J. "Capturing the Customer: Consumerism and Social Welfare." *Self, Agency and Society* 1, no. 1 (1997).

Codeluppi, V. *Consumo e comunicazione: Merci, messaggi e pubblicità nelle società contemporanee*. Milan: Franco Angeli, 1989.

Codeluppi, V. *I consumatori: Storia, tendenze, modelli*. Milan: Franco Angeli, 1992.

Codeluppi, V. "Il marketing e il nuovo consumatore." *Micro & Macro Marketing* 9, no. 1 (April 2000).

Codeluppi, V. *Lo spettacolo della merce: I luoghi del consumo dai Passages a Disney World*. Milan: Bompiani, 2000.

Codeluppi, V. *Il potere della marca: Disney, McDonald's, Nike e le altre*. Turin: Bollati Boringhieri, 2001.

Cohen, J.-L. *Frank O. Gehry. The Art of Architecture*. New York: Abrams, 2001.

Collier, B. "The Appliance of Science: The Fat Duck Radical Approach to Food." *Frieze* 58 (April 2001).

Colomina, B. *Privacy and Publicity: Modern Architecture as Mass Media*. Cambridge, Mass.: MIT Press, 1994.

Colour in Architecture. A. D. Architectural Design, vol. 66, nos. 3-4. London: Academy Editions, 1996.

Cometto, M. T. "Il baby boomer è triste. Che business."

Corriere Economia. Supplement to *Corriere della Sera,* 4 December 2001.

Connellan, T. *Inside the Magic Kingdom: Seven Keys to Disney's Success.* Austin: Bard Press, 1997.

Connelly, J. "Andrea Zittel." *Surface Magazine* (summer 2000).

Cook, G. *The Discourse of Advertising.* London: Routledge, 1992.

Cosseta, K. "Tra pietra e luce: la nuova boutique di Giorgio Armani a Paris." *Interni* 502 (June 2000).

Crawford, M. "The Architect and the Mall." In *You Are Here,* The Jerde Partnership International. London: Phaidon, 1999.

Crewdson, G. *Gregory Crewdson. Dream of Life.* Salamanca: Universidad de Salamanca, 1999.

Cruz, A., E. Smith, and A. Jones. *Cindy Sherman: Retrospective.* New York: Thames & Hudson, 1997.

Dannat, A. et al. "Sylvie Fleury." *Parkett* 58 (May 2000).

Davidson, C. C., ed. *Anything.* New York: Anyone Corp.; Cambridge, Mass.: MIT Press, 2001.

Davidson, M. P. *The Consumerist Manifesto.* London: Routledge, 1992.

Davis, M. *City of Quartz.* London: Verso, 1990.

Davis, M. *Ecology of Fear: Los Angeles and the Imagination of Disaster.* New York: Metropolitan Books, 1998.

Daza, R. *Looking for Mies.* Barcelona: Actar; Basel: Birkhäuser, 2000.

Dear, M. J. *The Postmodern Urban Condition.* Oxford: Blackwell 2000.

Debord, G. *Commentaires sur "La Société du spectacle."* Paris: Champ Libre, 1988.

Debord, G. *La Société du Spectacle.* Paris: Champ Libre, 1971.

Degon, R. *La Marque Relationelle.* Paris: Vuilbert, 1998.

Deitch, J., ed. *Form Follows Fiction.* Ex. cat. Museo d'Arte Contemporanea, Castello di Rivoli. Milan: Charta, 2001.

Deitch, J., and D. Friedman, ed. *Artificial Nature.* Athens, Geneva and New York: Deste Foundation for Contemporary Art, 1990.

Dewey, J. *L'arte come esperienza* (1934). Florence: La Nuova Italia, 1951.

Dick, P. K. *Do Androids Dream of Electric Sheep?* Garden City, N.Y.: Doubleday, 1968.

DiCorcia, P.-L. *Philip-Lorca diCorcia: Streetworks.* Salamanca: Universidad de Salamanca, 1998.

DiCorcia, P.-L. *Heads. Philip-Lorca diCorcia.* Göttingen: Steidl, 2001

Diller, E., and R. Scofidio. *Flesh. Architectural Probes.* New York: Princeton Architectural Press, 1994.

Di Pietrantonio, G., ed. *Camera Italia.* Ex. cat. VistaMare, Pescara, 2001. Rome: Magazzino d'Arte Moderna (Libri Perché/?), 2001.

Dolce, D., and S. Gabbana. *Animal. Dolce & Gabbana.* Photography by Ellen Von Unwerth, Helmut Newton, Herb Ritts, Steven Meisel, Mario Testino, and Bruce Weber. New York: Abbeville, 1998.

Donald Judd. Räume/Spaces. Ostfildern-Ruit: Cantz, 1993.

Douglas, M., and B. Isherwood. *The World of Goods: Towards an Anthropology of Consumption.* Harmondsworth: Penguin, 1979.

Douglas, M. *Purity and Danger: An Analysis of Concept of Pollution and Taboo.* Harmondsworth: Penguin, 1970.

Downey, J., and J. McGuigan, ed. *Technocities: The Culture and Political Economy of the Digital Revolution.* London: Sage, 1999.

Drabble, B. "Trading Places: Art and Global Economics." *Flash Art International* 220 (October 2001).

Du Gay, P., ed. *Production of Culture, Cultures of Production.* London: Sage, 1997.

Eberle, T. "Donald Judd." *Interview* 24. no. 4 (April 1994).

Edgell, S., K. Hetherington, and A. Warde, ed. *Consumption Matters: The Production and Experience of Consumption.* Oxford: Blackwell, 1996.

Einhorn, B. *Cinderella Goes to Market: Citizenship, Gender, and Women's Movements in East Central Europe.* London and New York: Verso, 1993.

Ellen Von Unwerth's Wicked. Kempen: te Neues Publishing Company, 1998.

Ellin, N. *Postmodern Urbanism.* New York: Princeton Architectural Press, 1999.

Escobar, R. *Metamorfosi della paura.* Bologna: Il Mulino, 1997.

Falk, P., and C. Campbell, ed. *The Shopping Experience.* London: Sage, 1997.

Fausch, D., P. Singley, R. El-Khoury, and Z. Efrat, ed. *Architecture: In Fashion.* Princeton: Princeton Architectural Press, 1994.

Favata, I. *Joe Colombo and Italian Design of the Sixties.* Cambridge, Mass.: MIT Press, 1988.

Featherstone, M. *Consumer Culture and Postmodernism.* London: Sage, 1991.

Ferguson, R., ed. *Jorge Pardo.* Ex. cat. Los Angeles: Museum of Contemporary Art; Chicago: Museum of Contemporary Art, 1997.

Ferrari, F., ed. *Carlo Mollino. Polaroid.* Turin: Allemandi, 1999.

Field, M. "Comme des alien." *Blueprint* (February 1999).

Field, M. *Future System.* London: Phaidon, 1999.

Fields, G. *Gucci on the Ginza: Japan's New Consumer Generation.* Tokyo and New York: Kodansha International, 1989.

Fine, B., and E. Leopold. *The World of Consumption.* London: Routledge, 1993.

Fishman, R. *Bourgeois Utopia: The Rise and Fall of Suburbia.* New York: Basic Books, 1987.

Forden, S. G. *The House of Gucci: A Sensational Story of Murder, Madness, Glamour, and Greed.* New York: Morrow, 2000.

Frank, T. *The Conquest of Cool: Business Culture, Counterculture, and the Rise of Hip Consumerism.* Chicago: University of Chicago Press, 1997.

Frank, T. *One Market Under God: Extreme Capitalism, Market Populism and the End of Economic Democracy*. New York: Doubleday, 2000.

Frank, T. "La felicità è un centro commerciale." *Le Monde diplomatique*, supplement to *Manifesto* (October 2001).

Frankel, S. *Visionaries: Interviews with Fashion Designers*. New York: Abrams, 2001.

Frantz, D., and C. Collins. *Celebration, U.S.A.: Living in Disney's Brave New Town*. New York: Henry Holt & Co., 1999

Frisa, M. L. "Gotico sublime." *Flash Art* 210 (June-July 1998).

Frisa, M. L. "Rubacuori." In *Espresso: Arte oggi in Italia*. Milan: Electa, 2000.

Frisa, M. L., M. Lupano, and S. Tonchi, ed. *Total Living*. Milan: Charta, 2002.

Frith, K. T., ed. *Advertising in Asia: Communication, Culture, and Consumption*. Ames: Iowa State University Press, 1996.

Fusaho, A. "Disneyland's Dreamlike Success." *Japan Quarterly* 35, no. 1 (January-March 1988).

Gaines, S., and S. Churcher. *Obsession: The Lives and Times of Calvin Klein*. New York: Carol Publishing, 1994.

Galassi, P. *Philip-Lorca diCorcia*. Ex. cat. New York: The Museum of Modern Art, 1995.

Galassi, P. *Andreas Gursky*. Ex. cat. New York: The Museum of Modern Art, 2001.

Gallo, P. *Nuovi negozi a Milano 2*. Milan: L'Archivolto, 1994.

Gallo, P. *Nuovi negozi in Italia 2*. Milan: L'Archivolto, 1994.

Garner, P. *Eileen Gray. Designer and Architect*. Cologne, Taschen, 1993.

Garner, P., D. A. Mellor. *Cecil Beaton: Photographs 1920-1970*. Paris: Stewart Tabori & Chang, 1996.

George, L. "Weird Wear." *Azure* (May-June 2001).

Ghent Urban Studies Team. *The Urban Condition: Space, Community and Self in the Contemporary Metropolis*. Rotterdam: 010, 1999.

Giacomoni, S. *L'Italia della moda*. Milan: Mazzotta, 1984.

Giancola, A., ed. *La moda nel consumo giovanile: Strategie & immaginari di fine millennio*. Milan: Franco Angeli, 1999.

Giddens, A. *Runaway World: How Globalization Is Reshaping Our Lives*. London: Routledge, 2000.

Gili Galletti, G. *Case paradiso: La costruzione dell'universo domestico ideale*. Barcelona: Gustavo Gili, 1999.

Gluckman, R., and H. Foster. *Space Framed: Richard Gluckman Architect*. New York: Monacelli, 2000.

Gobé, M. *Emotional Branding: The New Paradigm for Connecting Brands to People*. Oxford: Windsor Book, 2001.

Goldman, R., and S. Papson. *Sign Wars: The Cluttered Landscape of Advertising*. New York: Guilford, 1995.

Goldman, R., and S. Papson. *Nike Culture: The Sign of the Swoosh*. London: Sage, 1998.

Golub, J. *Albert Frey. Houses 1 + 2*. New York: Princeton Architectural Press, 1999.

Graham, S., and S. Martin. *Splintering Urbanism*. London: Routledge, 2001.

Grosjean, M., and J.-P. Thibaud, ed. *L'espace urbain en méthodes*. Marseille: Parenthèses, 2001.

Groys, B., D. Ross, and I. Blazwick. *Ilya Kabakov*. London: Phaidon, 1998.

Guillaume, V. *Courrèges*. Paris: Assouline, 1998.

Hall, T., and P. Hubbard, ed. *The Entrepreneurial City: Geographies of Politics, Regime and Representation*. Chichester: Wiley, 1998.

Hannerz, U. *Transnational Connections: Culture, People, Places*. London and New York: Routledge, 1996.

Hannigan, J. *Fantasy City: Pleasure and Profit in the Postmodern Metropolis*. London: Routledge, 1998.

Hardt, M., and A. Negri. *Empire*. Cambridge, Mass.: Harvard University Press, 2000.

Harvey, D. "Anxious America's Rush from Reality." *The Guardian*, 27 July 1996.

Harvey, D. "The New Urbanism and the Communitarian Trap." *Harvard Design Magazine* (winter/spring 1997).

Harvey, D. *The Condition of Postmodernity*. Oxford: Basil Blackwell, 1989.

Haskell, B. *Donald Judd*. Ex. cat. New York: The Whitney Museum of American Art, 1988.

Haye, C. "Totalitarianism Without Tears." *Frieze* 50 (February 2000).

Hazel, D. "Mall Maestros." *Shopping Centers Today* (December 2001), on the site of the International Council of Shopping Centers (www.icsc.org).

Helfand, J. *Screen: Essays on Graphic Design, New Media, and Visual Culture*. Princeton: Princeton Architectural Press, 2001.

Hicks, D. *David Hicks: Living with Design*. London: Weidenfeld and Nicholson, 1979.

Hines, T. S. *Richard Neutra and the Search for Modern Architecture*. Oxford and New York: Oxford University Press, 1982.

Hirsch, E., and R. Silverstone, ed. *Consuming Technologies: Media and Information in Domestic Spaces*. London: Routledge, 1992.

Hochenberry, J. "Inside Disney." *I.D. Magazine* (March-April 1998).

Holtzman, J. *Every Room Tells a Story: Pages from Nest*. New York: Nest Books, 2001.

Horst, P. et al. *Horst Portraits: 60 Years of Style*. New York: Abrams, 2001.

Howes, D., ed. *Cross Cultural Consumption: Global Markets Local Realities*. London: Routledge, 1996.

Huck, B. *Donald Judd: Furniture*. Ex. cat. Rotterdam: Museum Boijmans Van Beuningen, 1993.

Humphrey, K. *Shelf Life: Supermarkets and the Changing Cultures of Consumption*. London: Cambridge University Press, 1998.

Hunwick, P. "An Open and Shut Case." *Blueprint* 178 (December 2000).

Irace, F. *Gio Ponti: La casa all'italiana*. Milan: Electa, 1988.

Isozaki, A. *Shiro Kuramata. 1967-1987*. Tokyo: Parco, 1988.

Issey Miyake: Making Things. Ex. cat.. Paris: Fondation Cartier pour l'art contemporain, 1998.

Iyer, P. *The Global Soul*. London: Bloomsbury, 2000.

Jackson, L. *Architecture and Interiors of the 1950s*. London: Phaidon, 1994.

Jackson, L. *The Sixties*. London: Phaidon, 1998.

Jencks, C. *The Architecture of the Jumping Universe*. London: Academy, 1995.

Jodidio, P. *New Form: Architecture in the 1990s*. Cologne and London: Taschen, 1997.

Jones, J. "Been There, Celebrations of the Future." *Frieze* 51 (March 2000).

Joselit, D., J. Simon, and R. Salecl. *Jenny Holzer*. London: Phaidon, 1998.

Judd, D.R., and S. Feinstein, ed. *The Tourist City*. New Haven: Yale University Press, 1999.

Katz, D. *Just Do It: The Spirit of Nike in the Corporate World*. New York: Random House, 1994.

Katz, P. *The New Urbanism: Toward an Architecture of Community*. New York: McGraw-Hill, 1994.

Kennedy, S. *Pucci: A Renaissance in Fashion*. New York: Abbeville, 1991.

King, E. "The Future is Orange." *Frieze* 50 (February 2000).

King, E. "Lux Interior. Emily Kings Look Forward to the Future Systems Shopping Mall." *Frieze* (June-July-August, 2001).

King, M. "Malls." In *City A-Z*, ed. S. Pile and N. Thrift. London: Routledge, 2000.

Klein, N. *No Logo: No Space, No Choice, No Jobs. Taking Aim at the Brand Bullies*. London: Flamingo, 2000.

Koolhaas, R. *S, M, L, XL*. New York: Monacelli, 1995.

Koolhaas, R. et al. *Mutations*. Barcelona: Actar, 2000.

Koolhaas, R. and Harvard Design School. *Guide to Shopping*. Cologne: Taschen, 2001.

Koolhaas, R. "Junk Space." *Domus* 833 (January 2001).

Koolhaas, R. *Projects for Prada Part 1*. Milan: Fondazione Prada, 2001.

Lapidus, M. *Too Much Is Never Enough: An Autobiography*. New York: Rizzoli, 1996.

Lash, S., and J. Urry. *Economies of Signs and Space*. London: Sage, 1994.

Lash, S. "Informationcritique." In *Cities in Transition*, ed. A. Graafland. Rotterdam: 010, 2001.

Leach, N. *The Anaesthetics of Architecture*. Cambridge, Mass.: MIT Press, 1999.

Leach, W. *Land of Desire*. New York: Vintage Books, 1993.

Lehmann, U. *Tigersprung: Fashion in Modernity*. Cambridge, Mass.: MIT Press, 2000.

Lever, W. F. *The Post-Fordist City*. In *Handbook of Urban Studies*, ed. R. Paddison. London: Sage, 2001.

Levi, C. "Carlo Mollino: Spazio tempo e garçonniere." *Westuff* 10 (September-October 1987).

Levin, J. *GQ Cool*. London: Pavillon Books, 2000.

Lewis, D., and D. Bridger. *The Soul of the New Consumer*. London: Nicholas Brealey, 2000.

Libby, B. "If You Build It . . ." *Metropolis* (August-September 2001).

Linke, A. *4FLIGHT*. Milan: a+m Bookstore Edizioni, 2000.

Lipovetsky, Gilles. *The Empire of Fashion*. Princeton: Princeton University Press, 1994.

Lodi, S., A. Pioselli, and A. Pieroni. *Loris Cecchini*. San Gimignano and Siena: Galleria Continua, 2000.

Lofland, L.H. *The Public Realm: Exploring the City's Quintessential Social Territory*. New York: Aldine de Gruyter, 1998.

Loos, A. *Ins Leere gesprochen*. Paris: Crès, 1921.

Loos, A. *Trotzdem*. Innsbruck: Brenner, 1931.

Loos, A. *La civiltà occidentale. "Das Andere" e altri scritti*. Bologna: Zanichelli, 1981.

Lopiano-Misdon, J., and J. De Luca. *Street Trends*. New York: HarperBusiness 1998.

Lowe, M., and N. Wrigley. "Retail and the Urban." *Urban Geography* 21, no. 7 (2000).

Lupano, M. *Italo Rota: Il teatro dell'architettura*. Milan: Federico Motta, 1997.

Lury, C. *Consumer Culture*. Cambridge: Polity Press, 1996.

Lutgens, A. *Jake & Dinos Chapman: Hell*. Stuttgart: Hatje Cantz, 2001.

Luttwack, E. N. *La dittatura del capitalismo*. Milan: Mondadori, 1999.

Mac Lamprecht, B. *Neutra: Complete Works*. Cologne: Taschen, 2000.

Mackay, H., ed. *Consumption and Everyday Life*. London: Routledge, 1997.

Maffesoli, M. *La contemplation du monde: Figures du style communautaire*. Paris: Grasset, 1993.

Mamiya, C. J. *Pop Art and Consumer Culture: American Super Market*. Austin: University of Texas Press, 1992.

Man, B. *Life Style*. London: Phaidon, 2000.

Marcuse, P. "Commodifying the Garden of Eden." In *Scanscape: A Visual Essay About a Global Phenomenon*, ed. M. Räder. Barcelona: Actar 1999.

Marcuse, P., and R. van Kempen, ed. *Globalizing Cities: A New Spatial Order?* Oxford: Blackwell, 2000.

Martin, R., and H. Koda. *Christian Dior*. New York: The Metropolitan Museum of Art, 1996.

Mattelart, A. *Advertising International: The Privatisation of Public Space*. London: Routledge, 1991.

Mattsson, H. "Luxury Is Not Shopping, Rem Koolhas Presents the Coming Prada World Order in a New Bible." *NU: The Nordic Art Review* 3-4 (2001).

Matzner, F. *Tobias Rehberger: 005-000 (Pocket Dictionary)*. Ostfildern-Ruit: Hatje Cantz, 2001.

Mau, B. *Life Style*. Ed. K. Maclear and B. Testa. London: Phaidon, 2000.

Mauriès, P. *Fornasetti: Designer of Dreams*. Boston and London: Little Brown, 1991.

Mayer, R. "The Retail System." *Interior Design* (April 2001).

McGrory. "Fantasyland? No, Disney Builds the Real World." *Boston Globe*, 18 February 1996.

Meier, R. *Building the Getty*. Berkeley: University of California Press, 1999.

Memo, M. "Tokyo Disney, Toshi-Ga." *Gomorra* 1 (February 1998).

Milgrom, M. "Target AVL." *Metropolis* (May 2000).

Miller, D., ed. *Acknowledging Consumption: A Review of New Studies*. London: Routledge, 1995.

Miller, D. *A Theory of Shopping*. Cambridge: Polity Press, 1998.

Millet, C. "Les Films de Pierre Huyghe." *Art Press* 227 (1997).

Mitchell, K. "The Culture of Urban Space." *Urban Geography* 21, no. 15 (2000).

Mitchell, W. J. *City of Bits: Space, Place and the Infobahn*. Cambridge, Mass. and London: MIT Press, 1995.

Mitchell, W. S. *E-topia*. "Urban Life, Jim – But Not As We Know It." Cambridge, Mass.: MIT Press, 1999.

Monk, T. *The Art and Architecture of Paul Rudolph*. Chichester: Wiley-Academy, 1999.

Mooij, M. K. de. *Global Marketing and Advertising: Understanding Cultural Paradoxes*. Thousand Oaks, Calif. and London: Sage, 1998.

Moore, R., and R. Ryan. *Building Tate Modern*. London: The Tate Gallery, 2000.

Moore, R., and R. Ryan. *Building Tate Modern: Herzog & de Meuron Transforming Giles Gilbert Scott*. London: Tate Gallery, 2000.

Moos, S. von. "La sindrome di Disney." *Domus* 787 (November 1996).

Morin, E. *L'industria culturale*. Bologna: Il Mulino, 1963.

Morrow, B. "Gregory Crewdson." *Bomb Magazine* (fall 1997).

Moschino? Concept by L. Stoppini, text by M. Casadio. Milan: Skira, 2001.

Noever, P., ed. *Donald Judd: Architecture*. Ostfildern-Ruit: Hatje Cantz, 2002.

Oldenburg, R. *The Great Good Place: Cafés, Coffee Shops, Community Centers, Beauty Parlors, General Stores, Bars, Hangouts, and How They Get you Through the Day*. New York: Paragon House, 1989.

Ottman, K. "Io sono: Un nuovo umanesimo nell'arte e nel design americani." *Domus* 816 (June 1999).

Parr, M. *Common Sense*. Stockport: Dewi Lewis, 1999.

Pawley, M. *Future Systems: The Story of Tomorrow*. London: Phaidon, 1993.

Pawson, J., and A. Bell. *Living and Eating*. New York: Clarkson Potter, 2001.

Perkins, S. et al. *Experience*. London: Booth-Clibborn, 1995.

Peter Lindbergh: Selected Works 1996-1998. Paris: Assouline, 1999.

Philippi, S., ed. *Starck*. Cologne and London: Taschen, 2000.

Picchi, F. "Droog e Duck." *Domus* 833 (January 2001).

Pierre Cardin: Past, Present, Future. London and Berlin: Dirk Nishen, 1990.

Pinchon, J.-F., ed. *Rob. Mallet-Stevens: Architecture, Furniture, Interior Design*. Cambridge, Mass.: MIT Press, 1990.

Pine, B.J., and J. Gilmore. *The Experience Economy: Work Is Theatre & Every Business a Stage*. Boston: Harvard Business School Press, 1999.

Pitteri, D., ed. *Fabbriche del desiderio*. Rome: Sossella, 2000.

Plumb, B. *Horst: Interiors*. Boston: Bulfinch, 1993.

Pocock, P. "Interview with Thomas Ruff." *Journal of Contemporary Art* 6, no. 1 (1993).

Ponti, L. L. *Gio Ponti. L'opera*. Milan: Leonardo, 1990.

Poschardt, U. "Thomas Ruff." *Vogue Homme International* (fall-winter 2001).

Pountain, D., and D. Robins. *L'esprit "cool."* Paris: Autrement, 2001.

Poynor, R. "Adbuster: Guerriglia nell'era dell'informazione." *Domus* 828 (August 2000).

Puato, A. "Siate sexy, fateci guadagnare." *Corriere Economia*, supplement to *Corriere della Sera*, 4 December 2001.

Räder, M. *Scanscape*. Barcelona: Actar, 1999.

Radner, H. "Roaming the City: Proper Women in Improper Places." In *Spaces of Culture*, ed. M. Featherstone and S. Lash. London: Sage, 1999.

Ramakers, R., G. Bakker, ed. *Droog Design: Spirit of the Nineties*. Rotterdam: 010, 1998.

Ramonet, I. *Propagandes Silencieuses: Masses, télevisions, cinéma*. Paris: Galilée, 2000.

Rapaport, K. et al. *Vital Forms: American Art and Design in the Atomic Age, 1940-1960*. New York and London: Abrams, 2001.

Rapaport, K., and K.L. Stayton. *Vital Forms*. New York: Abrams, 2001.

Rashid, K. *Karim Rashid. I Want To Change the World*. London: Thames & Hudson, 2001.

Rassegna 73 (1988) (*Ri-vestimenti*) with articles by J. Rykwert, M. Wigley, G. Malossi, U. Volli, F. La Cecla, and C. Bertelli.

Rawstorn, A. "Good Chemistry." *I.D. Magazine* (March-April 1998).

Raz, A. E. *Riding the Black Ship: Japan and Tokyo Disneyland*. Cambridge, Mass. and London: Harvard University Asia Center, 1999.

Reddy, A. C. *The Emerging High-Tech Consumer: A Market Profile and Marketing Strategy Implications*. Westport, Conn.: Quorum, 1997.

Restany, P. " Back into the Pop Era: Pierre Restany Interviews Damien Hirst." *Domus* 806 (July-August 1998).

Rice, B. "The Selling of Life-Styles." *Psychology Today* (March 1988).

Rifkin, J. *The Age of Access*. New York: J. P. Tarcher/Putnam, 2000.

Rinaldi, P., ed. *Walter Albini: Lo stile nella moda*. Modena: Zanfi, 1988.

Risaliti, S. *Nina Saunders*. Ex. cat. Arezzo: Note arte-contemporanea, 2001.

Ritchie, M. "People in Glass Houses." *Frieze* 57 (March 2001).

Ritzer, G. *The McDonaldization of Society: An Investigation into the Changing Character of*

Contemporary Social Life. Thousand Oaks, Calif.: Pine Forge, 1995.

Ritzer, G. *Enchanting a Disenchanted World: Revolutionizing the Means of Consumption*. Thousand Oaks, Calif.: Pine Forge, 1999.

Rosa, J. *Albert Frey, Architect*. New York: Rizzoli, 1990.

Ross, A. *The Celebration Chronicles: Life, Liberty, and the Pursuit of Property Value in Disney's New Town*. New York: Ballantine Books, 1999.

Rüedi, K., S. Wigglesworth, and D. McCorquodale, ed. *Desiring Practices: Architecture, Gender, and the Interdisciplinarity*. London: Black Dog, 1996.

Rugoff, R. "Authentic Consumption: Ralph Rugoff Considers the Britishness of Bluewater, the UK's Largest Mall." *Frieze* 47 (June-August 1998).

Rymer, R. "Back to the Future." *Harper's* (October 1996).

Sack, R. D. *Place, Modernity and the Consumer's World: A Relational Framework for Geographical Analysis*. Baltimore: Johns Hopkins University Press, 1992.

Saltz, J. "A Short History of Rirkrit Tiravanija." *Art in America* (February 1996).

San Pietro, S., ed. *New Shops in Italy 4*. Milan: L'Archivolto, 1997.

San Pietro, S., ed. *New Shops 5. Made in Italy*. Milan: L'Archivolto, 1998.

San Pietro, S., ed. *New Shops in Italy 6*. Milan: L'Archivolto, 2001.

San Pietro, S., ed. *Nuovi negozi a Milano*. Milan: L'Archivolto, 1988.

San Pietro, S., ed. *Nuovi negozi in Italia*. Milan: L'Archivolto, 1990.

San Pietro, S., ed. *Nuovi negozi in Italia 3*. Milan: L'Archivolto, 1995.

San Pietro, S., ed. *Vetrine a Milano*. Milan: L'Archivolto, 1995.

Sassen, S. *The Global City: New York. London: Tokyo*. Princeton: Princeton University Press, 1991.

Sassen, S. *Globalization and Its Discontents*. New York: New Press, 1998.

Savan, L. *The Sponsored Life*. Philadelphia: Temple University Press, 1994.

Schafaff, J., and B. Steiner, ed. *Jorge Pardo*. Baden-Württemberg: Landesbank Baden-Württemberg; Ostfildern: Cantz, 2000.

Schjeldahl, P. "Silver Dream Machine." *Frieze* 37 (May 1997).

Schmitt, B. H. *Experiential Marketing: How To Get Customers To Sense, Feel, Think, Act, and Relate to Your Company and Brands*. New York: The Free Press, 1999.

Schwartz, H. *The Culture of the Copy*. New York: Zone Books, 1996.

Semprini, A. *Marche e mondi possibili*. Milan: Franco Angeli, 1993.

Semprini, A. *La marca: Dal prodotto al mercato, dal mercato alla società*. Milan: Lupetti, 1996.

Semprini, A., ed. *Il senso delle cose*. Milan: Franco Angeli, 1999.

Sennett, R. *Reflections on the Public Realm*. In *A Companion to The City*, ed. G. Bridge and S.

Watson. Oxford: Blackwell, 2000.

Sernini, M. *La città disfatta*. Milan: Franco Angeli, 1988.

Sernini, M. "I centri commerciali dieci anni dopo." *Commercio* 63 (1998).

Serraino, P., and J. Shulman. *Modernism Rediscovered*. Cologne: Taschen, 1994.

Seydel, J. "Theatre and Emotion in the Supermarket." *Mediamatic* 9, no. 4 (October 1999).

Shields, R., ed. *Lifestyle Shopping: The Subject of Consumption*. London: Routledge, 1992.

Shulman, J. *Architecture and Its Photography*. Cologne: Taschen, 1998.

Simmons, L., and P. Wheelright. "Peek-a-Boo Views." *nest* 10 (fall 2000).

Slater, D. R. "Going Shopping: Markets, Crowds and Consumption." In *Cultural Reproduction*, ed. C. Jenks. London: Routledge, 1993.

Slater, D. R. "Marketing Mass Photography." In *The Image and Visual Culture*, ed. J. Evans and S. Hall. London: Sage/Open University, 1999.

Slater, D. R., and F. Tonkiss. *Market Societies and Modern Social Thought*. Cambridge: Polity Press, 2000.

Slimane, H. *Visionaire 34 Paris Dior Homme Solitaire*. Visionaire Publishing, 2000.

Smart, B., ed. *Resisting Mc Donaldization*. London: Sage, 1999.

Smith, P. *You Can Find Inspiration in Everything*. London: Violette, 2001.

Smoodin, E., ed. *Disney Discourse: Producing the Magic Kingdom*. London and New York: Routledge, 1994.

Socha, M. "Less is Dior." *W* (January 2001).

Soja, E. W. *Thirdspace Journeys to Los Angeles and Other Real and Imagined Places*. Cambridge, Mass.: Blackwell, 1996.

Soja, E. W. *Postmetropolis: Critical Studies of Cities and Regions*. Oxford: Blackwell, 2000.

Sorkin, M. *Variations on a Theme Park: The New American City and the End of Public Space*. New York: Hill and Wang, 1992.

Sorkin, M. "New Urbanism's Perverse Vision of Stanislavsky's Method. Can New Urbanism Learn from Modernism's Mistakes?" *Metropolis* 1 (August-September 1998).

Sorkin, M. *Some Assembly Required*. Rochester: University of Minnesota Press, 2001.

Southgate, P. *Total Branding by Design: How To Make Your Brand's Packaging More Effective*. London: Kogan Page, 1994.

Sozzoni, C. "Oltre il trend: Pensiero-progetto." *Interni* 500 (April 2000).

Stafford, A. "Rirkrit Tiravanija." *Surface Magazine* 15 (1998).

Steele, J. *Architecture Today*. London: Phaidon, 1997.

Steiner, D. "A Diary of Disney's Celebration." *Domus* 787 (November 1996).

Steiner, D. "The Truman Show." *Domus* 816 (June 1999).

Steiner, D. "Herzog & de Meuron." *Domus* 828 (July-August 2000).

Steinglass, M. "Toilet Paper: A German Plumbing-Fixtures Company Creates a Magazine Awash in Bathroom Culture." *Metropolis* (April 2000).

Sterling, B. "La città virtuale" (1994). In *Parco giochi con pena di morte,* ed. W. Gibson and B. Sterling. Milan: Mondadori, 2001.

Steven Meisel: Four Days in LA: The Versace Picture. Ex. cat. London: White Cube, 2001

Stungo, N. *Charles and Ray Eames.* London: Carlton, 2000.

Suardi, S. "Il dinosauro: Mandarina Duck a Bologna." *Interni* 502 (June 2000).

Sudjic, D. *Rei Kawabuko and Comme des Garçons.* New York: Rizzoli, 1990.

Sudjic, D. *Equipment Stores: Architect David Chipperfield.* London: Wordsearch, 1992.

Sudjic, D. *John Pawson Works.* London: Phaidon, 2000.

Sudjic, D. "L'arte dello sguardo." *Domus* 835 (March 2001).

Sudjic, D. "Is the Future in Their Hands?" *The Observer,* 14 October 2001.

Teboul, D. *Yves Saint Laurent, 5, Avenue Marceau, 75116 Paris, France.* New York: Abrams, 2002.

Thall, B. *The New American Village.* Baltimore: The Johns Hopkins University Press, 1999.

Thomas, B. *Building a Company: Roy O. Disney and the Creation of an Entertainment Empire.* New York: Hyperion, 1998.

Tobias Rehberger. Ex. cat. Basel: Kunsthalle Basel, 1998.

Tomlinson, A., ed. *Consumption, Identity and Style: Marketing, Meanings, and the Packaging of Pleasure.* London: Routledge, 1990.

Torres, M. *Luoghi magnetici.* Milan: Franco Angeli, 2000.

Toscani, O. "Il mondo e la sua immaginazione." *Micromega* 5 (2001).

Trétiack, P. *Raymond Loewy and Streamlined Design.* New York: Universe/Vendome, 1999.

Tsuzuki, K. *Tokyo: A Certain Style.* San Francisco: Chronicle Books, 1999.

Twitchell, J. *Carnival Culture.* New York: Columbia University Press, 1992.

Vanderbilt, T. "Mickey Goes to Town(s)." *Nation,* 28 August 1995.

Vanderbilt, T. *The Sneaker Book: Anatomy of an Industry and an Icon.* New York: The New Press, 1998.

Vanderbilt, T. "It's a Mall World After All." *Harvard Design Magazine* (fall 1999).

Vansittart, K. "Make-up's Make Over." *Azure* (May-June 1999).

Veca, S. "Dialogo su Impero e democrazia." *Micromega* 5 (2001).

Venturi, R. *Iconography and Electronics Upon a Generic Architecture: A View from the Drafting Room.* Cambridge: Mass. and London: MIT Press, 1996.

Venturi, R., and D. Scott Brown. "Las Vegas postclassica." *Domus* 787 (November 1996).

Venturi, R., D. Scott Brown, and S. Izenour. *Learning from Las Vegas.* Cambridge, Mass.: MIT Press, 1972.

Vercelloni, M. "Eterotopie della compensazione: I parchi a tema Disney e le loro strutture alberghiere." *Domus* 787 (November 1996).

Versace, G., and I. Sischy. *Versace: Rock and Royalty.* New York: Abbeville, 1997.

Vesegack, A. von, and M. Remmele. *Verner Panton: The Collected Works.* Weil am Rhein: Vitra Design Museum, 2000.

Vidal, J. *Counter Culture vs. Burger Culture.* London: Macmillan, 1997.

Vinyets, J. "Per un altro marketing: Il nuovo design si basa sull'esperienza." *Domus* 826 (May 2000).

Virostek, G. "Profile: Kalle Lasn." *Blueprint* 167 (December 1999).

Volpe, M. "Il Grande Fratello prepara punizioni choc." *Corriere della Sera,* 10 September 2001.

Watts, S. *The Magic Kingdom: Walt Disney and the American Way of Life.* Boston: Houghton Mifflin, 1997.

Weaving, A., and L. Freedman. *Understanding Modern: The Modern Home As It Was and As It Is Today.* London: Quadrille, 2001.

Weber, J. "The Ever-Expanding, Profit-Maximizing, Cultural-Imperialist, Wonderful World of Disney." *Wired* (February 2002).

Weintraub, A., photography. *The Architecture of John Lautner.* Text by A. Hess. London: Thames & Hudson, 1999.

Wernick, A. *Promotional Culture: Advertising, Ideology and Symbolic Expression.* London: Sage, 1991.

Whitely, L. "How Consumer Demand Is Translated into Production: Marks and Spencer and Next." In *Components of Dress: Design, Manufacturing and Image-Making in the Fashion Industry,* ed. J. Ash and L. Wright. London: Routledge, 1988.

Whitney, D. *Philip Johnson: The Glass House.* New York: Pantheon, 1993.

Wilcox, C., ed. *Radical Fashion.* London: Victoria & Albert Museum, 2001.

Wilson, C. "Celebration Puts Disney in Reality's Realm." *USA Today,* 18 November 1995.

Wilson E. *Adorned in Dreams: Fashion and Modernity.* London: Virago, 1985.

Wodiczko, K. *Critical Vehicles.* Cambridge, Mass. and London: MIT Press, 1999.

Wojciechowski, E. "Look at Fashion in the Museum." *Frieze* 58 (April 2001).

Woznicki, K. "Anarchy in the New Economy." *NU: The Nordic Art Review* 3-4 (2001).

Wynne, D. *Leisure, Lifestyle and the New Middle Class: A Case Study.* London: Routledge, 1998.

Yayoi Kusama. Paris: Les presses du réel, 2001.

Yilmaz, D. "Openings. Tobias Rehberger." *Artforum* (January 1997).

Yoshida, N., ed. *Kazuyo Sejima 1987-1999. Kazuyo Sejima and Ryue Nishizawa 1995-1999.* Tokyo: Shinkenchiku-Sha, 1999.

Zancan, R. "Il Palais de Tokyo." *Arch'it files* (24 February 2002). (http://architettura.super-eva.it/files/20020224/index.htm).

Zdenek, F. *Andrea Zittel: Personal Programs.* Ex. cat. Deichtorhallen Hamburg, Hamburg. Ostfildern-Ruit: Hatje Cantz, 2000.

Zelevansky, L. et al. *Love Forever. Yayoi Kusama*. Ex. cat. Los Angeles: Los Angeles County Museum of Art, 1998.

Zijil, I. van. *Droog Design, 1991-1996*. Utrecht: Centraal Museum, 1997.

Zijil, I. van. *Gijs Bakker. Objects To Use*. Rotterdam: 010, 2000.

Zukin, S. *Landscapes of Power: From Detroit to Disney World*. Berkeley: University of California Press, 1991.

Zukin, S. "How to Create a Culture Capital: Reflections on Urban Markets and Places." In *Century City: Art and Culture in the Modern Metropolis*, ed. I. Blazwick. London: Tate Gallery, 2001.

CONTENTS

DESIGN COORDINATION
GABRIELE NASON

EDITORIAL COORDINATION
EMANUELA BELLONI

EDITING
HARLOW TIGHE

PRESS OFFICE
SILVIA PALOMBI ARTE&MOSTRE, MILANO

COVER
VANESSA BEECROFT, *PONTI SISTER*, 2001
PHOTO DUSAN RELJIN, © 2001 VANESSA BEECROFT,
COURTESY DEITCH PROJECT, NEW YORK

ISBN 88-8158-371-2

EDIZIONI CHARTA
VIA DELLA MOSCOVA, 27
20121 MILAN
TEL. +39-026598098/026598200
FAX +39-026598577
E-MAIL: EDCHARTA@TIN.IT
WWW.CHARTAARTBOOKS.IT

PRINTED IN ITALY

TOTAL LIVING

PROJECT PRODUCED AND PROMOTED BY
PITTI IMMAGINE

EDITED BY
MARIA LUISA FRISA
MARIO LUPANO
STEFANO TONCHI

RESEARCH COORDINATOR
EMANUELA DE CECCO

SENIOR EDITOR AND EDITORIAL COORDINATOR
FEDERICA CIMATTI

RESEARCH COLLABORATORS
BRUNELLA CACCAVIELLO
LIVIA CORBÒ
LORENZA PIGNATTI
BRADLEY RIFE
ANGELO TEARDO

GRAPHIC DESIGN
ALESSANDRO GORI

TRANSLATIONS
MICHAEL ROBINSON
RODNEY STRINGER

PRODUCTION SECRETARY
VALERIA SANTONI, FLORENCE
WAYNE NORTHCROSS, NEW YORK

PRESS OFFICE
FRANCESCA TACCONI WITH
ELISABETTA PAROLI, FLORENCE
ALESSANDRA BUOMPADRE, MILAN
ANDREA MUGNAINI (WEB SITE)

GENERAL ORGANIZATION
ELISABETTA BASILICI MENINI
CRISTIANA BUSI

PITTI IMMAGINE ORGANIZES AND PROMOTES FASHION FAIRS AND EVENTS. OVER 1500 BUSINESSES EXHIBIT AT ITS FAIRS, REPRESENTING THE CREAM OF THE ITALIAN, EUROPEAN AND INTERNATIONAL TEXTILE AND CLOTHING INDUSTRY. FOR MORE THAN TEN YEARS PITTI IMMAGINE HAS BEEN COMMITTED TO PROJECTS WHOSE AIM IS TO HEIGHTEN PEOPLE'S AWARENESS OF AND TO CIRCULATE A CONTEMPORARY ARTISTIC CULTURE RELATED TO FASHION AND COMMUNICATION. THE OPERATION FOCUSES ON TOPICS THAT LINK FASHION TO THOSE BROADER ANTHROPOLOGICAL, CULTURAL AND SOCIAL SPHERES IN WHICH THE POINTS OF EXCHANGE AND COMPARISON ARE MOST STRIKING.
THE CONCEPT FOR *TOTAL LIVING* SPRANG FROM THE REALIZATION THAT STYLES AND WAYS OF LIFE HAVE BECOME INCREASINGLY UNIFORM UNDER LABELS AND DEFINITIONS OF FASHION AS INDUSTRY AND CULTURAL FORM. BY ILLUSTRATING NEW FACETS OF LIFESTYLES, THE GOAL IS ALSO TO SURVEY THE MANY AND VARIOUS INTERCONNECTIONS BETWEEN FASHION, DESIGN, ARCHITECTURE, ART AND COMMUNICATION.

CHAIRMAN
GAETANO MARZOTTO

CEO
RAFFAELLO NAPOLEONE

COMMUNICATION AND SPECIAL PROJECTS DIRECTOR
LAPO CIANCHI

ARTISTIC PROJECTS COORDINATOR
FRANCESCO BONAMI

PRESS OFFICE COORDINATOR
CRISTINA BRIGIDINI

PUBLIC RELATIONS DIRECTOR
SIBILLA DELLA GHERARDESCA

MARKETING DIRECTOR
AGOSTINO POLETTO

ORGANIZATION AND SERVICES DIRECTOR
ANTONELLO GINANNESCHI

PITTI IMMAGINE SRL
VIA FAENZA, 111
50123 FLORENCE
TEL.+39-0553693407
FAX +39-0553693200
WWW.PITTIMMAGINE.COM

PITTI IMMAGINE WOULD LIKE TO THANK

A+M BOOKSTORE, MILAN
A/R MEDIA
ABBEVILLE PRESS, NEW YORK
UMBERTO ALLEMANDI & C., TURIN
ARCHITECTURE INTÉRIEURE CRÉÉ
GIORGIO ARMANI
BALLY
BIG
CANTZ, OSTFILDERN
CAP
HUSSEIN CHALAYAN
ENNIO CAPASA
RITA CAPEZZUTO
ROBERTO CAVALLI
COMME DES GARÇONS
NATHAN COOPER
ALESSANDRA DAL ZOPPO
DEITCH PROJECTS, NEW YORK
FRANCESCA DEL PUGLIA
DIESEL
DIOR HOMME
ANTONELLA DI MARCO
GIACINTO DI PIETRANTONIO
DOLCE & GABBANA
DOMUS
DOMUS ACADEMY, MILAN
LINDA DRESNER
DUTCH
PHILIPPE DUBOY
TODD EBERLE
EDICIONES UNIVERSIDAD DE SALAMANCA, SALAMANCA
ÉDITION DU REGARD, PARIS
EDIZIONI CONDÉ NAST, MILAN
ELLE DÉCOR
ESQUIRE
CESARE FABBRI
FASHION WORK LIBRARY, MILAN
CARLO FEI
GIANFRANCO FERRÉ
FLAIR
FLAMMARION, PARIS
FLAUNT
FONDATION CARTIER POUR L'ART CONTEMPORAIN, PARIS
FONDAZIONE PRADA, MILAN
FONDAZIONE SANDRETTO RE REBAUDENGO PER L'ARTE, TURIN
TOM FORD
GIANNI FRANCESCHI
LUIGI FRANCO ARTE CONTEMPORANEA, TURIN
GA DOCUMENT
GALERIE HAUSER & WIRTH & PRESENHUBER, ZURICH
GALERIE LELONG, NEW YORK
GALERIE THADDEUS ROPAC, PARIS
GALLERIA CONTINUA, SAN GIMIGNANO
GALLERIA MARABINI, BOLOGNA
ALEX GINZALEZ
MARIAN GOODMAN GALLERY, NEW YORK
MANUELA GRAGNOLI
DAVID GRANGER
GUCCI
HARPER & ROW, NEW YORK
HERMÈS
LISA HINTELMANN
LAUREN IANNOTTI
INTERNI
INVIEW
JAY JOPLING/WHITE CUBE, LONDON

CALVIN KLEIN
MICHAEL KUCMEROSKI
HELMUT LANG
LEHMANN MAUPIN GALLERY, NEW YORK
LES PRESSES DU RÉEL, DIJON
GIO' MARCONI, MILAN
MARNI
MARSILIO, VENICE
RAUL MARTINEZ
DAVID MAUPIN
ISSEY MIYAKE
ARNOLDO MONDADORI EDITORE, MILAN
MOSCHINO
NAVONE ASSOCIATI, MILAN
NEST
NIKE
NOTE ARTECONTEMPORANEA, AREZZO
KARLA OTTO
RICHARD PANDISCIO
LUCA PERONI
PHAIDON, LONDON
PRADA
PUCCI
R + W, MILAN
RALPH LAUREN
RIZZOLI INTERNATIONAL, NEW YORK
ANDREA ROSEN GALLERY, NEW YORK
ITALO ROTA
YVES SAINT LAURENT
JIL SANDER
SEPHORA
CARLO SISI
HEDI SLIMANE
PAUL SMITH
KATE SPADE
TASCHEN, COLOGNE
THAMES & HUDSON, LONDON
THE FACE
THE MONACELLI PRESS, NEW YORK
THE NEW YORK TIMES MAGAZINE
VALENTINO
VANITY FAIR
MARCO VENERI
VERSACE
FRANCESCO VEZZOLI
VIAFARINI, MILAN
VOGUE
VOGUE ITALIA
W
WALKER ART CENTER, MINNEAPOLIS
ZANFI, MODENA
ZWIRNER & WIRTH, NEW YORK